The ABCs of
Environmental Regulation

2nd Edition

Joel B. Goldsteen
PhD, AICP, NCARB, AIA

Government Institutes
An imprint of
The Scarecrow Press, Inc.
Lanham, Maryland • Toronto • Oxford
2005

 **Government Institutes**

Published in the United States of America
by Government Institutes, an imprint of The Scarecrow Press, Inc.
A wholly owned subsidary of
The Rowman & Littlefield Publishing Group, Inc.
4501 Forbes Boulevard, Suite 200
Lanham, Maryland 20706
http://govinst.scarecrowpress.com

PO Box 317 Oxford, OX2 9RU, UK

Copyright © 2003 by Government Institutes

British Library Cataloguing in Publication Information Available

Library of Congress Cataloging-in-Publication Data

Goldsteen, Joel B.
    The ABCs of environmental regulation: understanding the federal
programs/Joel B. Goldsteen.—2nd ed.
        p. cm.
Includes bibliographic references and index.
ISBN: 0-86587-949-4
1. Environmental law—United States. I. Title.
KF3775.G65 2002
344.73'046—dc21   2002033911

⊗™ The paper used in this publication meets the minimum requirements of
American National Standard for Information Sciences—Permanence of
Paper for Printed Library Materials, ANSI/NISO Z39.48-1992.
Manufactured in the United States of America.

SUMMARY CONTENTS

Section One: The Framework

Section Two: Air

Section Three: Water

Section Four: Waste and Tanks

Section Five: Safety

CONTENTS

Section One: The Framework

Chapter 1: Introduction

Chapter 2: Summary Perspectives

Chapter 3: National Policy

Chapter 4: Federal Agency Requirements

Chapter 5: Preventing Pollution

Section Two: Air

Chapter 6: Air Pollution

Chapter 7: Sound

Chapter 8: Aircraft Sound

Section Three: Water

Chapter 9: Water Pollution

Chapter 10: Drinking Water

Chapter 11: Oil Spills into Water

Chapter 12: Ocean Dumping

Chapter 13: Ocean Dumping and Ships

Chapter 14: Ocean and Paints

Chapter 15: Shore Protection

Section Four: Waste and Tanks

Chapter 16: Solid Waste

Chapter 17: Hazardous Waste

Chapter 18: Storage Tanks

Chapter 19: Federal Compliance

Section Five: Safety

Chapter 20: Workplace

Chapter 21: Chemicals

Chapter 22: Pesticides

Chapter 23: Land

Chapter 24: Nuclear Safety

Section Six: Responding to Contaminant Releases

Chapter 35: Ecosystem

Chapter 36: Wetlands

Chapter 37: Non-native Species

Chapter 38: Land

Chapter 39: Offshore

PREFACE

Environmental laws and regulations (and their programs) may be viewed as the outcomes of the legislation originally passed by the federal government. Many federal, state, and local environmental agency personnel work with legislators in the House of Representatives and Senate and executive branch staff under the Office of the President to develop this "protective blanket" of environmental legislation. The laws and framework are quite dynamic. As field personnel from the Coast Guard, Department of the Interior, Environmental Protection Agency, Department of Defense—Homeland Security, and others are confronted with threats to our environmental future, they respond as responsible guardians of the public interest. New provisions are added to the laws or regulations nearly every week.

Many federal environmental regulations have changed substantially since the publication of the first edition of this book. Changes have been made to requirements for Superfund cleanups, chemical safety provisions, site security for air, water regulations, medical waste restrictions, stormwater regulations for smaller cities, ship painting and restrictions, and wetlands protection provisions, to name a few examples. Furthermore, a new federal act restores previously contaminated downtown and gray areas of cities to ready-for-building conditions, new annual reporting requirements have been added to protect endangered species, and state governments and Indian tribes are now authorized and aided in developing programs to respond to contaminant spills.

Note that there are differences between regulations and programs. A regulation is a separate set of instructions about one subject that is required to be followed. The federal environmental regulations for air include thousands of separate instructions, or regulations. Together these regulations or instructions can be viewed as "the air program." But portions of the total set of regulations for air, let us say 277 separately published regulations located in scattered sections of an act, may be considered "the hazardous substance release program for industrial facilities." To date, there is no general agreement about the precise names, titles, divisions, or separate programs within the federal environmental framework. Most give names to programs at will, according to their need in communicating with others. For example, some lump together all storage tank programs into a category called "tank programs." Others divide storage tank programs into aboveground and underground storage tank programs. Still others place storage tanks under the overall program name of the Resource Conservation and Recovery Act (RCRA) or even the Solid Waste Disposal Act (SWDA). The SWDA with its RCRA amendments is the name of the federal act containing the sets of regulations about storage tanks.

It appears that no one category is universally accepted. For these confusing reasons, this book does not clearly divide the federal environmental regulatory framework into separate programs. If the reader wishes to do so, she or he may readily use the subtitles in the text or table of contents freely.

During my first attempts at teaching courses, students in law, geology, engineering, public administration, city and regional planning, and the environmental professions did not understand the comprehensive structure of the regulations and agencies until after almost an entire semester of study. Even then, I was not certain that a comprehensive understanding was conveyed because a satisfactory written compilation did not exist. Using the available materials, we had to study and discuss one area of environmental regulation at a time. I compiled, edited, and wrote this book in order to fulfill my need to have the federal laws and regulations in a form that my students could use to obtain that comprehensive understanding more quickly.

Still, this book cannot be considered a complete compilation or a volume guaranteed to meet a reader's specific need for information about a law or regulation. Only a direct reading of all of the acts currently in force and a careful review of the applicable sections of the Code of Federal Regulations (CFRs)—the rules, details, and fine-tuned or specific requirements of each act—can fulfill that kind of need. Even then, the federal regulatory agencies and government officials may need to be contacted because some changes may have been recorded as circulars, memos, addenda, or orders that could apply to an individual situation. In editing and compiling the information for the first and second editions, many decisions had to be made. Sections of the federal environmental regulations were selected from my own perspective and from my experiences in consulting, research, and teaching courses in federal and state environmental regulations to graduate students in civil engineering, environmental science, business administration, city and regional planning, architecture, landscape architecture, and hazardous materials management programs—the seven university environmental graduate programs with which I am associated.

I reviewed the selected federal environmental regulations word for word, as well as related library sources, agency handouts, Internet sites, and mailings. I made visits and phone calls to agencies and researched particular issues. I solicited, collected, reviewed, and took some of the photographs. When no source is noted on the photographs, they were obtained from the U.S. Environmental Protection Agency site files under the Freedom of Information Act. The sites shown in the photographs are intentionally not identified.

They have been selected to illustrate the subject only. The captions are explanations of this author's intent only and intentionally tell a different story from the text. Readers should not read the captions and expect to understand the content of the chapters or sections of the book.

Personal opinions or criticisms are not intended in this book; I intend only to attempt to more clearly and succinctly relate the laws and agency interrelationships (when relevant) and those subjects necessary to supplement that information. When issues arise during my explanations, I have taken care to present both sides—conflicting opinions. Parts of this manual are compiled and edited but not authored by me, especially the lists of requirements under the different regulatory provisions. Each chapter is a summary of a federal act which explains its contents, concepts, and substance. An overview of each chapter is provided prior to the text of the chapter (in outline format). A reader may obtain the essence of the information that follows from these abstracts.

The first chapter, *Understanding the Programs and Agencies*, provides an overview of the federal environmental framework. For the reader needing a comprehensive sweep, read it first. If a reader is only interested in an overview, then Chapter 2, *Overview of the Programs*, provides general information with brief explanations of environmental protection through the various programs. Other readers can easily turn to their chapter of choice.

There are many terms and acronyms within the laws. Some are commonly used by environmental professionals and government employees. All applicable acronyms are defined in each chapter the first time used. By using acronyms, the text avoids repeating long sets of identifier names of acts, tests, conditions, and agencies. For example, the Environmental Protection Agency is the EPA throughout the book. This method of abbreviation through acronyms has drastically shortened the book and made it more readable. Any time the reader becomes lost in the acronyms, she or he may turn to the glossary at the end of the book.

Section headings cluster the environmental regulations into subject areas, and chapter headings are provided to best explain the subject of those regulations explained therein. Endnotes are provided at the end of the book. These endnotes are intended to be used as a reference only. There is no need to refer to the endnotes while reading. For the reader desiring more detail or a pathway to get to more information, the section of the law or regulation is cited.

Today there is such a high interest and passion to use the Internet to find information that a warning is necessary. This author is quite cautious about the completeness and quality of information available on the Internet and worries about Internet site maintenance, accuracy, and completeness of the information placed there. Sites are often disguised as authoritarian or government-like. When searching for government information, reports, laws, federal register postings, or the Code of Federal Regulations, you will find yourself switching between web sites maintained by consulting companies and those of the government. Also, searches can lead you through many screens and then truncate prior to the sections or pages you want. The same environmental act can be presented with different sections missing on different government, university, or private company sites. Beware. For these reasons, please treat any Internet information as potentially incomplete, out of date, or even incorrect. More and more information is added daily, which increases this possibility. Any information that is important for the reader must be verified with written, published records—especially the federal regulations themselves.

Maneuvering around the Internet sites containing the Code of Federal Regulations (CFRs), which provide the detailed orders or procedures, is difficult. Search engines are slow and almost unusable on three of my computers, even on the one that is networked directly through our University's computers (and not a DSL telephone line). Consider using the CD-ROM versions of the Code of Federal Regulations. To date, I have not seen a better way to get this information than from the CD-ROMs available from the publisher of this book, Government Institutes. These products are much easier to navigate, in general, and quicker and easier to reach the additions or updated sections of the CFRs. Since direct public agency contact is suggested for the reader's important issues, semiannual updates of the CFRs may be satisfactory for searches in most instances.

BRIEFS OF FEDERAL ENVIRONMENTAL REGULATIONS

Over the past few years there have been changes to many of the environmental acts to shift enforcement emphases, modify regulatory structures, and add different areas of concern. This edition adds new materials, provisions, changes, and emphases to these laws and regulations that have been enacted by the federal government since the first edition.

Airport Noise Abatement Act

Aircraft and airports are regulated to reduce noise. Sound is measured for volume and distance, and the land uses around airports are restricted.

Antarctic Protection Act

The minerals of Antarctica are protected according to international treaties to ensure the continent's continued use for scientific studies and as a natural stratospheric ozone depletion laboratory.

Aquatic Nuisance Prevention and Control Act

Non-native species of plants and fish, as well as unintentional discharges, are regulated to protect existing habitats and waters.

Asbestos Hazard Emergency Response Act

Airborne asbestos is recognized as a health hazard and must be contained or removed if found to be unsafe. Removal management plans must be approved. Contractors require accreditation.

Atomic Energy Act

Radioactive materials and substances are regulated during mining, transport, handling, and disposal. Scientific research and demonstration projects are promoted. Licensing of activities is required.

Clean Air Act

Air quality is regulated. A list of contaminants contains ranges of allowable chemical substances. Both mobile (vehicles) and stationary (buildings and facilities) sources are required to comply with the air quality standards stated in the National Ambient Air Quality Standards.

Clean Water Act (in Federal Water Pollution Control Act)

Surface and ground water are protected for purity. Any discharge into waters requires a permit. There are pretreatment standards, restrictions on non-point contamination of sources, and limitations on effluents.

Coastal Wetlands Planning, Protection, and Restoration Act

Provisions for preservation, restoration, and protection of the Louisiana Coastal wetlands and its Mississippi Delta are established.

Coastal Zone Management Act

Land and water along coastal shorelines are protected through the many provisions of federal acts and agencies. Non-point pollution is controlled from sources such as agriculture, silviculture, urban runoff, and marinas.

Comprehensive Environmental Response, Compensation and Liability Act—Superfund

This act promotes local readiness to cleanup spills, requires open records for owners and operators of industrial buildings and facilities, and advances funds to clean abandoned and problem ownership sites. Hazardous substances of concern are those listed in other federal acts.

Emergency Planning & Community Right-To-Know Act (also Pollution Prevention Act)

This act promotes local readiness to spill cleanups and requires open records for owners and operators of industrial buildings and facilities. States are required to establish local government chemical emergency spill response programs that include public notice of pollution events. All existing chemical or biological substances contained in buildings and facilities must be reported to a public agency.

Endangered Species Act

There are many species that would not survive unless strict regulations are imposed. Monitoring and recovery plans of those species are required through this act. Scientific and management authorities are created to develop a list of endangered species.

Environmental Quality Improvement Act

Every federal agency must follow all environmental regulations. None are exempt from the rules that apply to the private sector.

Estuary Restoration Act

This act develops a national estuary habitat restoration strategy, provides financial assistance, restores threatened areas, and enhances monitoring and research of rivers, streams, and other water bodies.

Federal Facility Compliance Act

All government buildings and facilities must comply with the same controls, rules, and regulations as those for the individuals, business, industry, or local and state governments.

Federal Insecticide, Fungicide, and Rodenticide Act

All pesticides, herbicides, insecticides, fungicides, and rodenticides must be registered with the federal government prior to manufacture and distribution for sale. Provisions include certifying applicators, inspecting factories, labeling products, protecting trade secrets, and requiring scientific reviews.

Federal Land Policy and Management Act

Publicly owned lands are protected against contamination and degradation and management areas are designated and established. Wilderness area studies and resource inventories are required.

Forest and Rangeland Renewable Resources Planning Act

Ecological harmonies are to be maintained by replacing and replanting forests and rangelands. Timber cutting is restricted, and survey, research, and technical assistance is promoted.

Marine Mammal Protection Act

Federal agencies must prevent mammal extinction through cooperative research, planning, observing, and coordinating with commercial fishermen and public agencies of other countries.

Marine Protection, Research, and Sanctuaries Act

Ocean dumping is not allowed without a permit. Only recommended ocean sites can be used.

National Coastal Zone Monitoring Act

A national program is developed to achieve long-term water quality through consistently monitored coastal ecosystems. Uniform indicators are developed to create and continue effective remedial programs.

National Environmental Policy Act

This act establishes comprehensive environmental policies and goals for the United States through studies, reports, and environmental impact statements. Funds are provided for environmental research and education. Cooperation between the different federal agencies is mandated. Any activity on federal land must meet the requirements of this act.

Noise Control Act

Noise emission standards are issued for manufactured products, airplanes, and other vehicles. Product labeling is required.

Occupational Safety and Health Act

Workplace environments are regulated, and air contamination, dust, dirt, machinery safety, and aromatic chemicals are targets.

Ocean Dumping Act

Oceans are protected by zoning for disposal of wastes, sludge, and dredged spoils. Research is promoted.

Oil Pollution Act

Preventing oil spills into oceans and lakes is a major objective. Double-hulled vessels are mandatory for oil transport. Prompt ocean spill cleanups are required.

Organotin Antifouling Paint Control Act

Antifouling paint on vessel hulls are controlled for tin organotin biocide compounds. This kind of paint must be certified safe by the EPA prior to use to avoid toxic exposures to marine and freshwater organisms at very low levels.

Outer Continental Shelf Lands Act

Offshore oil and gas sources and production are regulated to prevent accidental pollution. Equipment and tools that are used offshore are required to be labeled, color-coded, and stamped.

Pollution Prevention Act

Any kind of pollution must be reduced, wastes must be recycled, and planning prior to releasing wastes is encouraged.

Prevention of Pollution from Ships

Water and waste discharges from ships are regulated. Commercial vessels are inspected, and plastic waste compacting and processing equipment must be installed. "No discharge zones" for cruise vessels are allowed to be designated by the state of Alaska.

Public Vessel Medical Waste Antidumping Act

Shorelines are protected against wash-ups from ocean dumping of medical wastes. Vessel loading and unloading is controlled.

Resource Conservation and Recovery Act

Wastes are listed according to different factors. Requirements are stated about hauling, minimizing, treating, storing, and disposing of solid and liquid wastes. Underground storage tanks are regulated.

Safe Drinking Water Act (in Public Health Service Act)

Surface and underground drinking supplies are protected from contamination using lists of primary and secondary drinking water standards.

Shore Protection Act

Vessels carrying municipal or commercial waste cannot operate in coastal waters without a permit and loading and cleanups of cargo are controlled.

Soil and Water Resources Conservation Act

Agricultural and grazing lands and their waters are protected through soil and water conservation provisions.

Solid Waste Disposal Act

Household, industrial solid (nonhazardous), hazardous, and hazardous medical wastes are regulated. State and regional waste plans and programs are restricted. Medical waste must be tracked. Underground storage tanks are regulated.

Surface Mining Control and Reclamation Act

Open pits, public hazards, and abandoned or existing mines are subjects for control. Coal mining is the primary target, but all mining is controlled. Mining research and reclaiming mines are promoted.

Toxic Substances Control Act

All chemical and biological substances to be sold are controlled through testing, safety procedure requirements, labeling, facility inspections, record keeping, and other regulations.

Wilderness Act

A National Wilderness Preservation System is established to limit the uses for, development of, and machinery usage in wilderness areas.

Section One

The Framework

CHAPTER 1
Introduction:
Understanding Programs and Agencies

Overview

❖ Public environmental policy is created by legislation, regulations, rules, administrative orders, memoranda, acts, and programs.

❖ Many departments of the federal government in addition to the U.S. Environmental Protection Agency (EPA) have environmental program responsibilities.

❖ State and local governments may have obligations or may elect to implement federal environmental regulations.

❖ Regional federal offices are scattered throughout the United States.

❖ Because environmental threats cannot be predicted, our current programs cannot anticipate all of our future needs.

Scope of Protection

The federal government enacts laws about the environment and implements them through regulations, rules, administrative orders, memoranda, acts, and programs.[1] Although not all of these restrictions are precisely defined, they remain the major methods used to implement public environmental policy as developed by the three branches of government (executive, legislative, and judicial).[2] In order to make certain that people follow these laws about the environment, enforcement methods are devised to compel citizens to willingly comply with their intent. At times the threat of police action or legal suits may be all that is necessary, but some programs may require field enforcement and policing.

A number of federal agencies are responsible for regulating the environment; the best known one is the U.S. Environmental Protection Agency. Other examples are the U.S. Department of Justice, which enforces and prosecutes the regulations; the U.S. Department of Commerce, which controls oceans and atmosphere; U.S. Department of Labor, which handles workplace environmental safety; U.S. Coast Guard, which protects and enforces regulations on the seas; and the U.S. Department of Agriculture, which safeguards food and promotes animal safety. In addition to these major federal agencies, there are other agencies and departments at all levels of government (city, county, and state) that regulate the environment. In this book, these other levels of

3

government are discussed only in relation to their responsibilities for federal programs. Many federal environmental regulations are passed down to the states for their implementation. In most instances states may volunteer or elect to take responsibility but must adhere to performance standards estab-

Exhibit 1: Sky, air, ocean, eroded rocks, and seacoast vegetation are just a few elements of this California coast that compose the natural environment. The federal environmental framework of regulations protects these esthetic and wilderness assests. (Photo: author)

lished in the federal regulations or be subject to a federal agency re-assuming program or management.

Most of the federal agencies, such as the U.S. Environmental Protection Agency, have regional offices outside of the Washington D.C. area. These offices may be considered field offices because they are closer to the sites and problems needing federal environmental protection. Each office generally contains community liaison contact persons who serve as conduits for complaints, inquiries, and other matters. They also employ information officers and enforcement officers for each of the EPA's programs and have small libraries with resources concerning the regulations. Regional office duties and responsibilities include working with the appropriate agencies of their region's state and local governments (cities and counties, etc.).

Office Locations of the EPA and States in Each Region[3]

EPA Headquarters
Washington D.C.

Region 1—Boston
Connecticut
Maine
Massachusetts
New Hampshire
Rhode Island
Vermont

Region 2—New York City
New Jersey
New York
Puerto Rico
Virgin Islands

Region 3—Philadelphia
District of Columbia
Delaware
Maryland
Pennsylvania
Virginia
West Virginia

Region 4—Atlanta
Alabama
Florida
Georgia
Kentucky
Mississippi
North Carolina
South Carolina
Tennessee

Region 5—Chicago
Illinois
Indiana
Michigan
Minnesota
Ohio
Wisconsin

Region 6—Dallas
Arkansas
Louisiana
New Mexico
Oklahoma
Texas

Region 7—Kansas City, KS
Iowa
Kansas
Missouri
Nebraska

Region 8—Denver
Colorado
Montana
North Dakota
South Dakota
Utah
Wyoming

Region 9—San Francisco
Arizona
California
Hawaii
Nevada

Region 10—Seattle
Alaska
Idaho
Oregon
Washington

Other significant EPA offices are

National Air and Radiation Environmental Laboratory (NAREL)—Montgomery, Alabama

National Enforcement Investigations Center Laboratory—Denver, Colorado

National Exposure Research Laboratory (NERL), Ecosystems Research Division—Athens, Georgia

National Exposure Research Laboratory (NERL), Environmental Sciences Division—Las Vegas, Nevada

National Exposure Research Laboratory (NERL)—Research Triangle Park, North Carolina

National Health and Environmental Effects Research Laboratory (NHEERL)—Research Triangle Park, North Carolina

National Health and Environmental Effects Research Laboratory (NHEERL), Gulf Ecology Division—Gulf Breeze, Florida

National Health and Environmental Effects Research Laboratory (NHEERL), Mid-continent Ecology Division—Duluth, Minnesota

National Health and Environmental Effects Research Laboratory (NHEERL), Western Ecology Division—Corvallis, Oregon

National Health and Environmental Effects Research Laboratory (NHEERL), Atlantic Ecology Division—Narragansett, Rhode Island

National Risk Management Research Laboratory (NRMRL), Subsurface Protection and Remediation Division—Ada, Oklahoma

National Risk Management Research Laboratory (NRMRL), Water Supply and Resources Division, Urban Watershed Management Branch—Edison, New Jersey

National Risk Management Research Laboratory—Cincinnati, Ohio

National Vehicle and Fuel Emissions Laboratory (NVFEL)—Ann Arbor, Michigan

Radiation and Indoor Environments National Laboratory—Las Vegas, Nevada

The environmental framework has been developed piecemeal by enacting laws that responded to contamination events or that anticipated potential spills and accidents. Many activities with potential environmental consequences have been neither regulated nor ignored but overlooked.[4] As a result, the framework cannot be considered comprehensive. A patchwork structure contains many programs and areas that are well regulated and many that are not. Picture the federal framework of environmental protection as a protective wall containing many solid areas, some holes, and other structurally unsound portions. For some areas of concern, the solid areas function well while in many other areas, the number of holes is alarming. Many future environmental threats have been anticipated; many cannot be predicted. Restricting vehicle emissions can help clean the air, but the methods used may lead to unanticipated contamination. Likewise, chlorine or other chemicals used in water purification may well be identified as problems in the future.

Programs, Laws, Acts, and Regulations

It is difficult to sort out the topics of the enacted laws from the federal acts themselves, or from the lists developed by federal agencies. The targets of the regulations—or *what* is regulated—can be confusing. Certainly, the media carrying pollution is approached or addressed in most of the regulations. Air, water, soils, food, animal, and human paths to pollution are both hard and soft. Hard paths are industrially-produced contamination.[5] Soft paths are people-produced contamination. Each path may well produce half of the total, but the precise amount cannot be pinpointed. Since the federal environmental regulations address both paths even in the same act, it would be difficult to divide any discussion about environmental controls into two distinct categories.

Controls on people and industries are intertwined, and either path affects the other. For example, strict controls are placed on the processing of sewage liquids so that they can meet safe standards and be returned to the streams and lakes. Pesticides are also highly controlled in their packaging and labeling to avoid dangerous human contact. Are these requirements for industry or people?

Air programs

As mandated by the Clean Air Act, air programs control or regulate the release or transmission of contaminants into the air. Noises transmitted through the air are also covered by the Noise Control Act or the Airport Noise Abatement Act. Some programs that were intended for other purposes could also be considered air programs such as programs restricting radioactive releases to the air, which are covered by the Atomic Energy Act, and contaminants emanating from waste storage areas, which are covered by the Solid Waste Disposal Act; the Comprehensive Environmental Response, Compensation, and Liability Act (CERCLA); the Surface Mining Control and Reclamation Act, the Federal Insecticide, Fungicide, and Rodenticide Act; or the Toxic Substances Control Act.

Water programs

These programs control or regulate releases or transmission of contaminants in the water, as explained in the Clean Water Act, Safe Drinking Water Act, and Oil Pollution Act. They may also regulate the containment of wastes, covered by the Solid Waste Disposal and CERCLA Acts; the Federal Land Policy and Management Act; the Surface Mining Control and Reclamation Act; the Forest and Rangeland Renewable Resources Planning Act; the Coastal Zone Management Act; or the Marine Mammal Protection Act.

Waste programs

Waste programs control or regulate the release or transmission of contaminants contained in wastes of all kinds, such as those wastes covered by CERCLA and the Resource Conservation and Recovery Acts (RCRA)[6], and through any media, such as those covered by the Noise Control or Airport Noise Abatement Acts. Some programs that were intended for other purposes could be considered waste programs, such as chemical inventories, which are covered by the Emergency Planning and Community Right-to-Know Act (EPCRA); the Toxic Substances Control Act; the Federal Insecticide, Fungicide, and Rodenticide Act; the Atomic Energy act; the Pollution Prevention Act; and the Surface Mining Control and Reclamation Act.

Other programs

Other programs have been enacted into law to regulate a variety of potential environmental, health, and safety hazards:

❖ Controlling leaks in underground storage tanks (Underground Storage Tank program in RCRA)

❖ Reporting chemical releases (EPCRA)

❖ Maintaining radiation safety or containing atomic energy (Atomic Energy Act)

❖ Securing federal facilities and construction (National Environmental Policy Act)

❖ Optimizing workplace safety (Occupational Safety and Health Act)

❖ Regulating pesticide programs (Federal Insecticide, Fungicide, and Rodenticide Act)

❖ Controlling potentially dangerous chemicals (Toxic Substances Control Act).

In summary, the federal environmental regulation framework controls both the industrial and people paths to pollution (hard and soft paths). It controls a number of programs through acts that cross boundaries of media and subjects of concern. The major programs divided into sections of this book are air, water, wastes and tanks, safety, responding to contaminant releases, and nature and natural resources. Each environmental program and act is presented to provide the scope and structure of the regulations. Methods of enforcement vary and change regularly. Additionally, the roles or emphases of each regulatory agency can vary depending on public policy changes.

CHAPTER 2

Summary Perspectives: Overview of Programs

Overview

❖ The Clean Air Act (CAA) is the primary air regulation. Under the CAA, no one is allowed to contaminate the air in any way. A contaminant list—the National Ambient Air Quality Standards (NAAQS)—is developed and published by the Environmental Protection Agency (EPA) providing ranges of allowable toxicity for certain chemical substances.

❖ The Clean Water Act (CWA) and the Safe Drinking Water Act (SDWA) are the major federal regulations controlling water purity. Surface and groundwater are protected under those acts.

❖ Waste programs are directed at household, hazardous and nonhazardous industrial solids, and hazardous medical wastes.

❖ Safety is promoted in the workplace under the Occupational Safety and Health Act (OSH).

❖ Chemicals are controlled via the Toxic Substances Control Act (TSCA) and their use as pesticides through the Federal Insecticide, Fungicide, and Rodenticide Act (FIFRA).

❖ Land is protected from poor mining and nuclear operational and storage problems.

❖ Nature and natural resources regulations protect wildlife, land, and shorelines.

❖ The Oil Pollution Act (OPA) regulates vessels and facilities to prevent oil spills into the ocean and waters and to promote prompt cleanups.

❖ Readiness programs to respond to spills are promoted in the Emergency Planning and Community Right-to-Know Act (EPCRA) and the Comprehensive Environmental Response, Compensation, and Liability Act (CERCLA)—Superfund.

Environmental Content Areas and Scope of Protection

Different acts, regulations, and controls developed over more than a century target protecting the environment. Keeping the air and water clean have been major priorities that have been handled according to available and known technologies. Protection from dangerous practices in waste storage and disposal are more recent concerns. Newer regulations address human and animal protection from noise, oil spills, ocean dumping, and shore protection.

Safety is another broad category that includes laws and regulations about protection from poor mining practices, workplace threats, pesticide contamination, and nuclear contamination. Widespread media reports have led to extensive regulations requiring special responses to releases of pollutants.

Threats to nature and natural resources are other categories that are addressed in many United States regulations. Wildlife, land, shorelines, wetlands, ecosystem management, aquatic nuisances, and wilderness lands are still other broad areas that are regulated.

List of Acts

Airport Noise Abatement Act

Antarctic Protection Act

Asbestos Hazard Emergency Response Act

Atomic Energy Act

Aquatic Nuisance Prevention and Control Act

Clean Air Act

Clean Water Act (in Federal Water Pollution Control Act)

Coastal Zone Management Act

Coastal Wetlands Planning, Protection, and Restoration Act

Comprehensive Environmental Response, Compensation and Liability Act—
    Superfund

Emergency Planning & Community Right-to-Know Act

Endangered Species Act

Estuary Restoration Act

Environmental Quality Improvement Act

Federal Facility Compliance Act

Federal Insecticide, Fungicide, and Rodenticide Act

Federal Land Policy and Management Act

Forest and Rangeland Renewable Resources Planning Act

Marine Mammal Protection Act

Marine Protection, Research, and Sanctuaries Act

National Coastal Zone Monitoring Act

National Environmental Policy Act

Noise Control Act

Nonindigenous Aquatic Nuisance Prevention and Control Act

Occupational Safety and Health Act

Ocean Dumping Act

Oil Pollution Act

Outer Continental Shelf Lands Act

Organotin Antifouling Paint Control Act

Pollution Prevention Act

Prevention of Pollution from Ships

Public Vessel Medical Waste Antidumping Act

Resource Conservation and Recovery Act

Safe Drinking Water Act (in Public Health Service Act)

Shore Protection Act

Soil and Water Resources Conservation Act

Solid Waste Disposal Act

Surface Mining Control and Reclamation Act

Toxic Substances Control Act

Wilderness Act

Air programs

The primary regulatory device controlling air pollution is the Clean Air Act (CAA). Individuals, businesses, industry, and state and local governments are restricted and prohibited from contaminating the air. Since it was enacted in 1967, the CAA has been amended to become even more strict. Most of the additions to the act require state government involvement. The EPA has directed its Health Effects Laboratory to work with the Centers for Disease Control and Prevention (CDC)[1] to regularly develop sound information for guiding state and local governments in protecting the air. As new scientific information has been discovered, regulations have increased or been modified and the amendments reflect these findings.

Penalties are assessed for violators of the CAA, and fines, prison sentences, and special operating requirements are mandated. A list of contaminants and their ranges of safety are developed and published by the EPA. This list is called the National Ambient Air Quality Standards, or NAAQS. Not only is toxicity a concern, but also visibility, acid rain, lower atmospheric ozone chemical content, and changes in air quality from mobile pollution sources (vehicles) and facilities all pose a threat to the health and safety of air. From time to time the NAAQS list is modified, ranges changed, and chemical and biological agents added or deleted. Each state must develop a state implementation plan (SIP) to ensure that their methods for keeping the air clean meet EPA requirements.

Water programs

The federal government regulates water by developing partnerships with different agencies. As the major regulatory agency for water programs, the EPA devises, develops, and enforces the environmental water laws passed by Congress. At times the EPA delegates specific duties to other agencies.[2] Although the EPA reviews, inspects, and approves the programs and actions of its partner agencies, it maintains field staff in its regional offices to administer many of the water rules and regulations. In some areas of water protection, other federal agencies like the U.S. Army Corps of Engineers, the U.S. Coast Guard, or the U.S. Department of Transportation have responsibilities for protecting water. The EPA allows states to administer many of its water programs under close supervision. States can further delegate water responsibilities to local governments.

The major statutes for water protection are the Safe Drinking Water Act (SDWA) and the Clean Water Act (CWA). In order to prevent or contain water pollution, the Clean Water Act lists the following requirements:[3]

❖ Discharges of chemicals, biological agents, or waste materials are not allowed into surface waters, groundwater, or soils.

❖ Prior to any releases of potential contaminants, individuals or companies must apply for a permit and be approved.

❖ The states can become the regulatory agency for the federal programs, if approved by the EPA.

❖ All limitations devised by the EPA must follow a prescribed method.

❖ The prescribed process must be followed for reporting, responding, and preventing spills.

❖ Any placing or discharging of dredge wastes (from scraping the bottom of water bodies) must adhere to approved permit provisions.

❖ Established enforcement methods must be used for violations.

As can be seen from these provisions, the Clean Water Act attempts to eliminate any discharge of contaminants into water to protect human life, fish, and wildlife.

The EPA has established dirty-substance-in-water standards for specific industries. These national effluent standards are based on the technical ability of an industry to comply considering its ability to continue to operate as an economically-sound industry. To properly administer the effluent standards, a permit system is used called the National Pollution Discharge Elimination System (NPDES). States may administer the permits or allow the EPA to do so. Dredging and filling of waters are regulated, and spills must be reported. Ocean discharges are also regulated. Permits and pretreatment of water are required prior to any discharges.

Special requirements are established for safe drinking water. The EPA regulates public drinking water under the Safe Drinking Water Act (SDWA), which protects people from contaminated or poisoned water by setting national standards for contaminant levels. Acceptable levels of contaminants are set for public drinking water systems, groundwater, and underground injection wells. Standards for drinking water near contaminated and Superfund sites must meet the SDWA requirements; thus, Superfund is tied to the SDWA. The number of contaminants regulated is an ongoing issue. Public health experts always question the cost and benefits of regular testing requirements for some chemicals, some tests for which are quite costly.

Purity of surface waters (rivers, lakes, bays, inlets, and oceans) are controlled by the Oil Pollution Act (OPA). This act is much more comprehensive than any other national or international oil pollution act. OPA attempts to prevent water pollution from oil spills from vessels and facilities by requiring clean up and removal of spilled oil and corporate and personal liability for costs. There are stringent operational requirements to prevent spills. A list of damages are specified that can be imposed on violators. As a result of this act, there have been major changes in the oil production, transportation, and distribution industries.

OPA defines the responsible parties, establishes a standard for measuring natural resource damages, defines financial responsibilities, requires that a fund be established from the five-cent-per-barrel federal tax on oil or petroleum products received at U.S. refineries, and establishes penalties for not complying with the act.

Waste programs

Household and industrial (nonhazardous) wastes are solid wastes. Typically, cities or counties arrange for weekly or twice-weekly household waste collection. They may use private companies or create their own waste collection departments of government. Industrial facilities usually contract directly with a private waste handling company to collect their industrial wastes. Both are regulated by programs developed in the Solid Waste Disposal Act (SWDA). There is more to solid waste environmental protection than meets the eye. Under the SWDA, state and regional solid waste plans that promote materials and energy recovery and conservation must be developed. Each state must consider its different geological, hydrogeological, and climatic circumstances to protect ground and surface waters from landfill contamination. All open dumps must be closed or converted to sanitary landfills. A sanitary landfill must be lined according to detailed engineering standards, include leaching pipes for methane collection and disbursement, and cover its wastes daily with earth cover. Most household wastes in the United States are deposited in sanitary landfills. Waste to energy (burning of household and industrial solid wastes to create electricity or gas) is promoted in the SWDA.[4]

Hazardous wastes, as expected, require much more careful handling. Those companies or persons that generate over 275 tons of hazardous wastes per year; transport hazardous waste; and ownes or operates treatment, storage, and disposal facilities are regulated under the Resource Conservation and Recovery Act of 1976 (RCRA) and its 1984 Amendments.[5] The act contains a number of provisions that prohibit the thoughtless handling and careless permanent storage of hazardous wastes.

Hazardous wastes must be reduced in quantity at their sources, neutralized with high technology equipment, or securely contained in land disposal areas to minimize present and future risks. In order to meet the act's expectations, the following requirements must be met:

❖ Hazardous wastes must be properly stored and managed
❖ State and regional solid waste plans must be developed
❖ Resource and recovery must be provided
❖ Federal responsibilities must be defined
❖ A medical waste tracking program must be implemented
❖ Requirements must be imposed on research, development, demonstration, and information dissemination regulating underground storage tanks

Federal facility compliance programs

Federally-owned facilities, such as military bases, airports, buildings, and munitions storage areas, can be fined by the EPA for violations of any environmental regulations. Prior to the Federal Facility Compliance Act of 1992 (FFCA), facilities owned by the federal government were exempt from the same penalties for polluting as the private sector. This act was created to ensure that the federal government complies with all waste regulations imposed on residents, private landowners, and operators. One federal agency can fine another for wrongdoing.[6] FFCA was an amendment to the Resource Conservation and Recovery Act (RCRA) and a part of the Solid Waste Disposal Act (SWDA). Unlike the RCRA controls for individuals and private companies in transporting, treating, storing, and disposing solid and hazardous wastes, the FFCA regulations relate to federally-owned facilities only. The facilities regulated include landfills, radioactive mixed waste sites, public vessels, waste munitions, and wastewater treatment works.

Toxic substance programs

The Toxic Substances Control Act (TSCA) has been amended since its initial enactment to increase the number of toxic substances controlled. A major objective of this act is to identify and control toxic substances before they can be introduced in the marketplace and affect the environment. In contrast, other federal regulations, such as RCRA, control toxic chemicals after they have been released. Within TSCA, there are four major sections:

1. Control of toxic substances

2. Response to asbestos hazard emergencies

3. Abatement of indoor radon

4. Reduction of exposures to lead

TSCA creates several enforcement tools for use by the EPA. Suspected dangerous chemicals can be identified and tested. The EPA can require the review and testing of any new chemical substances before their introduction. The EPA can also limit or prohibit the manufacture, use, distribution, or disposal of any existing chemical substances. Finally, the EPA can require record keeping and reporting on any new chemical substances and can require export notices and import certification.

Responding to contaminant release programs

The two acts summarized in this section develop environmental programs to respond to contaminant releases. Each requires public notice of risk and preventative action. The first act is the Emergency Planning and Community Right-to-Know Act (EPCRA), which requires states to establish and develop local chemical emergency preparedness programs and disseminate information about the hazardous chemicals located within their communities.[7] This act had been devised to disclose to the public potential risks from accidental chemical spills.[8]

There are four major components to EPCRA:

1. Emergency response planning

2. Emergency chemical release notices

3. Community right-to-know reports

4. Toxic chemical release inventory reports

Each of these four components has special reporting requirements. The requirements for disseminating this information enable states, towns, and cities to understand the potential chemical hazards around them. EPCRA requires the governor of each state to designate a State Emergency Response Commission (SERC) and appoint a local emergency planning committee (LEPC). The commission must designate emergency planning districts within each state to prepare and implement emergency plans. The owner or operator of a facility that produces, uses, or stores a hazardous chemical must notify the SERC and the LEPC immediately when a listed hazardous substance is released and exceeds the reportable quantity (RQ).

Material safety data sheets (MSDSs) must be prepared and available from each owner or operator of a facility storing a listed hazardous material. The MSDSs are required under the Occupational Safety and Health Administration's (OSHA) hazard communication standard regulations. They must be submit-

ted to the SERC, the LEPC, and the local fire department (LFD) having jurisdiction over the facility. Minimum threshold quantities are established by the
EPA for reporting hazardous chemicals at a facility.

Under EPCRA, owners or operators of certain manufacturing facilities
must submit annual reports on the amounts of listed toxic chemicals that are
released from their facilities. These reports must be submitted regardless of
whether the chemical or biological release is an accident or intentional and
routine. All releases to the air, water, or soil must be reported. Discharges
from publicly-owned treatment works (POTWs) and transfers to off-site locations for treatment, storage, or disposal are also required. In order to avoid
violations, any facility subject to reporting requirements under EPCRA must
develop and implement written complaint procedures, response plans, and
information management programs to avoid enforcement actions.

The second act is the Comprehensive Environmental Response, Compensation, and Liability Act (CERCLA) and is known both as CERCLA and as
Superfund.[9] As a primary feature of this act, the EPA receives combined taxes
from the petroleum and chemical industries, general tax revenues, and a specially-levied environmental tax on corporations. While originally established
with these funding mechanisms, the federal government has recently stopped
this taxing system and passed through more funding responsibilities to the
states citizen taxpayers. CERCLA regulates the releases of hazardous substances, provides for compensation for cleanups of hazardous waste spills until
responsible parties are identified, and addresses abandoned hazardous waste
disposal sites not controlled under existing laws.

Superfund is supposed to be used by the EPA to clean up sites before
parties responsible for a spill or release can be identified. Now other procedures are promoted by the EPA to do the same. Even though most EPA actions
under CERCLA relate to hazardous substance dangers, the act requires that
the EPA develop nationwide criteria for priority assignments for releases or
threats of releases. The EPA develops the criteria based on risks to public
health, welfare, and environment. In applying these risk criteria, the EPA
scores and ranks different sites for possible listing on the National Priorities
List (NPL). The NPL is part of the National Contingency Plan (NCP), and the
NCP is the major guide for CERCLA decisions about responses and actions.

The EPA can remove or remediate hazardous wastes. Removal means
that wastes are taken away. Remediate means that dangerous waste sites are
modified, treated, or redesigned to safely contain the wastes. Environmental
emergencies often result in removal of contaminants. Remedial actions are
usually considered to be long-term, permanent cleanups. The EPA recovers
its costs from potentially-responsible parties (PRPs) after the cleanup is done
or, after administrative or judicial proceedings, the EPA may require the PRP
to perform the cleanup.

The chapters that follow describe these programs and many others in greater detail and are necessary to fully understand the federal environmental framework and programs. Each act is discussed within its proper setting, characteristics, program concepts, and with a view to providing a first step toward comprehending the scope of each important regulation. The framework is set for federal environmental regulation.

CHAPTER 3

National Policy:
National Environmental Policy Act (NEPA)

Overview

❖ National Environmental Policy Act (NEPA) establishes comprehensive environmental policies and goals for the United States.

❖ There is a national policy that promotes improving environmental conditions. State and local governments have the primary responsibilities to implement this national policy.

❖ NEPA specifies research and development requirements and budgets.

❖ NEPA creates a national environmental oversight committee, a science advisory board, and an environmental health task force.

❖ NEPA establishes programs, grants, funds, assistance programs, and demonstration projects.

❖ NEPA creates an environmental database of information on geographical areas of concern.

❖ NEPA requires reporting by the Environmental Protection Agency (EPA) to Congress, state, and local governments.

National Environmental Policy Act Acronyms

CEQ—Council on Environmental Quality

EPA—Environmental Protection Agency

EQR—Environmental Quality Report

NEPA—National Environmental Policy Act

NEPA, Need and Background

NEPA promotes safe, healthful, productive, and esthetically and culturally pleasing surroundings without environmental degradation. Prior to this Act, environmental protection was not a national goal nor was it viewed in a comprehensive way. There were a number of independent, somewhat unrelated acts and regulations. There was no responsible federal agency, commission, or consortium that had far-reaching environmental protection duties. Population growth was seen to be a problem because it was accompanied by high-density urbanization, industrial facility expansions, exploitation of natural resources, and expanding technological advances. Since environmental degradation was occurring, there was a need to maintain and restore environmental quality in the United States.

Congress recognized through NEPA that man and nature must safely and productively coexist. All practical means were to be used to improve and coordinate federal plans, functions, programs, and resources. Also, people became responsible for their own share of preserving and enhancing the environment.

NEPA established a Council on Environmental Quality (CEQ) with the needed personnel, experts, consultants, and advisory committees. Also, a Commission on Population Growth and the American Future was also created about the same time NEPA was created. This commission (and the CEQ created under NEPA) conducted and sponsored studies to provide information to all levels of government about problems with population growth and its implications for the future.

Structure and Public Policies

NEPA encourages research and new findings leading to new knowledge of natural resources and ecological systems. State, local, and federal agencies must promote improvements to environmental conditions. Congress declared in the Act that there is a need for a national policy to promote environmental safety and protect public health. By creating a committee called the Council on Environmental Quality (CEQ), the act established a group of environmental advocates with special powers.[1] The duties and functions of the CEQ are as follows:[2]

❖ Assist and advise the president

❖ Prepare the annual report (Environmental Quality Report)

❖ Review and appraise federal programs and activities

❖ Recommend and develop new national policies about the environment

❖ Conduct studies, research, and analyses

❖ Document and define changes in the natural environment; respond to the President if requested

Council members, appointees of the President, have the responsibility to look out for a safe and healthful environmental future on behalf of all citizens. Personnel, experts, and consultants may be engaged by an Office of Environmental Quality to carry out its functions.

Concepts, ideas, and policies promoted by NEPA are quite focused. Nature and man are to live in harmony with regard to influences from population growth, urbanization, industrialization, resource exploitation, and technological advances. NEPA recognizes that there is no reliable method of locating private or public research on environmental issues by geographic location. For this reason, a database is developed to detect trends in environmental quality, to provide information to the public, and to identify areas of critical environmental concern.[3] The federal government must work closely with the state and local governments. Financial and technical assistance is to be provided to relevant groups, companies, and public agencies in order to achieve these goals. All means must be used to improve and coordinate federal plans, functions, programs, and resources and to meet these goals:

1. The responsibilities of one generation cannot be passed on to the next.
2. Healthy, safe, and esthetically pleasing surroundings are to be maintained.
3. The environment can not degraded by unintended consequences.
4. Historical, cultural, and natural features are to be preserved, thus supporting diversity and variety of choice.
5. Population increases must be accompanied by preservation of resources in the interest of achieving higher standards of living and better quality of life.
6. Recycling of vanishing resources is to be encouraged, and the quality of renewable resources must be improved.[4]

In order for our society to reach these goals, each citizen must accept the responsibility to preserve and enhance the environment. All policies, regulations, and laws must respect NEPA, and all agencies of government must follow these agreed-upon practices:

❖ Interdisciplinary approaches from the natural sciences, social sciences, and city and regional planning for the man-built environment

❖ Methods and procedures that are appropriate for environmental decision-making (not only economic and technical considerations)

❖ Statements on the environmental impact, adverse environmental effects that cannot be avoided, alternatives, relationship between short- and long-term impacts of an action, and any irreversible or irretrievable commitments of resources which would be involved in the proposed action should it be implemented. Statements can be developed by the state or federal government. Every major federal action must contain an environmental impact statement. Alternative courses of action must be suggested if there are unresolved conflicts.

Interdepartmental environmental protection

The act requires the participation of different departments and agencies for implementing environmental programs. For example, some pollution emergencies are handled by the EPA with help from the U.S. Coast Guard, and any violations of laws or regulations, contamination events, or related environmental problems are pursued and prosecuted by the EPA Office of Criminal Investigation. A National Enforcement Training Institute is created under NEPA to train environmental lawyers, inspectors, civil and criminal investigators, and technical experts.

Federal Domestic and Foreign Policy

Under NEPA, the global and long-range character of environmental problems must be consistent with federal foreign policy and other national policies. Information about restoring, maintaining, or enhancing the quality of the environment must be made available to states, counties, municipalities, institutions, and individuals. An Environmental Quality Management Fund is established to finance study contracts and federal interagency environmental projects. When resource projects are planned or developed, ecological information must be reviewed carefully, applied, or developed.

All agencies of the federal government are required to conform to the provisions of NEPA.[5] Each year, the President must transmit to Congress an Environmental Quality Report that explains the condition of major natural, manmade, or altered environmental media (air, water, and land). The report to Congress must include trends in the quality, management, and use of these media and the effects of those trends on the social, economic, and physical characteristics of the United States in view of increased population. Finally, the report to Congress has to contain a program to solve the problems of existing programs and activities and enact needed legislation.[6]

Under NEPA, a Citizens Advisory Committee on Environmental Quality is established. This committee has a membership composed of business, industry, science, agriculture, labor, and conservation organizations, state and local governments, and other groups as considered advisable. The role of the Citizens Advisory Committee on Environmental Quality is to consult with the presidential CEQ.

Good Science and Innovative Technology Promoted

Full-scale pollution control technology demonstrations are to be developed, arranged, and implemented by the EPA administrator. Funds from the EPA budget are assigned to research and development as needed by the various program offices for air, water, hazardous materials, pesticides, solid waste, toxic substances, radiation, and noise. A science advisory board is established to give advice as needed to the EPA and other agencies and departments. The science advisory board can use any criteria documents, standards, or regulations of the EPA, and use all of the technical and scientific capabilities of the federal agencies and national environmental laboratories to determine the adequacy of the scientific and technical basis of any proposed criteria. NEPA's science advisory board works closely with the EPA's Scientific Advisory Panel.

The EPA must identify and coordinate environmental research, perform research, and develop and demonstrate activities that may need to be more effectively coordinated to avoid duplication. The agency must determine the steps to be taken under existing law and promote coordination between other public agencies. Older Americans who have relevant experiences and talents are to be engaged in projects of pollution prevention, abatement, and control.[7] Additionally, the EPA must develop any new legislation needed to ensure such coordination between agencies.[8] In providing this new science knowledge as mandated by NEPA, the CEQ consults with the Office of Science and Technology Policy to coordinate research activities and reports to the President and Congress. The EPA is required to review journals or scientific proceedings to develop a database of environmental research articles. This database must be indexed according to geographic location.[9] Reports are to be made available promptly to the House and Senate—particularly two committees: Science, Space, and Technology (House of Representatives) and Environment and Public Works (Senate)—whenever requested.[10]

Chronology of the National Environmental Policy Act (NEPA)

1969, The National Environmental Policy Act of 1969, 42 USC 4321–4370e

1970, NEPA Amendment, Pub. L. 91–190, 42 USC 4321–4347

1975, NEPA Amendment, Pub. L. 94–52

1975, NEPA Amendment, Pub. L. 94–83

1982, NEPA Amendment, Pub. L. 97–258, 4(b)

1995, Certain Commercial Space Launch Activities, Pub. L. 104–88

2000, Necessity of Military Low-Level Flight Training to Protect National Security and Enhance Military Readiness, Pub. L. 106–398, s317

CHAPTER 4

Federal Agency Requirements: Environmental Quality Improvement Act (EQIA)

Overview

- ❖ Every federal agency involved with public works must follow all environmental laws.
- ❖ The President's office provides professional and administrative staff for an Office of Environmental Quality. The Chairman of the Council on Environmental Quality (CEQ) serves as the Director of the Office, and the President appoints a Deputy Director.

Environmental Quality Improvement Act Acronyms

CEQ—Council on Environmental Quality

EPA—Environmental Protection Agency

EQIA—Environmental Quality Improvement Act

OEQ—Office of Environmental Quality

Agency Compliance Is Mandated

In this act, Congress declares that people have caused changes in the environment which affect basic relationships; many of these changes have been negative, and population increases combined with urban concentrations of buildings and facilities contribute directly to polluting and degrading the environment. The purpose of EQIA is to ensure that each federal agency involved with public works (water and sewer supply, treatment, disposal, etc.) follows all environmental laws.[1]

An Office of Environmental Quality is established within the Executive Office of the President whose role is to provide professional and administrative staff for the Office of Environmental Quality (OEQ).[2] A director and deputy director of the Office of Environmental Quality are created along with the powers and charges to engage personnel, experts, and consultants to carry out its functions. State and local governments are given the primary responsibilities to implement this national policy.[3]

The Chairman of the Council on Environmental Quality serves as the Director of the Office of Environmental Quality. A Deputy Director is appointed by the President and serves as a part of the executive branch of government. Experts, consultants, and staff personnel can be engaged as necessary. Functions of the Office are to

❖ Provide professional and administrative staff and support for the CEQ
❖ Assist other agencies in assessing the effectiveness of existing and proposed facilities, programs, policies, and other activities of the federal government
❖ Promote the advancement of environmental scientific knowledge and the use of technology
❖ Coordinate different federal agencies to develop and interrelate environmental standards
❖ Collect, collate, analyze, and interpret data and other information about environmental quality, ecological research, and methods of evaluation

Reports and funding

Each Environmental Quality Report required under the EQIA shall be transmitted to Congress and referred to each standing committee which has jurisdiction over any of the subject matter. An Environmental Quality Management Fund is established to finance studies, contracts, and federal interagency environmental projects.[4]

Chronology of the Environmental Quality Improvement Act (EQIA)

1970, Environmental Quality Improvement Act, 42 USC 4371–4375

1970, Federal Water Pollution Control Act Amendments, Title II of Pub. L. 224

1977, Executive Order 11991 42 FR 26967, 3 CFR, 1977 Comp.

1982, EQIA Amendments, Pub. L. 97-258 4(b) 96 Stat. 1067 (established by NEPA (42 USC 4343).

CHAPTER 5

Preventing Pollution:
Pollution Prevention Act (PPA)

Overview

❖ Prevention is the best way to decrease the potential for pollution.

❖ Pollution must be reduced at its source as much as possible.

❖ Wastes that cannot be recycled must be safely treated.

❖ Incentives to industry are provided by the EPA.

❖ Federal agencies must be open and forthcoming in reporting emissions and disclosing materials by complying with the Community Right-to-Know laws (EPCRA) and all pollution prevention requirements applicable to industries and individuals.

❖ States may receive 50 percent matching grants for technical assistance programs that promote source reduction by business.

❖ The Common Sense Initiative (CSI) involves community participation in helping to create ideas to improve source reduction.

❖ The Excellence in Leadership (XL) program allows industries to meet the regulations through innovative pilot projects.

❖ A National Environmental Performance Partnership System (NEPPS) transfers some of the responsibilities for pollution prevention to the states.

Pollution Prevention Acronyms

CSI—Common Sense Initiative

ELP—Environmental Leadership Program

EPA—Environmental Protection Agency

EPCRA—Community Right-to-Know

NEPPS—National Environmental Performance Partnership System

PIT—Permits Improvement Team

PPA—Pollution Prevention Act

TRI—Toxic Release Inventory

XL—Excellence in Leadership

Preventing Pollution

This act promotes a somewhat new approach for the federal government in protecting health and the environment.[1] PPA recognizes that millions of tons of contaminants are produced and released, and tens of billions of dollars per year are spent to control these releases. Prevention is part of the cure, and preventing pollution is easier than dealing with it later. Changes may save industry money and reduce the cost of raw materials, equipment control systems, and liability costs to workers and residents around industrial facilities. A national objective is promoted to prevent pollution first. Industry is accused of having missed the opportunity to reduce or prevent pollution through changes in production, operations, and the use of less harmful raw materials. If this prevention approach were initiated, then cost savings would occur, environmental protection would increase, and risks to workers and residents around buildings and facilities would decrease. Under this program, strategies are developed by the EPA to encourage industry, public agencies, and citizens groups to innovate, develop, and implement methods to promote the reduction of pollution at its source.[2]

Requirements

Under the PPA, owners and operators must prevent and reduce pollution at its source whenever feasible. Pollution that cannot be prevented or wastes that cannot be recycled must be safely treated. Premeditated disposal or release into the environment may be used only as a last resort. The EPA maintains a separate office to review and advise their single-medium program offices on how to promote this multimedia approach. Strategies to prevent pollution include

❖ Establishing standard methods of measuring source reduction

❖ Considering changes to existing environmental regulations

❖ Coordinating source reduction efforts at the EPA and other federal offices

❖ Helping businesses adopt source reduction methods

❖ Identifying measurable pollution prevention goals

❖ Establishing technical advisory panels

❖ Developing training programs

❖ Appointing inspection officials

❖ Reducing barriers to adopting source reduction methods

❖ Developing waste auditing procedures

❖ Establishing a Source Reduction Clearinghouse to serve as an information center for different approaches

❖ Establishing an annual award program that recognizes companies that are successful and innovative in source reduction.[3]

EPA Support to Owners, Operators, and States

States may be awarded matching fund grants from the EPA for their technical assistance programs that promote the use of source reduction programs by business.[4] Owners or operators of facilities that are required to file an annual toxic chemical release form must include a source reduction and recycling report. The Environmental Leadership Program (ELP) of the EPA encourages companies to adopt source reduction efforts. National risk reduction goals are stated in the ELP materials; corporations are asked to voluntarily develop their own "Corporate Statement of Environmental Principles." Public recognition of source reduction is promoted by the ELP's "Model Facility Program." This program is open to all facilities that develop Corporate Statements of Environmental Principles and submit data confirming their reduction of sources as listed in the toxic release inventory (TRI).

A Source Reduction Clearinghouse is established with this function: compile information in a computer data base about management, technical, and operational approaches to source reduction. The EPA operates the Clearinghouse to become a center for source reduction technology transfer; to outreach and educate through the states to further the adoption of source reduction methods and technological innovations; and to collect and compile information reported by those states receiving grants under the EPA's technical assistance programs.

Source reduction reporting

Each owner/operator of a facility that is required to file an annual toxic chemical release form must include a Source Reduction and Recycling report for all toxic chemicals. Each chemical must be separately reported. The report must state the annual quantities entering any waste stream or released into the environment prior to recycling, treatment, or disposal; the amount of the chemical recycled on site or elsewhere during that year; and the specific source reduction practices used for that chemical during that year (equipment, technology, process, or procedure modifications; reformulating or redesign of products; substitution of raw materials; improvement in managing, training, inventory controls, materials handling, or other operational phases of industrial facilities).

CSI, XL, and NEPPS programs

There are other ways that EPA supports pollution prevention. One is the Common Sense Initiative (CSI), which differs from the pollutant-by-pollutant approach. It protects the environment by focusing on industries rather than the pollutants themselves. The first phase of the CSI is targeted to six industries:

❖ Automobiles

❖ Electronics

❖ Iron and steel

❖ Metals (plating and finishing)

❖ Oil

❖ Printing

This approach assembles community residents, industry executives, and state and local officials to work together to improve source reduction. The EPA has yet another program called Regulatory Reinvention. As a part of the effort to reinvent government, the Excellence in Leadership (XL) program is created to enable industries to meet regulatory requirements through pilot projects, source reduction, and otherwise technologically innovative approaches. For example, a Permits Improvement Team (PIT) spearheads a process for obtaining public opinions, using performance-based standards, submitting data, and streamlining permitting methods by issuing group permits and granting minor (de minimis) exemptions.

In transferring some of the responsibilities for pollution prevention to the states, a National Environmental Performance Partnership System (NEPPS) has been established. Annual agreements are negotiated between a state and the EPA regional office to establish the state's goals and indicators for environmental protection.[5]

Chronology of Pollution Prevention Act (PPA)

1990: Pollution Prevention Act, 42 USC 13101–13109

Section Two

Air

CHAPTER 6

Air Pollution:
Clean Air Act (CAA)

Overview

❖ A permit is required for any building or facility that can release contaminants into the air.

❖ Many duties are delegated to the states, such as creating regional air quality plans called state implementation plans (SIPs).

❖ The Act divides concerns into two potential sources of pollution: mobile and stationary.

❖ There are both national primary and national secondary air quality standards.

❖ Lists of contaminants are developed that become the National Ambient Air Quality Standards (NAAQS).

❖ Permits are required for all existing and new stationary sources of potential pollution.

❖ A nonattainment area is one that does not meet the NAAQS for a particular contaminant.

❖ Regulated chemicals and compounds are ground level and stratospheric ozone, NO_x, VOC, lead, PM-10, PM-2.5.

❖ There is a national goal to eliminate any cause of impaired visibility.

❖ Upper stratospheric ozone is protected by phasing out certain chemical substances (a global issue).

❖ Lower stratospheric ozone (ground level breathable ozone) is considered a national problem related to motor vehicle exhausts and other factors.

❖ Motor vehicle requirements are strict; lower emissions are promoted in the CAA.

❖ Industrial facilities may buy, sell, or trade portions of their emissions as a method to stimulate overall air emission reductions.

❖ Hazardous air, poisonous air, and reduced visibility are other areas of concern regulated by the CAA.

Clean Air Act Acronyms

AQRVs—Air quality related values

BACM—Best available control measures

BACT—Best available control technology

BART—Best available retrofit technology

CAA—Clean Air Act

CAMS—Continuous air monitoring system

CFC—Chlorofluorocarbon

CO—Carbon monoxide

CTGs—Control technique guidelines

CWA—Clean Water Act

DOJ—Department of Justice

DOT—U.S. Department of Transportation

EPA—Environmental Protection Agency

FIP—Federal Implementation Plan for a state

HCFC—Hydroclorofluorocarbon

HOV—High occupancy vehicle

LAER—Lowest achievable emission rate

LEV—Low Emission Vehicle Program, or national LEV

MACT—Maximum achievable control technology

MWe—Megawatts of potential electric output capacity

NAAQs—National Ambient Air Quality Standards

NASA—National Aeronautics and Space Administration

NCA—Noise Control Act

NOAA—National Oceanic and Atmospheric Administration

NO_x—Nitrogen oxides

NSPS—New source performance standards

PM—Particulate matter

PSD—Prevention of significant deterioration

RACT—Reasonably available control technology

SIP—State Implementation Plan

Regulating Air

The major regulation protecting air quality in the United States is the Clean Air Act (CAA).[1] It controls air emissions by requiring individuals, businesses, industries, and government agencies to avoid, reduce, or eliminate air contamination from areas, facilities, and stationary and mobile sources. Its goal is to prohibit any kind of air contamination.[2] New scientific information about the air has been periodically added to the regulations, and many changes, additions, amendments, and new provisions have been made over the three decades that the CAA has been in effect. Particular concerns have been the failure to confront problems of acid rain, ozone, and other toxic agents. Since the CAA was first enacted, it increased each state's responsibilities for the federal clean air requirements.[3] Every three years, the EPA prepares and transmits a comprehensive report to Congress on the measures to reduce pollutants and sources taken by the Agency and the states.

Exhibit 2: Smoke stacks from industrial facilities, process lines, and buildings spew visible and invisible emissions. The visible smoke from the left stack may be harmful or harmless; however, air regulations require that any emission must be approved by the government.

Sources of Air Contaminants

Regardless of the source of the air contaminant—government, industry, or a single individual—strict penalties are assessed for violations. Sources are classified as stationary or mobile, and both are subject to the requirements of the CAA.

Stationary Source. A stationary source is any source of an air pollutant except those emissions of an internal combustion engine for transportation purposes or from a non-road engine or vehicle. This means that buildings, structures, equipment, installations, or substance-emitting activities all belong to a single industrial classification. A stationary source operates on one or more contiguous properties under the control of one owner or operator.

Mobile Source. A mobile source is any other source, including a stationary source used for storage related to transportation.[4] Naturally-occurring hydrocarbon reservoirs are not included.[5] Violators are prosecuted with fines or prison sentences, or their facilities are placed under special operating restrictions.

Major source. A major source of hazardous air pollutants is "any single source (or group of stationary sources located within a contiguous area) that emits or has the potential to emit, at least ten tons per year of any combination of hazardous air."[6] The major source must have single ownership and the owner or operator must demonstrate technical methods to reduce the facility's pollution potential.

Exhibit 3: Careful thought and engineering are required prior to constructing a chemical (or other) manufacturing facility. Provisions of the Clean Air Act require that a permit application include details of backup systems, methods of scrubbing gases prior to venting to the air, design and as-built drawings of mechanical equipment, valves, connections, and process flow.

Maximum Achievable Emissions Limitations and Other Protection Programs

Standards are established by EPA for the maximum degree of technical reductions that can be achieved according to economic situations, energy consumption, and environmental factors. The limitations are called the maximum achievable control technology (MACT). Standards are based on the best technology currently available for the particular source category or for the best performing group of sources. There is a minimum level for existing source MACT in terms of the arithmetic mean of the best performing 12 percent of sources in the same category when there are 30 or more sources in that category—or the best performing five sources if there are fewer than 30 sources in that category. The MACT standards have these industrial source categories:

❖ Aerospace manufacturing

❖ Agricultural chemicals production

❖ Aluminum production

❖ Coke ovens

❖ Ferroalloys production

❖ Gasoline terminals and pipeline breakout stations

❖ Halogenated solvent cleaning

❖ Industrial cooling towers

❖ Magnetic tape manufacturing operations

❖ Oil and natural gas production

❖ Petroleum refinery sources

❖ Pharmaceutical production

❖ Polymer and resin production

❖ Printing and publishing

❖ Resin, polymer, and inorganic chemical production

❖ Steel foundries

❖ Wood furniture manufacturing

If a source has been voluntarily reduced by 90 percent or more in emissions before the MACT standard had been implemented, that source may be eligible to extend the compliance deadline. Case-specific MACT standards may be established for a source category if the EPA fails to establish a federal standard.[7] Coke ovens are not required to achieve emission limitations until January 2020, but by January 2007, coke ovens that are rebuilt or replaced must be more stringent in their air controls than they are now. The EPA must perform risk assessments to determine the appropriate levels and emission standards.

Prevention of significant deterioration program [8]

The PSD program protects national parks, wilderness areas, monuments, seashores, and other areas of special national or regional natural, recreational, scenic, or historic value from any air pollution or exposure to media affecting NAAQS. It preserves, protects, and enhances air quality. Economic Impact Analyses are required to include a cost-benefit analysis for a criteria air pollutant; hazardous air pollutant; emissions from mobile sources; or limitations for emissions of sulfur dioxide, nitrogen oxide, or any ozone-depleting substance. Before a major new source of potential air contamination can be constructed in an attainment area, a permit must be obtained.[9] This PSD program requires that the owner or operator explain

❖ How the source will comply with national ambient air quality levels

❖ How it will prevent adverse impacts on federally classified areas, such as national wilderness areas or national parks greater than 5,000 acres[10]

❖ How it will use the best available control technology (BACT) for each pollutant that it will emit

BACT is the maximum amount of emission reductions possible considering economics, energy needed to reduce the emissions, and the facility location. A BACT review is applied to any regulated pollutant from a source that could be emitted in a significant amount under the PSD rules.[11] In most all instances the BACT is as strict as an applicable new source performance standard (NSPS) for that source.

In most instances, the amount of allowable deterioration (PSD) that a new source can consume and the allowable BACT are state responsibilities. The EPA allows states which have developed PSD permitting programs as part of their SIPs to determine the BACT with broad discretion. For this reason and many others, BACT is often quite controversial. If the source is located near a national park or other classified area, then the BACT must address how it will adversely impact the air quality related values (AQRVs) for that area. Federal land managers must receive pre-application notices for any source proposed within 60 miles of such classified areas.

Risk identification program

Because the MACT standards are based on technology, public health is protected by identifying the risks of the technology used. A risk identification program sets priorities for regulating hazardous air pollutants in different source categories and geographic areas.[12] Public access to information about off-site consequences must be made available. Risk management plans should contain information about off-site worst-case release scenarios or alternative release scenarios.

Accidental release controls

Regulated hazardous pollutants and extremely hazardous substances are a major concern. Owners and operators must prepare risk management plans for each substance that could accidentally be emitted from a facility into the air. Annual audits and safety inspections may be required by the EPA to help prevent leaks and accidents.[13]

Acid rain controls

Sulfur dioxide (SO_2) and nitrogen oxides (NO_x) are regulated to decrease the potential for creating acid rain. To prevent acid rain, emission allowances and trading programs for SO_2 are established with tracking, trading, monitoring, excess emissions penalties, offset plans, and an administrative appeals process. An allowance may be granted to emit one ton of SO_2. Facilities may not emit more than the allocated, purchased, or traded allowances for a given calendar year. If a facility exceeds this amount, then the unit's owners or operators will be subject to penalties. Eligible parties can purchase, trade, or receive a pro rata share of the money collected. NO_x emission rates are tied to categories of coal-fired electric utility boilers with a second set of NO_x emission standards applied to the remaining categories of boilers.

The acid rain program uses a new system which gives market allowances to electric utilities. The EPA holds yearly auctions of allowances for a small part of the annually allocated allowances. Private parties can also offer their allowances for sale in the EPA auctions.[14]

Visibility protection and air quality

As a national goal, the CAA attempts to eliminate any manmade visibility impairment in Class I areas, including international parks, national wilderness areas above 5,000 acres, national memorial parks above 5,000 acres, and national parks exceeding 6,000 acres. All areas in a state that are not established as Class I are Class II areas.

To accomplish this goal, the states must develop their own requirements to apply the best available retrofit technology (BART) and other strategies as part of the state implementation plan process. There are federal SIP criteria for improving visibility and eliminating visible plumes.[15] Visibility is also one of the criteria applied under the prevention of significant deterioration (PSD) permit program.[16] The U.S. Forest Service and the National Park Service guide local Federal Land Managers in deciding whether proposed new sources would have an adverse impact on the air quality-related values (AQRVs).

The PSD program protects these and any other areas from any air pollution or from exposure to other media affecting NAAQS. It preserves, protects, and enhances air quality in national parks, wilderness areas, monuments, seashores, and other areas of special national or regional natural, recreational, scenic, or historic value.

Fuels, Additives, and Mobile Sources of Emissions

Vehicle fuels and their additives are regulated. If there is a potential for emission of an ozone-depleting substance or sulfur dioxide, nitrogen oxide, criteria air pollutants, hazardous air pollutant, or an emission from mobile sources, then a cost-benefit analysis must be performed and submitted to the EPA.

Certainly, poor air quality has been unequivocally connected to motor vehicles—automobiles, buses, and trucks. These sources and others are mobile sources of air contamination. Beginning in 2003, automobile manufacturers are required to reduce the amount of tailpipe emissions by 50 percent (from 1993). For the model years beginning 2003, light-duty vehicles and light-duty trucks with a loaded weight of 3,750 pounds or less must meet more stringent emissions standards than now. Also, vehicle fuels and fuel additives are regulated. Guidelines for emission standards are called control technique guidelines (CTGs). A federal implementation plan may be developed. A 30-day minimum is required for public participation prior to the EPA enacting any mobile source emissions' regulation. An economic impact analysis, under the CAA, must include a cost-benefit analysis (considering the health, safety, and welfare of residents; economy; and environment) which considers these items:

Exhibit 4: There are exposed stacks, pipes, equipment, and vents in every city, suburb, and small town in the United States. Owners and operators must bear extra costs to comply with environmental regulations.

❖ Criteria or hazardous air pollutants

❖ Any technology-based standard

❖ Any risk-based standard for either category of pollutants

❖ Emissions from mobile sources

❖ Limitations for emissions of sulfur dioxide or nitrogen oxide

❖ Limitations on the production of any ozone-depleting substance

One new program aimed at reducing air pollution from new motor vehicle engines is the National Low Emission Vehicle Program (called "National

LEV").[17] As a voluntary program to reduce air emissions, motor vehicle manufacturers and the northeastern states can commit to meeting tailpipe standards that are more stringent than the EPA mandates.[18] Heavy-duty trucks and motorcycles are treated the same as automobiles and SUVs; they may not exceed 4.0 grams per brake horsepower hour (gbh) of NO_x from gasoline and diesel-fueled heavy-duty trucks. Refueling onboard vapor recovery systems are required. The major emission control components of trucks and light-duty vehicles and engines shall be eight years or 80,000 miles of use, whichever comes first. At any time, the EPA can determine and require further emissions reductions.

A reformulated fuel program requires using blended gasoline in certain carbon monoxide and ozone nonattainment areas to reduce volatile organic compounds (VOCs) and toxic exhaust emissions.[19] Another clean fuel vehicle program uses alternative fuels such as methanol, ethanol, natural gas, and reformulated gasoline. This program has a California pilot program to produce and sell 300,000 clean fuel vehicles. The plan requires the use of clean fuel vehicles by any operator of ten or more vehicles in carbon monoxide and ozone nonattainment areas. Both a registration system and extensive testing of fuels and additives are required to determine health risks. The clean fuels program supports conventional emission control technology to obtain the required emission reductions.[20]

Another program provides information about methods to reduce or control transportation-related pollutants in the interest of decreasing these sources that influence human health. The methods to reduce or control pollution include

❖ Improved mass transit systems
❖ Bus and High Occupancy Vehicle (HOV) lanes
❖ Employer transportation management plans and incentives
❖ Trip-reduction ordinances
❖ Traffic flow improvement programs to achieve emission reductions
❖ Fringe and transportation corridor parking facilities serving multiple occupancy vehicle programs or transit service
❖ Programs to restrict vehicle use in downtowns during peak times
❖ Programs to provide all kinds of high-occupancy and shared ride services
❖ Programs to restrict portions of road surfaces to non-motorized vehicles or pedestrian use
❖ Bicycle storage facilities and lanes
❖ Programs to reduce extended vehicle idling
❖ Programs to reduce vehicle emissions caused by extreme cold start conditions

❖ Programs to permit flexible work schedules by employer sponsorship

❖ Mass transportation planning and ordinances for new shopping centers, special events and other centers of vehicle activity

❖ Programs for new construction and reconstruction of paths and tracks for pedestrian and non-motorized transportation

Another important program is the Pilot Design Program, which is used in five metropolitan areas and administered by DOT with funding from the Related Agencies' Appropriations Act (2000). Each program is developed according to recommendations by the National Telecommuting and Air Quality Steering Committee and local design teams are to promote protocol development in the five metro areas; advertise telecommuting, emissions reduction, and pollution credits strategies; recruit employers; and gather data on emissions reductions. Grants are awarded.

Exhibit 5: This aerial view of a refinery shows the large land area and typical arrangement of tanks and other facilities. Many oil and chemical refineries are surrounded by buildings and large populations. For this reason, environmental protection is warranted.

Acid in the air

Acidic compounds and their ingredients in the atmosphere are a threat to all media (water, soils, wildlife, food) natural resources, ecosystems, materials, and visibility. Most acid sources originate from the combustion of fossil fuels and form sulfur and nitrogen oxides.[21]

Utility companies can be sources releasing acidic compounds and ingredients. Each existing utility unit (an electric power generating facility) is subject to an annual sulfur dioxide tonnage emission limitation. With a base year of 1985, the allowable annual sulfur dioxide tonnage limitation is increased as bonuses. Coal and oil-fired units are controlled, too, for utility units. Phase II sulfur dioxide requirements are increased from 2000 to 2009, with the EPA allowing up to 530,000 more annual tons under Phase II bonus allowances. In addition to these Phase II and bonus allocation allowances, another bonus of 50,000 annual tons may be multiplied by the unit's pro rata share of the total number of basic allowances allocated for all units located in the states of Illinois, Indiana, Ohio, Georgia, Alabama, Missouri, Pennsylvania, West Virginia, Kentucky, and Tennessee.[22] Electricity-generating coal- or oil-fire facilities that produce below 75 MWe (megawatts of potential electric output capacity) and above 1.2 lbs/mmBtu (million British thermal units, a measurement of energy) cannot exceed a unit baseline formula multiplied by an emission rate.[23]

Beginning in 2000 through 2009, the overall amount of emissions must be reduced each year. For specific units started after 1986 and 1995, there are different reduction requirements. Also, units that are coal- or oil-fired have different allowances. For nitrogen oxides (NO_x), emission reduction program limitations apply to coal-fired utility units. There are emission limitations, revised performance standards, alternative emission limitations, and emissions-averaging between two or more units.

First and second phase permit applications and applications for permits for new units must contain a compliance plan. For units owned by multiple owners, a certificate of representation must be filed by an owner regarding the holding and distribution of allowances and the proceeds of transactions involving allowances. Any permits that could affect air in contiguous states trigger a requirement to notify all states whose air quality may be affected within 50 miles of that source.

Ozone*

Ozone, an air contaminant that is harmful to public health, is a pale blue, relatively unstable molecule composed of three oxygen atoms. The ozone molecule is angular, polar, and diamagnetic. Both oxygen bond lengths (1.28 angstroms) are identical. It is formed from molecular oxygen (O_2) by ultraviolet and extreme ultraviolet decomposition followed by recombining atomic oxygen (O) with O_2. It may also be formed without ultraviolet stimulation by passing an electrical discharge through gaseous oxygen. Ozone has a unique odor that is often noticed during electrical storms or around electrical transformers or power lines. The density of ozone is about 2.5 times that of O_2. At

---

* The following material on ozone is taken from the following NASA website: http://daac.gsfc.nasa.gov/campaign_docs/ATM_chem./ozone_atmosphere.html. 6/14/2002.

-112 degrees C it condenses to a deep blue liquid. It is a powerful oxidizing agent and, as a concentrated gas or a liquid, is highly explosive. Concentrations of ozone are located in both the lower and upper atmosphere.

The ozone layer is located at an altitude between 12 and 18 miles from the surface of the earth. Approximately 90 percent of the ozone in the atmosphere resides here (the stratosphere). Ozone in the stratosphere is concentrated about 50 times greater than the ozone located in the lower atmosphere close to earth.[24] Stratospheric ozone absorbs the bulk of solar ultraviolet radiation, or wavelength, in the upper atmosphere.[25] These wavelengths are harmful to life because they can be absorbed by the nucleic acid in cells. Without this blocking of wavelengths, ultraviolet radiation would reach earth's surface and damage animal, marine, and plant life and have devastating environmental effects. For example, a large amount of solar ultraviolet radiation could result in a dramatic increase in cancers of many types. Upper atmospheric ozone, therefore, is helpful, not harmful.

In contrast, lower atmospheric ozone is the layer of atmosphere closest to earth which contains the highest total atmospheric mass. The more ozone here, the more harm. We breathe it. In this lower area, ozone can damage lungs and is harmful, not helpful. Ozone is also a photochemical oxidant that mixes with other air contaminants and damages rubber, plastic, vegetation, and animal life. In many major metropolitan areas, ozone reacts with hydrocarbons from vehicle emissions to form secondary organic pollutants.[26] Some ozone-nitrogen compounds are eye and throat irritants.[27] Elevated ozone concentrations are between 30 and 50 parts per billion by volume with measurements made of concentrations three to eight times greater than natural background levels.

Ozone pollution shifts with weather changes. Rural and open spaces hundreds of miles away from those metropolitan areas producing the most ozone-related pollution can be affected. Forests may be stressed and foliage killed. During summer heat waves, record ozone concentrations have been recorded in Acadia National Park, the Smoky Mountains, and the Shenandoah Mountains. These rural areas are far removed from industrial regions and polluted cities. The ozone pollution recorded in Acadia most likely originated in New York City. The ozone pollution in Virginia may have migrated from refineries on the Gulf Coast.

Agriculture is affected by lower atmospheric ozone concentrations as well. Crops are lost. The most significant cause of agricultural loss in the United States is photochemical oxidants; their damaging effects on vegetation and crops have been confirmed in the eastern United States, areas in Canada, and much of Europe. Ozone alone or in combination with sulfur dioxide (SO_2) and nitrogen dioxide (NO_2) accounts for 90 percent of the annual crop losses in the U.S. that are caused by air pollution.

Lower atmospheric ozone

Lower atmospheric ozone is regulated through both mandatory and voluntary requirements. An ozone nonattainment area is an area within a geographic boundary that reaches high levels of ozone for certain time periods. A high level of ozone ranges anywhere from 0.121 to 0.280 parts per million and over. Marginal, moderate, serious, severe, and extreme are the broad classifications and nomenclature for ozone nonattainment areas.[28]

Stratospheric ozone protection

There are two classes of substances: I, chlorofluorocarbons (CFCs), halons, carbon tetrachloride, methyl chloroform; and II, hydrochlorofluorocarbons. Each depletes the upper atmospheric ozone and potentially increases global warming. Anyone who produces, imports, or exports Class I or II substances must file a report with the EPA. Phaseout of the production and consumption of Class I substances was set for 2001, but use in medical devices and aviation safety devices is still allowed. Manufacture, production, or sale of any Class I substance in quantities greater than the annual limits specified by the EPA is prohibited. In Title VI of the CAA, global warming and ozone depletion are handled through a program that phases out ozone depleting substances.

Exceptions are made for the production of medical substances and aviation substances used for aircraft safety. Beginning in 2000 (and 2002 for methyl chloroform), all Class I substance production is banned. In addition, there are strict regulations about the safe use, disposal, release, and recycling of Class I and II substances from appliances, industrial refrigeration, motor vehicle servicing, and nonessential products and the labeling of products made with Class I and II substances. A trading system is allowed for substitutions of these materials.[29] By 2015, production and consumption of Class II substances must be stopped. By 2020, the use of refrigerants of this class in appliances manufactured prior to 2020 must be ended. Production allowances are allowed for interpollutant transfers by 2020 on an ozone-depletion, weighted basis.

A safe alternative policy must be developed for Class I and II substances which replaces chemicals, product substitutes, or alternative manufacturing processes to reduce overall risks to human health and the environment. Technology status reports about developing alternative systems or products needed to manufacture and operate appliances without Class II substances are due in 2015. The EPA can give transfer allowances of Class I and II substances to other parties. CAA is obligated to terms and conditions of the Montreal Protocol. The EPA, NASA, and NOAA can determine together that the global production, consumption, and use of Class II substances are contributing to atmospheric chlorine loading in excess of the projections noted in the Montreal Protocol. By 2015, no person can introduce any Class II substance into interstate commerce unless it has been used, reconverted, and recycled; used and entirely consumed (except for trace quantities) in the production of other chemicals; or used as a refrigerant in appliances manufactured prior to January 2020. Also, by 2015 no owner or operator can produce any Class II substance in an annual quantity greater than the quantity of the substance produced during the baseline year.

Air Emission Standards

The EPA is required to establish hazardous air pollutant emission standards for different kinds of sources. Maximum amounts of emission reductions are required. Methods that may be used include reductions in volume; total elimination; manufacturing processes to eliminate, collect, or capture treatment when released from a process, stack, storage or fugitive emissions point; or creating new design standards. Both existing and new sources must be reduced according to averages developed by the best-performing 12 percent of existing sources.

Existing and new sources of possible air contamination are regulated through a number of devices. A list of contaminants and their ranges of safety are developed and published by the EPA. This list is called the National Ambient Air Quality Standards (NAAQS). From time to time the list is modified, ranges changed, and chemi-

Exhibit 6: A new addition to a facility may include new storage tanks, pipes, valves, and other connectors. Each addition has the potential to modify a process that had been previously approved in a permit.

cal and biological agents added or deleted. For this reason, interested persons must keep informed about the NAAQS.[31] For example, explosives were recently deleted from the list of regulated substances, and gasoline used as fuel and in naturally-occurring hydrocarbon mixtures prior to industrial processing were deleted.[32] If an agent or compound from the list can be identified for a source, there is a chance for such a contaminant to be released. Thus, the source is subject to federal regulation.

Meeting the National Ambient Air Quality Standards (NAAQs)

Ambient air is the composition of specific pollutants measured at one location and time.[33] The primary NAAQSs are meant to protect public health, and the secondary NAAQSs are established to protect the public welfare. There are difficulties in establishing these factors of safety because people, animals, birds, fish, and plant life differ so much within each species. A small amount of one air contaminant can greatly affect one person but not another. Six pollutants are identified in the NAAQS: sulfur dioxide (SO_2), nitrogen oxides (NO_x), particulate matter,[34] carbon monoxide (CO), ozone, and lead (Pb). Pollutants that must meet national standards (NAAQS) are ozone, carbon monoxide, and particulate matter PM-10.

Nonattainment areas

A location or region that does not meet NAAQS for a pollutant is a nonattainment area for that pollutant. For example, the most common ozone nonattainment areas are metropolitan areas. Lower atmospheric ozone caused by automobile emissions and stagnant air devoid of major breezes, air inversions, or other releases of contaminants from major industrial facilities increases ozone concentrations. Any EPA-designated ozone nonattainment area must meet specific requirements:

❖ All reasonable available control measures for stationary sources must be adopted (with a minimum of reasonably available control technology [RACT] for existing sources).[35]

❖ There must be annual incremental reductions for the emissions of nonattainment pollutants.

❖ An inventory must be developed of current emissions in the area.

❖ Permits must be modified for new and other major stationary sources.

❖ Any new emissions must be quantified to help create an emissions budget for each nonattainment area.

❖ Automatic implementation measures must be indicated in the State Implementation Plans (SIPs).

❖ Contingency actions must be specified if the area fails to make reasonable progress to attain NAAQS by the stated date.

❖ Other techniques like modeling, inventorying, and planning may be allowed by EPA.[36]

Ozone nonattainment areas can be marginal, moderate, serious, severe, or extreme. Marginal areas had been required to meet ozone NAAQS by 1993; moderate areas had to meet them by 1996, and serious areas by 1999. Severe areas must meet ozone NAAQS by 2005, and extreme areas such as California by 2010. For both moderate and serious areas, each state must submit its SIP provisions containing items related to vehicle miles traveled and oxygenated gasoline controlled by commerce. Milestones must be demonstrated and achieved by each state for serious areas.

Carbon monoxide (CO) nonattainment areas are moderate or serious. Moderate areas had to meet the NAAQS by 1995 and serious areas by 2000. Particulate matter (PM-10) nonattainment areas are moderate only and had to meet NAAQS by 1994. NAAQs for CO must be met in the SIP for serious areas by reducing the total emissions tonnage of CO by at least five percent per year. PM-10 must be reduced by RACM (reasonably available control measures) and BACM (best available control measures). New air monitoring data is to be collected for PM-2.5. SIPs must be submitted to EPA by states if there are any areas designated as nonattainment with respect to NAAQs.

Some releases are exempt from the notification requirements of reportable quantities. For example, releases of radionuclides that naturally occur in the soil on large tracts of land like golf courses or parks are exempt. Releases from land disturbances from farming, construction, or mining extraction are not reportable although there are some exceptions.[37] Reports to EPA must be made for uranium, phosphate, tin, zircon, hafnium, vanadium, monazite, and rare earth mines. Dumping and transporting coal and fly ash, bottom ash, and boiler slags also are excluded.

While the EPA has been lenient with many metropolitan areas that have been nonattainment areas in the past, there is good reason to believe that the EPA will begin to apply even greater compliance pressures on state and local governments. Now, however, the CAA does not infringe upon the existing authority of counties or cities to plan or control land use. The EPA has an important role in promoting consistent state and local government air quality. Without a uniform system of standards, there could be increased costs to companies, consumers, and government agencies. For example, myriad requirements could be crippling to manufacturers who would be required to adjust their production machinery throughout the country according to different ordinances or regulations. Promoting clean air by encouraging state and local governments to adopt national standards helps everyone in the long run.

Before new major stationary sources (or major modifications) are constructed, a nonattainment permit must be granted. Both prevention of significant deterioration (PSD) and nonattainment permits may be required for areas that can be considered attainment for some regulated pollutants and nonattainment for others.[38] States administer the nonattainment permit program. Major new or modified existing sources must commit to achieving the lowest achievable emission rate (LAER). This rate is the most stringent emission limit contained in a state implementation plan or one that is achieved in practice by the same or similar source category. A state's permit program must require that offsets of potential nonattainment pollutants be secured from nearby facilities. The EPA can determine baseline emission levels against which any offset credits are issued.[39] Offset ratios are set for ozone, carbon monoxide, and particulate material nonattainment areas.

States may enter into joint planning for nonattainment areas that cross borders. Each state has to submit its SIP for national primary and secondary ambient air quality standards to the EPA. The SIP should contain the content of the plan, any revisions, new sources, indirect source review program, and supplemental or intermittent control systems. An owner or operator of a new or modified major stationary source can comply only by reducing the emissions from the same or other sources in the same nonattainment area; however, a state may allow the owner or operator to have a compensatory emission reduction in another nonattainment area. Any person can propose an innovative technological system of continuous emission reduction to the EPA—as long as the state agrees with the system. Waivers can be granted.

State Implementation Plans

Specific emission limits for the National Ambient Air Quality Standards (NAAQS) are controlled by the federal government by requiring state implementation plans (SIPs). Each state must develop and enact a comprehensive statewide plan to keep its air clean. They must address major fuel burning sources.[40] States must enforce and comply with their own state air plans, state implementation plans, and permit programs.

Under the CAA, each state must formally adopt its own plan after public hearings and notices. The SIP contents may vary from state to state, such as "moderate area" and "serious area" designations for air pollution. However, there are minimum criteria by which the state's SIP becomes the major means for the federal government to control pollution. The SIP must include these elements:

❖ Emission limitations with controls, economic incentives, and timetables

❖ Air quality data classifying areas of attainment or non-attainment

❖ Programs enforcing emission limitations

❖ Prohibition of emissions that interfere with attaining and maintaining the NAAQS

❖ Compliance with interstate and international pollution abatement requirements

❖ Assurance of the financial capability of permit applicants, maintenance of adequate state environmental personnel, and enforcement authority for the designated control authority

❖ Emission monitoring with periodic reports from stationary sources

❖ Adequate contingency plans to restrict emissions after the fact

❖ Methods to change the plan in response to any changes in NAAQS

❖ Ways to meet EPA's requirements for new sources of air pollution (and operating existing sources which do not attain the NAAQS)

❖ Programs of pre-construction review and notice to prevent significant deterioration (PSD) of major new sources and to operate existing sources in areas that do not attain the NAAQS

❖ Models for air quality containing supportable data

❖ Methods for owners or operators of major stationary sources to pay fees covering permit review

❖ Local government consultation and participation in developing the SIP

A model does not need to be followed by a state as long as the above requirements are included. After the EPA approves the SIP, both that state and the EPA are responsible for enforcing it. In order for the EPA to approve a SIP, it must be considered complete by meeting specific guidelines.[41] For example, there must be reductions in CO (five percent per year), ozone, and other pollutants for serious areas in a state. If the EPA does not act within six months, the SIP is automatically considered complete. Once complete, the EPA has 12 months to approve it. If only part of the SIP is approved, revisions to other parts may be recommended and later approved. The SIP is considered a dynamic plan that needs to be updated as local conditions and federal requirements change.

Revisions must be submitted to the EPA within three years of the EPA's adoption of any new NAAQSs. If the EPA believes that a SIP is not adequate for maintaining an NAAQS, then the state may be given a deadline to submit a revision.[42] According to the CAA, the EPA must also notify the public about any SIP inadequacies. A finding of SIP inadequacy is a "SIP call."

If a state receives disapproval for its SIP, the EPA is required to enact a Federal Implementation Plan (FIP) for that state. Any SIP deficiencies can result in federal sanctions. Examples of sanctions may be freezing highway funds or eliminating additional emission offsets for new or modified sources seeking new source permits. Sanctions can be assessed at the time of a SIP finding of deficiency or any time thereafter. Offsets can be defined as a reduction of the emissions in a major source that is countered by an equal or greater decrease in the quantity of emissions of another hazardous air pollutant.

Federal departments or agencies cannot support, provide financial assistance, or approve any activity that does not conform to a SIP. Also, all state and federal policies, programs, and actions must conform to a state's SIP. For example, highway and transportation plans, programs, and projects; U.S. Army Corps of Engineers actions; and other such matters are actions which must conform. The transportation conformity issues (mobile sources of air contamination) are particularly stringent with regard to air emissions, as would be expected. All SIPs need to provide for increases in the number of motor vehicles. In this way, air monitoring becomes quite important.

Exhibit 7: Technicians may set up air measuring stations in resonse to spills or releases to the atmosphere. Measurements may be automated and taken at periodic times or over continuous periods.

Monitoring the air

Monitoring or watching and measuring potential contaminants or pollutants is required for industrial emissions. Enhanced monitoring is the use of a monitoring method that is different but can provide similar data to EPA's recommended methods. Enhanced or increased emissions monitoring is required only to determine if a facility meets government specified emission limits. Monitoring plans are required to identify those industrial emission levels above acceptable limits, to provide scheduling information for improvements, or to reduce emissions. For example, when 85 percent of the allowable emissions are reached for particulate matter, an industrial process must engage additional air scrubber equipment. A common method of air monitoring is the continuous air monitoring system (CAMS) by which electronic data is collected regularly or periodically and later reviewed by owners, operators, or public agencies.

New Source Performance Standards (NSPS)

The federal government controls air emissions from new sources differently than the way it controls old sources. By accepting the principle that retrofitting old sources of emissions could be cost prohibitive, if an old source is reconstructed or modified, it must meet the new more stringent source performance standards.[43] Categories of new sources are given sets of standards for emissions. EPA has listed about 60 different source categories.[44] For these categories, the best technology is used to develop the amount of emission reduction required. New source performance standards (NSPS) can be established as equipment, design, or work or operating standards when specific emission limits are not feasible. An NSPS only applies to a facility when construction begins after the date of the proposal of the NSPS.

Under the CAA, a large new facility or other source of air pollution is subject to a preconstruction review prior to award of a permit. If the location of the new source is in a nonattainment area for a pollutant, the new source permit may be rejected. If the new source is located in an attainment area, it is subject to a permit considering the prevention of significant deterioration (PSD) of air quality. If a potential source could emit at least 250 tons of pollution per year or at least 100 tons per year of one of 28 designated source categories, the source is subject to the nonattainment permit program. The nonattainment program applies if a source can emit at least ten to 100 tons per year of the nonattainment pollutant. The pollutant in question and the seriousness of the nonattainment problem where the source is located are considerations in awarding the permit.[45] The maximum capacity of a source or facility to emit a pollutant according to its design is based on federal emissions limits such as those limits established in a state implementation plan.

Reconstructed and modified buildings or facilities

When rebuilding, making additions, or replacing parts of an existing facility or when expenditures for a project are 50 percent or more of the cost for a comparable new facility, a reconstruction rule is triggered. If triggered, the reconstruction rule does not necessarily require that an NSPS be used. If the reconstructed or modified facility is considered not feasible for economic or technical reasons, the EPA may determine that an NSPS is not appropriate. When reconstruction exceeds the 50 percent limit, the NSPS rules apply.

Any increases in emissions that result from modifications or changes may be allowed in certain instances. Nonattainment permit programs and the NSPS are triggered if there is a physical or operational change resulting in increased emissions of the regulated pollutant. Activities such as repair, replacement, or maintenance are not considered to be a facility modification. When a facility initiates operations, the EPA will not calculate an emissions increase for the modification but will calculate a past-to-future actual comparison. The EPA excludes all pollution control projects from the new source permitting rules. If there is equipment failure, the rules for modification of facilities are not triggered. The EPA determines whether a specific project causes increased emissions as a test for new source review. If a facility meets BACT or LAER levels of emission reductions, then the EPA may exclude it from the modification rule.

States must include a preconstruction review of minor new or modified sources in their SIPs. Minor new sources defined on an SIP can become a way for owners or operators to comply with federal and state air controls. By applying the minor new source review rules to facilities, operating limits on industrial facilities are lowered. States develop their own minor new source review programs in coordination with their SIP.

Air Permits for Sources

Existing and new source owners or operators are required to apply for and receive operating permits. The source can be an industrial building that makes cast metal products, a blast furnace, an electrical generating station, a paint shop, a commercial bakery, or anything that emits gases or other airborne contaminants. In other words, any facility that has the potential for air pollution requires a permit. A facility may apply for an expedited permit if necessary. A single air permit may be issued for a facility with multiple sources. During the permit application process, a method of air pollution control for that building, process, facility, or operation must be developed. Review and comment are made by the EPA or the state agency responsible for air pollution control. As architects of their own operating permits, the owner or operator is involved in deciding about the provisions of his own permit. In this way, the potential for accidental air emissions and high company costs may be minimized. All accidental releases of regulated substances are to be prevented through detection and prevention that include monitoring, record keeping, reporting, training, vapor recovery, secondary containment, and other design, equipment, work practice, and operational requirements.

Generally, the comprehensive operating permit program is the major method for CAA enforcement. Permits usually specify that owners and operators monitor the source periodically or continuously. Any changes in operations or equipment must be documented and materials submitted to the appropriate governmental agency for review and approval, then included as an amendment of new condition of the specific operating permit. New sources are even more tightly regulated than existing sources. New source facilities may not begin operating without first receiving a permit describing all operating stipulations.

Operating Permit Program

There is a preconstruction permit program for new and modified sources, a state implementation plan operating permit program, and a comprehensive operating permit program for most sources of air pollution. The comprehensive operating permit program is developed and administered by the states and based on EPA minimum requirements.[46] Sources subject to permits must prepare and submit applications for approval or be in violation of federal law.

There are a number of features of the operating permit program. Sources that require a permit are a major source (one emitting or having the potential for emitting 100 tpy or more of any air pollutant including fugitive emissions), a designated source category (classification of industrial operation, etc.), or any other source defined by a state or the EPA. States must develop, comply, and enforce their SIP and permit programs. They must review and ensure adequate air control and must implement plans for major fuel burning sources. States can develop exceptions for low levels of emissions, small-sized facilities, and low production rates.

A permit application must contain information about source plans compliance with all applicable requirements. If a state does not implement an air pollution permit program of their own, the EPA imposes a federal operating permit program. Within 60 days, the state or the EPA permit review authority must determine whether the application is complete. During the time that a permit application is being reviewed, the applicant has an "application shield" which allows temporary operations. The application must contain

❖ Description of air pollution control equipment

❖ Certification of truth, accuracy, and completeness of the application

❖ Compliance status statement

❖ Emission rates listed in tons per year

❖ Emissions of all pollutants for which the source is major

❖ Emissions of regulated air pollutants

❖ Monitoring and measurement methods

❖ Identification of emissions

Within 18 months after receiving the application, the permitting authority must take action on the permit. Fixed terms of the permits cannot exceed five years. Each permit must include

❖ Compliance monitoring, testing, reporting, and record keeping

❖ Compliance schedule and regular progress reports

❖ Compliance certification

❖ Emission limitations and standards

❖ Fees (according to an approved state permit fee schedule)

❖ Inspection and entry requirements for the permit authority

❖ Monitoring, measuring, and record keeping requirements

❖ Opportunity to request a public hearing on the draft permit

❖ Procedures for public notice and comment

❖ State-only requirements clearly noted

❖ Statement that permit can be modified, revoked, reopened, reissued, or terminated

❖ Sulfur dioxide emission prohibitions exceeding any allowances

The EPA may provide technical assistance to an owner or operator of a stationary source and help to develop voluntary industry standards to reduce accidental releases. In addition, the EPA may collect, publish, and disseminate information about the methods for preparing hazard assessments.

State and EPA reviews of permit applications

The state permitting agency provides the EPA with copies of each air permit application, draft permit, and final permit. The EPA may comment on any of these phases of the submittal. Notice of each draft permit must be given to any affected state before public notice is given.[47] If the EPA objects to a proposed final permit within 45 days of receipt, the state permit agency cannot issue the permit. If the state agency fails to revise and resubmit the proposed permit to the EPA within 90 days of receiving the objection notice from the EPA, the EPA must then issue or deny the permit. If the EPA does not object, any person may petition the EPA to object within 60 days after expiration of the 45 day EPA review period.[48]

A permit shield means that compliance with the permit is considered compliance with the CAA. This shield is optional with each state, and the permitting agency can expressly require that a permit shield applies. If the permit does not expressly state this, no shield is assumed.

Permit revisions

A state agency or the EPA may approve revisions to a permit only if the change could not be performed without violating the existing permit. There are a few categories of permit revisions; minor and significant permit revisions and the administrative permit amendment categories are the most common.

An Administrative Permit Amendment is a simple revision correcting typographic errors, changes in name, more frequent monitoring, or new requirements needed from a preconstruction review permit. No public notice is required for these administrative permit amendments. No permit shield is allowed.

A Minor Permit Revision may be allowed with only limited review requirements. No public review is required for this kind of revision, but the EPA and affected states must be notified. This revision cannot violate any of the permit term requirements. It cannot violate source requirements, and the change may be made immediately.[49]

A Significant Permit Revision is one that cannot qualify as an administrative or minor permit revision. The same procedures must be followed that are used for applying or renewing a permit.

An Alternative Operating Scenario allows some freedom in operations. A permit can specify a number of anticipated facility operating scenarios. An owner or operator would give notice to the state agency or the EPA that it has changed its operating scenario, and no permit revision would be required. The EPA prefers that permit revisions be avoided, if possible, through such a method.[50]

States must create a fee schedule that provides sufficient revenue to cover permit program costs.[51] State fee schedules can include service fees, application fees, emission fees, and others. The EPA expects a state to collect at least $25.00 per year per ton of the actual emissions of each regulated pollutant emitted.

Exhibit 8: Equipment at some facilities can rust or deteriorate faster if it is exposed to certain chemical substances or gases. These discards provide evidence of the importance of regular replacement and repair to ensure continued compliance with the terms of a permit.

Emissions trading

States are required by the EPA to allow sources to trade emissions according to the source's cap as stated in the permit. This requirement provides operational flexibility through the trading of emissions. Some states have developed programs whereby industrial facilities, including public utility facilities, may accumulate credits for not producing their expected amounts of air pollution. These credits refer to a hypothetical area of effect around their facility, like an imaginary bubble. Within the area of effect, facilities that do not emit the expected tons per year of contaminants may sell those credits to another facility that exceeds their own allocated amounts of air pollution. Buying and selling of credits becomes an incentive for any facility to reduce its emissions.[52] For example, there is a sulfur dioxide allowance program for existing and new units. There is an allowance transfer system with interpollutant trading and a tracking system.

Enforcing the Clean Air Act

The operating permit program allows the government to identify a source's clean air requirements—the methods of operation, industrial processes, monitoring procedures, record keeping requirements, limits for pollutants, etc. A single air permit may be issued for a facility with multiple sources. Permit applications are required to have a compliance plan for the source. The state or the EPA reviews and approves or disapproves them. All facilities must operate according to their provisions stated in the approved permit. Both the EPA and the states encourage expedited permitting. The permit conditions provide a basis for enforcing the CAA without going to the courts. Air permit programs may be carried out by the EPA or delegated to the states or another agency. Each permitting authority is required to submit copies of each permit application for EPA review. It should be noted that the CAA administrative enforcement provisions are modeled after the Clean Water Act (CWA). The model provides for administrative penalties up to $200,000 or more. Enforcement of the CAA must not infringe upon the existing authority of counties and cities to plan or control land use as granted by the states.

Owners and operators of each source which has a new electric utility steam-generating unit must submit both a permit application and compliance plan. The EPA promotes clean coal technology regulatory incentives.

Violators of the permit process (either violators of permits or those who do not apply for a permit) are given notice, and the violator has 30 days to request a hearing. Agreements are reached much more quickly when the DOJ can be bypassed. A field citation program is used for minor violations. Field citations allow inspectors to issue small fines of up to $5,000 per day per violation. Violators can pay or request a hearing. Private citizens can seek civil penalties, and the EPA can pay up to $10,000 to anyone who provides information leading to criminal or civil convictions.

Criminal penalties can be given for violating the CAA. A knowing violation of the CAA is a felony. Enforcement can be made against individuals, corporations, or partnerships. Crimes connected to record keeping are subject to fines and jail terms. Persons who make misstatements can be criminally prosecuted. Failure to pay any fees owed the government under the CAA is a criminal act and subject to fines and imprisonment.

Knowing or negligent releases of air toxins which place others in danger of death or serious bodily injury are subject to criminal penalties. Penalties could be assessed as high as $250,000 per day with 15 years imprisonment. Corporations could be fined as much as $1,000,000 per day. If an individual honestly does not have knowledge about a release, he or she may still be subject to a fine up to $100,000 and up to a year in prison. Corporations that do not have knowledge of a release may be fined as much as $200,000.

Compliance audits are regular inspections of the premises and operating procedures as developed by the applicant and agencies and stated in the permit(s) for a facility. Companies or facilities desiring to adhere to federal environmental regulations typically initiate an internal compliance program. A practice of regular audits ensures detecting and correcting problems and is considered by the courts to be mitigating actions against any assessed penalties. Any permitted facility should report any departure from a permit requirement.[53] The EPA designates national priority sectors for enforcement attention. For example, one year the priority sector may be petroleum refining, dry cleaning establishments, and strip mining. The next year it may be another set of targets.

Chronology of the Clean Air Act (CAA)

1955, Air Pollution Control Act, Ch. 360, 69 Stat. 322

1963, Clean Air Act, Pub. L. 88-206, 77 Stat. 392

1965, National Emissions Standard Act, Pub. L. 89–675

1967, Air Quality Act of 1967, Pub. L. 90–148, 81 Stat. 465

1970, Clean Air Act Amendments of 1970, Pub. L. 91–604, 84 Stat. 1676, 42 USC 7401 et seq.

1977, Clean Air Act Amendments of 1977, Pub. L. 95–95, 91 Stat. 685

1981, Steel Industry Compliance Extension Act of 1981, Pub. L. 97–23, 95 Stat. 139

1986, Radon Gas and Indoor Air Quality Research Act of 1986, Pub. L. 99–499

1990, Clean Air Act Amendments of 1990, Pub. L. 101–549, 104 Stat. 2399

1998, Border Smog Reduction Act of 1998, Pub. L. 105–286, 112 Stat. 2773

1999, Chemical Safety Information, Site Security and Fuels Regulatory Relief Act, Pub. L. 106–40, 113 Stat. 207

CHAPTER 7

Sound:
Noise Control Act (NCA)

Overview

❖ Noise is increasing and becoming a growing danger to the nation.

❖ Sources are machinery, vehicles, equipment, appliances, and other commercial products.

❖ National uniformity of treatment of noise is promoted in the Noise Control Act (NCA).

❖ Noise emission standards are provided by the EPA for manufactured products.

❖ Aircraft and military equipment are not covered under this act.

❖ Records, product labeling, and warranties of products are required of manufacturers.

❖ Noise control education projects are promoted under the NCA.

❖ The Office of Noise Abatement and Control is established in the EPA.

Noise Control Act Acronyms

BAT—Best available technology

DOL—Department of Labor

DOT—Department of Transportation

EPA—Environmental Protection Agency

NCA—Noise Control Act

NASA—National Aeronautics & Space Administration

Policy Statements and Products Regulated

Uncontrolled noise is a growing danger to the health, safety, and welfare of the national population, especially in urban areas. The major sources of noise are motor vehicles and equipment, machinery, appliances, and other commercial products. Primary responsibility for controlling noise lies with state and local governments. In order to create a uniform treatment, federal controls are required under the NCA. All manufactured products are regulated except aircraft (and their engines, propellers, and equipment), any military weapons and equipment designed for combat, NASA equipment, and research rockets.[1]

An Office of Noise Abatement and Control is established within the EPA.[2] The purpose of the office is to investigate, study, and classify the causes and sources of noise. Its objectives are to

❖ Determine the effects of noise at different levels

❖ Project any growth of noise levels in urban areas

❖ Study the psychological and physiological effects of noise on people

❖ Study the effects of sporadic extreme noise (such as jet noise near airports) as compared with constant noise

❖ Study the effects of noise on wildlife and property

❖ Study the effects of sonic booms on property and values

❖ Consider all other matters related to noise

Research, Public Information, and Quiet Communities

The EPA, in coordination with other federal agencies, uses grants, contracts, and federal actions to help state and local governments develop their own noise control programs. They provide education about noise and public health through school curricula, volunteer organizations, radio and television programs, and various publications. They conduct research about the control, measurement, and effects of noise (psychological and physiological) on people, animals, wildlife, and property. The determination of dose-response relationships suitable for decision making is emphasized. Noise technology is promoted through demonstration projects. Monitoring equipment is to be used by state and local noise control programs. The economic impact of noise on property and human activities is another research topic. Economic incentives, including noise emission charges, are considered as a means to help control noise.

State and local governments can apply for grants to help them carry out these noise controls:

❖ Determine the extent of the noise problem in a jurisdiction

❖ Plan and establish a noise control capability (including equipment purchases)

❖ Develop noise abatement plans around airports, highways, and rail yards

❖ Evaluate methods to control noise and demonstrate the best available technologies for each jurisdiction

A national noise environmental assessment program identifies trends in noise exposure and response, ambient levels, and compliance data to determine the effectiveness of noise abatement actions. Regional technical assistance centers are associated with universities and private organizations.[3]

Control methods

The EPA consults with other federal agencies to develop and maintain scientifically-based criteria for noise and to coordinate all noise research and controls with the other agencies. Public health effects from noise are the major interest for the research used in developing the noise criteria. Reports must be developed on noise sources and the technology to control them.[4]

Noise emission standards are developed for commercial products such as construction equipment, transportation equipment including recreational vehicles (snow mobiles, water vehicles, motorcycles, etc.), motors or engines, and electrical and electronic equipment. Standard limits that are established for each product must consider the amount of use of such product (alone or in combination with other noise sources), the degree of noise reduction achievable through the best available technology (BAT), and the cost of complying with those standards. The Department of Transportation (DOT) requires railroad carriers to limit their equipment noise through BAT, taking into account the cost of compliance. Motor carriers must meet the EPA standards in the same way as railroads.

Manufacturers' warranties

Each manufacturer of noise-producing products must warrant to the final purchasers that the products have been designed, built, and equipped to operate at or below the sound level required by the EPA at the time of its manufacture. Any costs that manufacturers incur from adding sound deadening devices or changes to the product cannot be transferred to any dealer. No advertisements for the products can contain the costs or dollar values of the noise emission control devices unless they can be attributed to the Bureau of Labor Statistics (BLS) of the U.S. Department of Labor (DOL). This provision of the act deters the potential for exaggerated advertising claims.

Manufacturers must maintain records, submit reports to the EPA, and develop information about their products. Testing may be required by the EPA to verify any claims made in reports or records. Penalties and violations may be assessed if records, reports, and information about the product is not provided.

Removal of sound deadening devices is prohibited, as are modification of products, or changes to the operating characteristics to increase sound. Even if performance is increased, products can only have sound deadening devices removed for maintenance purposes.[5] There are criminal penalties for violating the NCA that cannot exceed $25,000 per day of violation, imprisonment, or both the monetary penalty and the imprisonment.

Low noise emission products

The EPA must determine which products qualify as low noise emission products according to the NCA. A low noise emission product is one that emits noise below EPA-specified noise reduction standards. A Low Noise Emission Product Advisory Committee recommends the products, and the EPA makes such decisions. These products are considered suitable for use by the public. A certificate may be issued for such products. Federal government agencies are required to purchase low noise emission products in lieu of other products as long as these products do not exceed 125 percent of the retail price of competing products. The EPA may test noise levels for items purchased by any federal agency.

State and local agency limitations

State and local governments cannot change the federal noise limits. Noise limits for a product may not be changed even if a component is added to a product. State and local governments cannot license, regulate, or restrict the use, operation, or movement of any product regulated for noise beyond those limitations set in the NCA. A state or local government can, at any time, petition the EPA to change a noise requirement. The state and local governments are able to require product labeling and information about products in any way as long they conform with EPA requirements.[6]

Chronology of the Noise Control Act (NCA)

1972, Noise Control Act, 42 USC 4901–4918

1978, Noise Control Act (Quiet Communities Act of 1978), Pub. L. 95–609, 92 Stat. 3079

1994, NCA Amendments, Pub. L. 103–272, 108 Stat. 1379

CHAPTER 8

Aircraft Sound:
Airport Noise Abatement Act (ANAA)

Overview

❖ The EPA works with the DOT to regulate noise from airports and aircraft.

❖ A single system of measuring noise is uniformly applied to airports and their surroundings.

❖ Land uses that are compatible with airport noise are identified, such as warehousing, manufacturing, and open space uses. Residential use is to be avoided.

❖ Noise exposure maps related to runways and operations are required for airports.

❖ Noise compatibility programs are required along with soundproofing and the acquisition of certain residential buildings and properties.

❖ Limits are placed on the amount of damages from noise that can be awarded.

Airport Noise Abatement Act Acronyms

ANAA—Airport Noise Abatement Act

DOT—Department of Transportation

EPA—Environmental Protection Agency

NASA—National Aeronautic & Space Administration

Airport Noise

The activities that people perform in certain locations have a strong connection to the amount of airport noise that can be tolerated. Residential land use has the least tolerance for noise for many reasons. Not only do people sit in their backyards but also many dwelling units are constructed of less dense building materials which have a greater tendency to transmit sound to their interiors. Another concern of the ANAA[1] is reducing noise in certain occupied areas, such as national parks and other special places.[2]

In consultation with state and interstate agencies, the EPA regulates a single system of measuring noise that can be used to relate noise exposure to human reactions. The EPA develops standards for aircraft and aircraft engines with the International Civil Aviation Organization. Land uses that are compatible with individuals with varying exposures to noise must be identified. In most cases, industrial uses—especially warehousing which employs the fewest numbers of people—and recreational land uses are deemed compatible with airport use. Labor-intensive industries are not compatible.

Noise, public health, and exposure

Noise exposure maps must be prepared in consultation with public planning agencies for the areas surrounding the airports; they must comply with the criteria stated in the ANAA and must be submitted to the DOT. Planning grants are available to help communities prepare them. When there are any changes in airport operations or runway changes, the maps must be revised to indicate any changes in land use compatibility. Noise exposure maps and related information cannot be used as admissible evidence in civil actions asking for relief for noise resulting from the operation of an airport, however.[3]

Noise compatibility programs should be indicated on the airport map and should be implemented at the airport. The noise program may include

❖ Preferential runways
❖ Restrictions on the use of the airport to a type or class of aircraft based on the noise characteristics of the aircraft
❖ Construction of barriers and acoustical shielding
❖ Soundproofing of public buildings
❖ Changes in flight procedures for landings and takeoffs
❖ Acquisitions of land, air rights, easements, development rights, and other interests to ensure land use compatibility.[4]

A noise program will not be approved by the DOT unless it reduces incompatible uses and prevents the introduction of additional incompatible uses. A 1999 study determined the threshold of noise affecting public health, the effectiveness of airport noise abatement programs, community and school impacts, and the effectiveness of the FAA noise assessment programs.[5]

Soundproofing and property acquisition

The DOT may make grants available to help soundproof or acquire residential buildings if the noise exposure contours so indicate. Updated noise maps may qualify an airport for these acquisition grants. A number of restrictions apply to these grants, and funds are always limited. For these reasons, airport owners (such as local governments) may need to apply their own revenues to conform to the intent and requirements of the ANAA.[6] Airport noise compatibility planning grants may be made to a sponsor of an airport for the research necessary to prepare and submit a noise exposure map and related information or for a noise compatibility program.

One legal note should be noted about the ANAA. Noise exposure maps and related information that is submitted to DOT may not be admitted into evidence or used in a civil action asking for relief for noise resulting from airport operations. Additionally, all foreign air carriers must comply to noise standards for aircraft of the United States (subsonic, not supersonic).[7]

Quiet aircraft technology

Quiet aircraft technology is promoted in a research program for both propeller and rotor-driven aircraft. The design of the blades is a concern because certain pitches and curves in the blades can add quiet but at the same time promote inefficiencies in power and fuel consumption. The goal of the research program is to apply high technology that is cost beneficial and to determine if more research is necessary to supplement existing research activities. If NASA determines that additional research is necessary and can contribute to developing quiet aircraft technology, then the DOT and NASA will do so.

Chronology of the Airport Noise Abatement Act (ANAA)

1980, Airport Noise Abatement Act, USC 47501–47510,

1994, Abatement of Aviation Noise, Pub. L. 103–272 1(e), 108 Stat 1284

2000, ANAA Amendments, Pub. L. 106–181, 114 Stat 178

Section Three

Water

CHAPTER 9

Water Pollution:
Clean Water Act (CWA)

Overview

❖ The CWA protects people, fish, and wildlife from contaminated water.

❖ Many federal, state, and local agencies have responsibilities under the CWA.

❖ Prior to any release of potential contaminants into soil, surface water, or ground water, individuals or companies must apply for a permit and be approved for that release.

❖ Dredge wastes from the bottoms of water bodies cannot be deposited without a permit.

❖ Waste water from industry or public water treatment plants must meet purity standards.

❖ If a pollutant is discarded from a single place, it is a point source.

❖ Water discharge permits (National Pollution Discharge Elimination System [NPDES] permits) must be obtained prior to releasing contaminants into surface or ground waters.

❖ Limits on chemical or biological discharges called "national effluent guidelines" are established.

❖ States can establish their own standards of water quality as long as the state standards are greater than the EPA standards.

❖ Pretreatment of wastewater is required for industrial wastes discharged into a public sanitary sewer system.

❖ Dredge and fill permits are required for surface waters and are managed by the U.S. Army Corps of Engineers.

❖ Spill prevention plans are required under the CWA.

❖ Oil spills are covered under both the CWA and the Oil Pollution Act (OPA).

Clean Water Act Acronyms

BAT—Best available technology

BCT—Best conventional technology

BMP—Best management practices

BOD—Biochemical oxygen demand

BPCT—Best practical control technology

BPJ—Best professional judgment

BPT—Best practical control technology

CCMP—Comprehensive conservation management plan

CSO—Combined sewer overflow

CWA—Clean Water Act

CZMP—Coastal Zone Management Program

DMR—Discharge monitoring report

DOI—Department of the Interior

DOT—Department of Transportation

EPA—Environmental Protection Agency

FDF—Fundamentally Different Factors

FWPCA—Federal Water Pollution Control Act

ICT—Individual Control Technologies

MOU—Memorandum of Understanding

MPRSA—Marine Protection Research and Sanctuaries Act

NEP—National Estuary Program

NOAA—National Oceanic and Atmospheric Administration

NPDES—National Pollution Discharge Elimination System

NRS—National Response System

NSPS—New source performance standards

OPA—Oil Pollution Act

POTW—Publicly-owned treatment works

SPCC—Spill Prevention Control and Countermeasure Plan

TIE—Toxicity identification evaluation

TRE—Toxicity reduction evaluation

TSP—Trisodium phosphate or tribasic sodium phosphate

USDA—U.S. Department of Agriculture

WET—Whole effluent toxicity

Regulations for Water

The federal government regulates water by developing partnerships with different agencies and encouraging states to prevent, reduce, and eliminate pollution. The Environmental Protection Agency (EPA) is the major agency implementing the environmental water laws passed by Congress. In some instances, a federal agency other than the EPA is given responsibilities for an environmental program. For those cases, there may be delegation of some duties to state and local agencies, or cooperation with the EPA may be mandatory. The EPA may also delegate specific duties to other agencies. Although the EPA reviews, inspects, and approves the programs and actions of these partner agencies, it also maintains field staff in its regional offices to administer many of its water-related rules and regulations. In some areas of water protection, the U.S. Army Corps of Engineers, U.S. Coast Guard, or the U.S. Department of Transportation have responsibilities.

Exhibit 9: Surface and ground waters can easily receive contaminants from different sources. Concern for purity demands that no one discharge a liquid or solid without first obtaining a permit. (Photo: author)

Regrettably, there is no clear pattern of responsibilities, nor is there any particular logic that can lead the reader toward intuitively selecting the appropriate agency which has responsibility for her or his water area of interest. For example, the EPA allows states to administer many water programs under the EPA's close supervision. It allows the states to further delegate water responsibilities to their own local governments.

Water pollution is regulated by the EPA and its designated state agencies by applying these restrictions:[1]

❖ No discharges of chemicals, biological agents, or waste materials are allowed into surface waters, groundwater, or soils.[2]

❖ Prior to any release of potential contaminants, individuals or companies must apply for a permit and be approved for that release.[3]

❖ States can become the regulatory agency for the federal programs, if approved by the EPA.[4]

❖ All environmental controls and limitations devised by the EPA must follow a prescribed method.[5]

❖ There is a prescribed process for reporting, responding, and preventing spills.[6]

❖ Any placing or discharging dredge wastes (from scraping the bottoms of water bodies) must adhere to approved permit provisions.[7]

❖ Enforcement methods are established for violations.[8]

As can be seen from these provisions, the Clean Water Act attempts to eliminate the delivery of pollutants into water and tries to protect human life, fish, and wildlife.

Important definitions within the CWA

Surface waters are streams, rivers, lakes, rivulets, and creeks. **Ground waters** are waters embedded under the surface of the earth within rock formations. Some ground waters move similar to an underground river, and others are fairly still but contain enough pressure to allow occasional springs to bubble up from the surface. **Ocean waters**, or seas, are composed of vast saltwater bodies or bays and estuaries that transition the ocean water to the land. The Great Lakes may be considered as either ocean or surface waters because of their vast expanses in comparison to most all other lakes.

Ground water can mix with surface waters and vice versa. Similarly, ocean waters can invade fresh surface and ground waters and contaminate them for use as drinking water. Ocean or sea waters can enter bodies of fresh water through inlets or travel through underground rock formations into aquifers (rock bearing water) as a result of tides.

If a pollutant is introduced (or discharged) into a body of water, it is an **addition**. Discharges of water from dams are not considered additions of pollutants. If a pollutant is discarded from an observable single place as a single route of contaminants, it is defined as a **point source**. A place, spot, industrial machine, or storage or manufacturing area can be a point source. This term can be applied to industrial waste streams, process water, cooling water, or storm water runoff in channels, pipes, ditches, or drainage ways. A point source can also be a vehicle, such as a tanker (ship, train, or truck). **Sheet runoff** is a term that implies runoff of rain mixed with chemicals or other agents that originate on large land areas, such as paved areas. Sheet runoff is not classified as a point source.

All the waters in the United States are **navigable waters**. They include tidal waters, interstate commerce waters, lakes, rivers, streams, or wetlands that are used for recreation, commercial fishing, and industrial uses. Also, tributaries of all of those waters mentioned and the impoundments and wet-lands associated with them are navigable waters.[9] EPA does not have jurisdiction over groundwater with regard to point source discharges, but many states have declared that ground waters are part of their regulated bodies of water and so regulate them.[10] **Wetlands** are saturated or flooded land areas that support vegetation common to swamps, marshes, bogs, and similar areas.[11]

The CWA was preceded by the Federal Water Pollution Control Act (FWPCA). In that act, the EPA established national effluent standards for specific industries. **Effluent standards** are the acceptable amounts, given in ranges of measurement of chemicals or substances, that can be safely released into the environment. The standards are based on the technical ability of a particular industry to comply to that standard compared to its ability to continue its operation as an economically-sound industry.

Pollutants include the following:

Dredged debris and material

Solid waste

Incinerator residue

Sewage

Garbage

Sewage sludge

Munitions

Chemical wastes

Biological materials

Radioactive materials

Heat

Wrecked or discarded equipment

Rock

Sand

Cellar dirt

Industrial, municipal, and agricultural waste discharged into water [12]

New Source Performance Standards (NSPS)

A new source is somewhat difficult to define. According to the CWA, a new source is one that began after the publication by the EPA of proposed regulations about standards of performance, or after the publication of the final NSPS for an industry.[13] NSPSs try to express the highest amount of reduction of effluents that may be achieved by applying the BAT standard. The

EPA can require the installation of advanced treatment technology in new facilities, but it avoids this requirement in older facilities where it may be economically unreasonable.

Standards of water quality

States establish water quality standards according to uses and criteria for protection. The CWA requires the classification of all waters in the state according to use: drinking water supply, fish and wildlife needs, recreation, industrial use, agricultural use, or others.[14] According to the EPA, state standards must maintain water as fishable and swimmable wherever possible and must not allow water degradation. State criteria for water quality must be based on EPA water quality criteria, but a state may examine the unique local water body's characteristics and develop its own numerical criteria. A water quality standard is an assigned number representing a pollutant's contaminant level that cannot be exceeded. For example, arsenic in a stream for trout cannot exceed 0.2 milligrams per liter. Some chemical-specific standards are listed in permits. Each owner or operator who obtains a permit is limited to the amount of contaminated discharge allowed and cannot exceed the standard set in the permit.

States are required to develop a list of their impaired water bodies and submit them to EPA.[15] An impaired water body is one in which applied technology cannot improve it and water quality standards cannot be met. In these cases, point sources of toxic contaminants are identified and individual control technologies (ICSs) are applied.

Limitations on toxicity

Releases of radiological, chemical, or biological warfare agents; high-level radioactive waste; or medical waste are not allowed, and there are limits for effluent discharges. For effluent and point discharges, the EPA determines toxic criteria and lists them as pollutants.[16] Aquatic species are exposed to one or more concentrations of an effluent in a laboratory to determine the short- and long-term effects of their exposure. Whole effluent toxicity (WET) limitations require toxicity testing on a permitted facility's effluent. Monthly or quarterly toxicity tests may be required after a permit is issued. Any change in the death rate of the tested aquatic species could be the result of a violation of the permit. In some WET limitations, toxicity identification evaluation (TIE) or toxicity reduction evaluations (TRE) may be required. The EPA requires states to coordinate biological assessments with chemical limitation and toxicity tests.

Trading of pollutants in effluents for watersheds

Any facility that can lower its amount of pollution by meeting water quality standards at a lower cost can accumulate credits by doing so. These credits can be traded between companies through sale or barter within the same watershed. Traders must meet the technology requirements for their own facility. The trading may be point-to-point source trading, intra-plant trading, pretreatment trading, point-nonpoint source trading, or nonpoint-nonpoint source trading.

Clean lakes

Each state must report eutrophic conditions of any publicly-owned lakes to the EPA and provide a description of the methods to control pollution sources to those lakes. States must also report methods to mitigate high acidity and to remove toxic metals and other toxic substances mobilized by high acidity. A list of publicly-owned lakes which have impaired uses, do not meet water quality standards, and in which water quality has deteriorated must also be filed with the EPA.

Financial assistance for lake improvements may be provided by the EPA to a state. Lake improvement demonstration programs are established for cost-effective technologies to

❖ Control pollutants and enhance water quality

❖ Control nonpoint sources

❖ Evaluate consolidated pollution control strategies and methods to remove and dispose contaminated lake sediments

❖ Develop improved methods to remove silt, stumps, aquatic growth, and other obstructions

❖ Construct and evaluate silt traps and other devices to prevent or abate the deposit of sediment in lakes

❖ Demonstrate the costs and benefits of using dredged material from lakes in reclaiming despoiled land

Water treatment

Grants and pilot programs are available for treatment works.[17] Assistance grants are available to treat wastewater and ensure water supplies to Mexican border communities, Indian Tribes, Pacific Islands, and the Virgin Islands. Every treatment works constructed or improved with CWA grants is required to file annual reports with the EPA.

There is a pilot program to fund alternative water source projects. Grants may be awarded to an entity if it has state authority to develop or provide water for municipal, industrial, and agricultural uses that are experiencing critical water supply needs. By definition, an alternative water source project is one that provides municipal, industrial, or agricultural water supplies in an environmentally-sustainable manner by treating wastewater or by conserving, managing, reclaiming, or reusing water or wastewater. An alternative water source project may not include water treatment or distribution facilities.

States may be awarded sewer overflow control grants that they may give to local governments for planning, designing, or constructing treatment works that intercept, transport, control, or treat municipal combined sewer overflows and sanitary sewer overflows. Combined Sewer Overflows (CSO) are such a widespread problem that the CWA requires EPA to report its progress in implementing its policies, programs, and enforcement. If there are periods of heavy rainfall, the volume of wastes mixed with water can exceed sewer pipe capacities or water treatment facilities. These overflows can contain toxic materials as well as human wastes and may travel into surface or ground water. Currently, about 800 cities have combined sewer systems.

National Pollution Discharge Elimination System

The CWA Amendments regulate storm water and water quality and establish a revolving loan fund to construct sewage treatment plants.[18] Any discharge of a pollutant by any person or company is prohibited under the CWA unless a permit is issued and the release or discharge is allowed according to provisions of that permit. This permit program, the National Pollution Discharge Elimination System, requires that anyone wishing to discharge contaminants from any point source into any waters must apply for a permit and have it reviewed and approved. If a permit application is approved, the applicant (owner or operator) has the right to discharge for as long as five years. Typically, the permit establishes limits on the discharge quantities and composition as a condition of approval. The owner or operator must adhere to all provisions approved in the permit.[19]

Exhibit 10: Liquid, solid, or hazardous waste treatment plants may need to discharge their clean water from wastes elsewhere. Standards are imposed on all such fluids that must be monitored, measured, recorded, and reported.

Applying for permits

The NPDES permit requires that an applicant develop and submit information about the facility, place, point source, composition of the discharge, and other material. When a permit application contains unusual conditions or features, informal meetings may be requested to develop terms and conditions. At times the EPA or the responsible state agency will issue a pre-draft permit, sometimes with a 14-day limit. A draft permit may be issued accompanied by a Fact Sheet or a Statement of Basis explaining its calculations and any special considerations. The government agency publishes a notice of intent to issue the draft permit and accepts comments from the public. There may be a public hearing on the permit.

Applicants can appeal a negative decision on the permit or its provisions within 30 days of the decision. An administrative law judge (from the EPA Environmental Appeals Board or a state agency) usually decides the appeal. When the state issues or denies a permit, the state procedures for appeal must be observed. The EPA Environmental Appeals Board hears and decides appeals for permits issued or denied by federal agencies.

States issuing NPDES permits

States may be authorized by the EPA to issue NPDES permits.[20] After issuing authorization to a state, the EPA issues a Memorandum of Understanding (MOU) which specifies pertinent guidelines and provisions of the state's authorization.[21] For the remaining states not authorized to issue NPDES permits, the ten EPA regional offices issue them. Any state program is required to be as strict as the EPA program and must include methods of calculating contaminants from the sources and standard procedures for issuing the permits. Appeal procedures and other individual state requirements may vary as long as the state program adheres to the NPDES concepts.[22] Any state-issued NPDES permit is subject to EPA review. If not agreeable, the EPA may object and issue its own permit for the discharge. The EPA can withdraw approval of a state NPDES permit program at any time and take over its operation.

When a state does not have the authority to grant an NPDES permit, the EPA requires the state to certify that the discharge authorized in the permit complies with the state's standards.[23] A state has a deadline for response to the EPA. If it does not meet that time deadline, the EPA assumes that the state has waived its certification veto.

Permit requirements, purposes, and procedures

Water discharge permits have the major purpose of limiting offensive substances from contaminating surface and groundwater. The permits typically have discharge chemical ranges (or limits), monitoring requirements,

reporting requirements, operating and maintenance procedures and requirements, spill procedures, and methods for bypassing the discharge if an emergency occurs. Often a permit may require an owner or operator to perform
the best management practices (BMPs). These BMPs ensure that the release
of contaminants is minimized.[24] Monitoring is a self-policing activity, but reports on discharges must be submitted to the state or the EPA on discharge
monitoring reports (DMRs).

All discharges must be chemically or biologically treated to meet levels
that are prescribed by EPA for that industry or for those discharge conditions.
This limitation ensures the quality of effluent and is based on available technology. If the water body receiving the effluent cannot purify any remaining
low-level contaminants, then the discharge must be treated to meet the levels
of quality to ensure a reason-
able degree of cleanliness.
The permits have both maximum limits for the time period of the permit and also
maximum limits for monthly
averages. Another limit is
placed on discharges under
the NPDES. This limitation is
technology-based for over 50
industrial facilities according
to their category (such as process water, cooling water, and
wastewater). These limits are
called national effluent
guidelines. The limits are
part of the NPDES permit

Exhibit 11: Well casings require periodic inspection by workers
to determine leaks, functioning of pumps, or blockages.

and are enforced under the permits. If the category is not covered by an applicable effluent guideline, a permit may be issued with provisions established
using best professional judgment (BPJ).[25] A BPJ is a somewhat intuitive decision by the permit reviewer.

One program for reducing water pollution from industrial discharges is
through the use of the best practical control technology (BPT). The BPT hinges
on the permit reviewer's relating the economics or costs of the technology to
the discharge requested for approval. It is the average of the best conditions
achieved by an industry. Another level of pollution control is the best available technology (BAT). A BAT is a standard which applies to any pollutant
except quantities of dissolved oxygen from decomposing organic matter (BOD),
industrial process solids or liquids of trisodium phosphate or tribasic sodium
phosphate (TSP), fecal coliform, acidity or alkalinity (pH), or oil and grease.
BATs are "maximum feasible pollution reduction for an industry."[26]

A more lenient method and level of pollution control that can be applied to an NPDES permit is the best conventional pollutant control technology (BCT). BCT is a reasonableness-of-cost test for permit applicants. Reasonable costs to the industry are balanced against environmental protection. This system dilutes the permit conditions by connecting the costs and availability of a different potential control technology to a conventional method of pollution control. The BCT makes the assumption that more conventional methods will be less costly to an applicant and, therefore, more likely to be administered.

The holders of NPDES permits must report their compliance or violations to the state agency or federal agency on standardized DMRs. Violations of all permit limitations on discharges must be explained. Noncompliance must be reported within 24 hours, and any anticipated noncompliance must be reported as well. CWA is a strict liability statute, which means that intent is irrelevant and liability is connected to a violation. Negligence and purposeful intent does not matter.

Anyone who has an interest that can be affected by the release of contaminants can initiate a civil action. Violations of NPDES permits, OPA violations, or other regulations can be settled under a consent agreement. There may be penalties, fees and costs, compliance schedules, payment of money to support an environmental activity in the public interest, or other requirements.

Permit Enforcement

For any facility that requires a permit for operation, an innovative production process or control method may be initiated if the resulting effluent reduction is greater than listed in the permit. A potential for significantly lower costs to the facility or innovations that could provide industry-wide improvements and applications are important criteria for choosing a new process. As with any NPDES permit, applicants must meet effluent limitation guidelines, procedures for elimination pollution discharges, and secondary treatment requirements. Nonpoint sources of pollution are to be identified and evaluated. Some purposes of national discharge standards are to enhance the operational flexibility of vessels of the Armed Forces, to stimulate the development of innovative vessel pollution control technology, and to compel the U.S. Navy to build environmentally-sound ships.

During the permitting process, industry is expected to promote best management practices. States are required to develop and maintain water quality and related agreements with the U.S. Department of Agriculture (USDA) and the Department of the Interior (DOI) to achieve and maintain water quality. In fulfilling this requirement, states must develop a list of navigable waters and strategies to keep them free of pollution.

A National Response System (NRS) requires that the Coast Guard create a National Response Unit in Elizabeth City, North Carolina. A list of spill removal resources, personnel, and equipment is maintained there and available to the public. A number of different Coast Guard strike teams exist in different Coast Guard districts.

Marine sanitation devices on vessels are required to treat "graywater" produced from galley, bath, and shower waters. These devices have federal standards of performance. Additional maritime safety from pollution events is promoted through testing and maintaining marine guidance systems. Studies and placement of main sector laser lighting, cold cathode lighting, and ultraviolet enhanced vision technology are promoted to guide marine vessels and traffic.

Changing the NPDES permits (Variances)

There are only a few possible ways to change the conditions of a permit. Changes are called variances. One kind of variance is the fundamentally different factors (FDF) variance. The FDF allows a change from limitations normally set by the NSPS. This kind of variance cannot be issued to allow changes in water quality limitations. Factors that could be fundamentally different are

❖ Kinds of pollutants in the discharge

❖ Volume of the discharge

❖ Non-water-quality environmental impacts of control and treatment of the discharge

❖ Energy requirements of the treatment technology

❖ The age, size, land availability, and configuration related to the discharger's equipment, facilities, and processes

Dredge and fill permits and the 404 permit program

Disposing dredged or fill material into water is not covered under the NPDES permit program of the CWA. If a point source, such as a bulldozer, pushes waste material into surface waters, a permit is required by the U.S. Army Corps of Engineers (Corps).[27] The Corps can designate areas for this kind of disposal as a condition for award of the 404 permit. Any land area that may be a wetland requires a 404 permit prior to any discharge of waste materials. This permit must be obtained prior to discharging or placing dredge and fill material, but the permit is not required for dredging operations. Even if dredged materials are redeposited into the wetlands, a 404 permit is required. Violations of the section 404 permit requirement can result in monetary and criminal penalties.

Input from the community is required by the Corps prior to the awarding of a 404 permit. A Public Interest Review may be required to help evaluators maintain a balance between conservation, esthetics, economic benefits to the applicant, historic values, protection of fish or wildlife, flood prevention, water supply and quality, and other factors. The EPA guidelines are followed in each Corps review. If any alternative to the release is possible, then a discharge cannot be approved.[28] Also, no deterioration in the aquatic ecosystem can result from the discharge into the water. In addition, the Corps must obtain certification from the state and consult with the EPA and the Fish and Wildlife Service prior to granting the 404 permit.

An applicant who desires a 404 permit must do all possible to lessen adverse effects from the proposed fill. The Corps has tried to avoid the loss of wetlands resulting from its approvals of 404 permits and discharges that result. They have initiated a No Net Loss Policy. If there is degradation or disappearance of a wetland, the wetland must be restored or new wetlands created.

For any discharge determined by the Corps to have minimal environmental impact, a nationwide permit or a general permit may be issued. A list of about 36 activities has been devised for nationwide permits, including back filling utility lines, bank stabilization, oil and gas structures, hydropower projects, survey activities, minor road crossings, outfall structures, and maintenance. About 13 activities of the nationwide permit, are "technically self-executing," but contact with the Corps is very important for anyone planning an activity within a wetland area.[29]

Discharges

Storm water discharges

Storm water runoff (rain water surface runoff, snow melt runoff or the drainage of either of these) is considered to be a multiple-point source discharge of contaminants. Industrial processes can contaminate storm water runoff, so storm water discharge from industrial processes and discharges from separate municipal storm sewer systems are controlled by the EPA. Discharges from any point source are connected to industrial activity based on the North American Industry Classification system (NAIC codes).[30]

There are two kinds of storm water discharge permits—general and individual. An applicant can apply for an NPDES permit by filing a notice of intent to be covered by a general permit. Both the EPA and some states issue their own versions of general permits. For example, the EPA issued a multi-sector general storm water permit that applied to 11,000 facilities in 29 industrial segments in the unauthorized states and territories.[31] Under this multi-sector permit, programs and facilities that fall within one of the 29 industrial sectors can qualify for a five-year permit. Approval of the general permit under the multi-sector permit program is based upon an applicant developing and submitting an acceptable, site-specific pollution prevention plan.[32] A facility owner or operator must submit an individual storm water permit application if the facility does not qualify for a general permit. Detailed facility information and quantitative data on discharge sampling during storm events are required for an individual permit.[33]

In order to best control the discharge of pollutants from industrial facilities into storm water, careful planning and design decisions are required. By planning to avoid pollution, it is expected that a storm water management plan be developed that contains best management practices (BMPs). BMPs may be general, industry specific, or site specific.

Heat or thermal discharges

Under the CWA, heat is a pollutant because it can kill marine life and vegetation. Some industrial facilities and processes cannot avoid depositing heat into water, so heat is regulated according to the limitations of current technology. Heat dischargers are required to develop scientific data that can prove that they will not harm the aquatic system.[34]

Ocean discharges

Marine environment and habitats must be protected and must not be degraded by a release of a contaminant or a thermal discharge. Changes in ecosystem diversity, productivity, or ecological stability in the discharge area are not allowed, as well as any threat to human health either from direct exposure to pollutants or from consuming exposed aquatic organisms. Also, no loss of esthetic, recreational, scientific, or economic value can occur as a result of a discharge.

Dumping in oceans is protected by the Marine Protection Research and Sanctuaries Act (MPRSA). Only the dumping of material dredged off surface water bottoms is allowed, but a permit is required. Under the MPRSA, the U.S. Army Corps of Engineers (Corps) can issue permits to transport dredge materials for ocean disposal. More than 140 disposal sites for dredge material are already designated by EPA.[35] Besides the Corps, the Coast Guard regulates ocean dumping and the discharge of sewage from ships.[36] NPDES permits are not issued for discharges into the seas or contiguous zones of the seas or the oceans unless the applicant complies with special criteria.

Publicly owned treatment works discharge

The CWA Pretreatment program covers industrial wastes not directly discharging into waters but into a public sanitary sewer system. None of these kinds of wastes can be discharged into a public sewer without government approval. Industrial users of a publicly owned treatment works (POTWs) require permits, orders, or executed contracts from the POTW or the municipality, not the state or the EPA. There are general and specific prohibitions, standards according to the category of waste, and locally imposed quantity limits for contaminants to be deposited into POTWs. The general pretreatment program limits do not allow industrial users to introduce any pollutant that might leave the POTW in a condition that could violate a requirement of the NPDES permit. Industrial users cannot discharge a contaminant into a POTW that could cause it to violate the NPDES permit of that POTW. For example, an industrial user cannot release an excess of any substance that could affect the chemical composition of the byproduct of sewage sludge from the POTW. There are specific prohibitions against discharging any of these pollutants to the POTW:

❖ Explosive or incendiary matter

❖ Matter that is corrosive or damaging

❖ Solid or viscous contaminants that could obstruct the flow

❖ Heated matter that could harm an ecosystem

❖ Any contaminant that could cause worker health and safety problems

Removal credits are given to industrial facilities that discharge wastes into POTWs with contaminant levels less than levels required if discharged directly into waters. To get the removal credits, an owner or operator of an industrial facility must meet BAT control or get credit for the level of removal of a pollutant consistently achieved by the POTW.

Local governments are to endorse and enact more stringent requirements than the EPA, especially to prevent toxic fumes and to encourage reduction of other kinds of air emissions. A pretreatment enforcement program is the responsibility of the municipality operating the POTW, but the EPA and the states retain enforcement authority. A POTW which has an approved pretreatment program may make modifications at any time to reflect changing conditions at the POTW.[37]

Grants and loans to states are provided to any municipality or any intermunicipal, interstate, or state agency for the construction of POTWs.[38] To qualify, an entity must produce an intended use plan, audits, reports, and fiscal controls. The intended use plan includes

❖ A list of construction precautions on the state's priority list for POTWs

❖ Long- and short-term goals and objectives in using the water pollution control revolving fund

❖ Information about the activities to be supported, project categories, discharge requirements, financial terms, and communities to be served

❖ Assurances and specific proposals

❖ Criteria and methods to distribute the funds

Nonpoint source discharges [39]

Agricultural runoff is the most common nonpoint source discharge and it generates the highest quantities of pollutants entering our waters, such as nutrients, salts, pesticides, and silt. The nonpoint source discharge program depends on state administration. States are required to submit state management programs and timetables to the EPA to reduce the amounts of nonpoint source discharges.

Protection Programs

Coastal Zone Management Program (CZMAP)

Land and water along the coastal shorelines are protected from nonpoint sources of pollution through the CWA and the Coastal Zone Management Program. The CZMAP program is administered by the EPA and the National Oceanic and Atmospheric Administration (NOAA).[40] There are 29 coastal states, and each must submit coastal nonpoint pollution control plans to the EPA and the NOAA. Penalties are levied and federal grants can be lost if a state does not comply.

The EPA must publish performance criteria for monitoring and assessing coastal recreation waters, which do not include inland waters or waters upstream of the mouth of a river or stream which has an unimpaired natural connection with the open sea. A list of discrete coastal recreation waters adjacent to beaches or other public points of access that do not meet water quality performance criteria is required to be maintained. Other public agencies at different levels of government must be notified and are required to monitor and protect public beaches and waters. A database for pathogens, pathogen indicators, and substances with the potential to carry human infectious disease in coastal recreation waters is maintained. The EPA also provides technical assistance to state and local governments to develop assessment and monitoring procedures for floatable material.

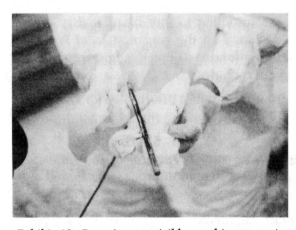

Exhibit 12: Deposits are visible on this measuring instrument. Even though the level of the water is the purpose of the probe, contaminants may be viewed on the instrument.

No later than 2004, the EPA must submit a report to Congress that includes recommendations about the need for additional water quality criteria for pathogens and their indictors; an evaluation of Federal, state, and local government efforts to implement this Act; and recommendations to improve methods and techniques for monitoring coastal recreation waters.

National Estuary Program (NEP)

The National Estuary Program, which is under the CWA, was created to protect and promote nationally significant bays and estuaries. As one of the major ways to control nonpoint pollution, the NEP requires a Comprehensive Conservation and Management Plan (CCMP). Each state's governor can nominate an estuary of national significance and request development of a CCMP for that estuary. This kind of CCMP typically includes industrial facilities, transportation, waste management, and enforcement provisions. Such a plan usually recommends approaches to correct and prevent problems for estuaries. There are currently 28 estuaries included in the NEP.

Surface water area protection programs

The CWA has targeted surface water areas such as the Hudson River (a reclamation demonstration project), the Chesapeake Bay (restoration of waters), the Great Lakes (water quality), Long Island Sound (dumping, runoff, and sediments); Lake Champlain (dumping, runoff, and sediments); Lake Ponchatrain (dumping, runoff, and sediments); and harbor dredging in many states.

The Chesapeake Bay Agreement joins a number of local, regional, and state government agencies with both formal and voluntary agreements to restore and protect the bay ecosystem and living resources.[41] The agreements are based on acknowledgements that there has been deterioration from pollution, excessive sedimentation, shoreline erosion, population growth, and building development impacts in the watershed. Maryland, Virginia, Pennsylvania, Delaware, and Washington, D.C. are committed to work with the EPA to develop and implement a comprehensive program that establishes a Chesapeake Bay Commission. The purposes of the commission are to develop a cooperative program as a model for managing estuaries and to study the nutrient loading results from dredge material disposal.

Similarly, water quality is promoted for the Great Lakes to attain the goals of the Great Lakes Water Quality Agreement of 1978 (amended 1987), particularly with respect to toxic pollutants. The Great Lakes are defined as Ontario, St. Clair, Erie, Huron, Superior, Michigan and their connecting channels (Saint Mary's River, Saint Clair River, Detroit River, Niagara River, and the Saint Lawrence River to the Canadian Border. The Great Lakes states are Illinois, Indiana, Michigan, Minnesota, New York, Ohio, Pennsylvania, Wisconsin. A Lakewide Management Plan is required as well as a Remedial Action Plan in accord with Great Lakes Water Quality Agreement.

Long Island Sound programs are established with a Management Conference of the Long Island Sound Study. Studies are to be made and a CCMP developed in response to

❖ Population growth

❖ Nutrient removal in sewage treatment plants

❖ Contaminated sediments and dredging activities

❖ Nonpoint source pollution abatement

❖ Land use activities in the Long Island Sound watershed

❖ Wetland protection and restoration

❖ Atmospheric deposition of acidic and other pollutants into Long Island Sound

❖ Water quality improvements for fish and wildlife

❖ Adequate state water quality program supplements

❖ Options for long-term financing of wastewater treatment projects

❖ Water pollution control programs

Lake Champlain programs are established with a Management Conference similar to the Long Island Sound programs but include Vermont, New York, and Quebec.

Sediment surveys, monitoring, and environmental dredging are priorities on the Brooklyn Waterfront, NY; Buffalo Harbor and River, NY; Ashtabula River, OH; Mahoning River, OH; Lower Fox River, WI; Passaic River and Neward Bay, NJ; Snake Creek, Bixby, OK; Willamette River, OR.

Lake Pontchartrain Basin is protected with restoration projects and related scientific and educational projects to restore the ecological health of its basin. Other wet weather watershed pilot projects are established to demonstrate the efficacy of treatment works improvements and innovations, treatment works for wet weather discharge control, watershed management, and storm water best management practices. Funds are allocated for FY 2002, 2003, and 2004 at $10, $15, and $20 million, respectively.

Exhibit 13: Stream flow may be controlled to prevent erosion or floods. If potential contaminants are located within stream banks, rapid water movement can threaten public health.

Preventing, Reporting, and Responding to Spills into Waters

A facility may be required to develop plans and keep records about preventing and responding to spills of oil and hazardous substances if the facility drills, produces, gathers, stores, processes, refines, transfers, distributes, or consumes oil or might release oil in harmful quantities into water.[42] Such plans are Spill Prevention Control and Countermeasure (SPCC) Plans. Some facilities are required to have a Facility Response Plan. This plan is quite detailed and must consider a worst-case oil spill.[43]

While not required to be submitted to the relevant state or federal agency, the SPCC plan must be filed and available to regulators at all times at the facility. The plan must be evaluated once every three years. In the SPCC plan, a number of detailed descriptions are required, as well as reports of recent spills and predictions of the direction, flow rate, and total quantities of oil that might result from a spill. Responsible parties and owner or operator contact persons for the facility must be identified in the SPCC plan.

Oil Pollution Act (OPA) and Facility Response Plans

Under the Oil Pollution Act (OPA), onshore facilities that are not involved in transportation matters must prepare a Facility Response Plan if they handle, transport, or store oil or if they could cause harm to the environment by the potential discharge into the water, shorelines, or economic zone around the facility. Substantial harm is defined for transferring oil over water to or from vessels storing more than 42,000 gallons, or storing at least one million gallons of oil. In the latter case, Facility Response Plans for worst case scenarios must be prepared:

❖ If there is no secondary containment for aboveground storage

❖ If fish and wildlife or other sensitive environmental settings could be harmed

❖ If a discharge could shut down water purification at a public drinking water intake

❖ If there has been a reportable spill greater than 10,000 gallons within the past five years

Facility Response Plans must contain these elements:

❖ Person assigned the authority to implement the plan

❖ Description of the actions to be taken for spills

❖ Spill containment plans

❖ Plans for evacuating the facility

❖ Methods for immediate communication to federal officials

❖ Available equipment and personnel to respond to a discharge

❖ Personnel training plans

❖ Equipment testing procedures and frequencies

The EPA can require facilities other than substantial harm facilities to prepare and submit a Facility Response Plan. In their review of a facility, the EPA considers

❖ Method of transfer of oil from facility to vehicle or process line

❖ Site-specific characteristics

❖ Proximity to water purification plants

❖ Spill histories

❖ Oil storage capacities

❖ Proximity to fish and wildlife environments

❖ Other factors

Under OPA, if a substantial harm facility does not submit a Facility Response Plan, it cannot operate.

Spill notices and responding to spills

The National Response Center must be notified of any harmful quantities of spills under OPA.[44] The harmful quantity is defined as those amounts producing a film or sheen on the water, sludge or emulsion under the surface or shorelines, or a quantity violating the water quality standard. Under the reporting requirements, the EPA has designated about 300 hazardous substances with the required reportable quantities. If a spill occurs in a facility holding a NPDES permit, notification may not be required if the permit contains effluent limitations, recurrent operations at a pointsource, or a treatment system exists.

Owners or operators of facilities are responsible for penalties and cleanup costs. There may be civil or criminal enforcement or monetary damages. Local and state governments may enforce the OPA and the CWA, but the federal government more actively enforces both acts.

Chronology of the Clean Water Act (CWA)

1948, Federal Water Pollution Control Act (FWPCA), 62 Stat. 1155; Pub. L. 845

1952, FWPCA Amendments, Ch. 927, 66 Stat. 1155

1960, FWPCA Amendments, Pub. L. 86–624, 74 Stat. 411

1965, FWPCA Amendments, Pub. L. 89–234, 79 Stat. 903

1972, Federal Water Pollution Control Act of 1972, or the Clean Water Act, Pub. L. 92–240, 86 Stat. 47

1977, Clean Water Act of 1977, Pub. L. 95–217, 33 USC 1251

1981, Municipal Wastewater Treatment Construction Grant Amendments of 1981, Pub. L. 97–117, 95 Stat. 1623

1983, CWA Amendment, 33 USC Section 1251 (a)(2)

1985, CWA Amendment, 33 USC Section 1251 (a)(1)

1987, Water Quality Act of 1987, Pub. L. 100–4, 33 USC 1254

1988, Massachusetts Bay Protection Act of 1988, Pub. L. 100–653, 102 Stat. 3835 1990, Great Lakes Critical Programs Act of 1990, Pub. L. 101–596, 1, 104 Stat. 3000, 33 USC 1269

1994, Ocean Pollution Reduction Act, Pub. L. 103–431, 108 Stat. 4396.

1998, National Ocean Survey Hydrographic Services Improvement Act of 1988, Pub. L. 106–541, 114 Stat. 2679

2000, Alternative Water Sources Act of 2000, Pub. L. 106–457, 114 Stat. 1975

2000, Lake Ponchartrain Basin Restoration Act of 2000, Pub. L. 106–457, 114 Stat. 1273

2000, Long Island Sound Restoration Act, Pub. L. 106–457, 114 Stat. 1269

2000, Chesapeake Bay Restoration Act of 2000, Pub. L. 106–457, 114 Stat. 1267

CHAPTER 10

Drinking Water:
Safe Drinking Water Act (SDWA)

Overview

❖ Public water systems and underground drinking water sources are protected.

❖ Contaminants are any physical, chemical, biological, or radiological substance or matter in water.

❖ The EPA has responsibility for administering the SDWA.

❖ National primary and secondary drinking water standards are developed, and a database is maintained.

❖ Maximum contaminant levels are recommended.

❖ EPA has guidelines for water conservation plans for public water systems.

❖ Groundwater is protected; technologies applied to keeping groundwater pure must be proven and field tested.

❖ State well water protection is ensured through the regulations.

❖ Public notices must be distributed to alert the immediate population about contaminated water.

❖ Water works infrastructure improvements may be improved with state revolving funds partially financed with federal moneys.

❖ A continuing research program identifies groups at risk from exposure to contaminants in drinking water.

❖ Radon and arsenic in water are targeted.

Safe Drinking Water Act Acronyms

BAT—Best available technology

CERCLA—Comprehensive Environmental Response, Compensation and Liability Act

CWA—Clean Water Act

FIFRA—Federal Insecticide, Fungicide, and Rodenticide Act

MCLG—Maximum contaminant level goal

MCL—Maximum contaminant level

POTW—Publicly-owned treatment works

PQL—Practical quantification level

RCRA—Resource Conservation and Recovery Act

RMCL—Recommended maximum contaminant level

SDWA—Safe Drinking Water Act

SRF—State revolving fund

TDS—Total dissolved solids

UIC—Underground injection control

USDW—Underground sources of drinking water

Background

The Safe Drinking Water Act (SDWA) was part of the Public Health Service Act and preceded the Clean Water Act (CWA). Under the act, national standards for levels of contaminants—any physical, chemical, biological, or radiological substance—in drinking water were established, and water wells and sole-source aquifers were protected.[1] Under the Comprehensive Environmental Response, Compensation, and Liability Act (CERCLA), the goals for safe water stated in the SDWA are adopted for contaminated and abandoned hazardous waste sites. The same drinking water standards are also adopted for corrective action at waste sites designated for cleanup under the Resource Conservation and Recovery Act (RCRA).[2]

The SDWA regulates drinking water by establishing a national primary drinking water standard and setting a secondary drinking water standard. These standards create a uniformity for municipal drinking water purification plants. The primary standard regulates contaminants that may cause adverse health effects; the secondary standards are advisory only (unenforceable) and are limited to protecting the public from odor or unusual appearance in drinking water. A single contaminant might be subject to both primary and secondary standards under the SDWA. When there is an urgent threat to public health, the EPA can promote an interim national primary drinking water standard for a contaminant or issue a health advisory for contaminants that are not subject to a national primary drinking water standard.

National primary drinking water regulations apply to every public water system in each state unless the system has only distribution and storage facilities (no collection or treatment facilities), or obtains its water from a public water system subject to the SDWA, or does not sell water to any person, or is not a carrier in interstate commerce.[3] Drinking water fountains and coolers are also regulated. They must be completely lead-free (no lead solder or tanks); lead or lead-compound tanks have been recalled under the Consumer Product Safety Act. Federal agencies must comply with all provisions of the SDWA. Administrative penalties or civil actions may be issued against a federal agency.

The act specifies that the EPA must propose and promote recommended maximum contaminant levels (RMCLs) and a final primary drinking water standard.[4] Under the 1986 amendments, the EPA set MCLs for 83 priority contaminants with the intent to add 25 more every three years. Requirements were set for disinfecting, filtration, and other types of treatment; groundwater protection; strengthened enforcement; and required monitoring of unregulated contaminants in public water systems. Provisions are made for technical assistance to smaller publicly-owned treatment works (POTWs) with histories of chronic noncompliance.[5]

Under some of the latest amendments to the Safe Drinking Water Act, an additional $725 million has been added to the drinking water revolving loan fund. There is also a user right-to-know modification, water source protections, special contaminant revised requirements (radon, arsenic, and others), health-effects drinking water research, and state funding for improvements to infrastructure.[6]

Exhibit 14: Common sources of drinking water are rivers, streams, lakes, and wells. Since purifying water is costly, regulations attempt to keep water free from contamination prior to its entering the treatment plant. (Photo: author)

Standards for Contaminants

Arsenic, sulfate, and radon are major concerns in the SDWA. Also, lead pipes, solder, and flux are prohibited in any public water systems or in any building or facility providing water for human consumption. Other water contaminants are regulated for safety; regular review of the regulations is necessary for a POTW to remain in compliance with the act.

A list of contaminants that are not regulated but are known to occur in public drinking water systems must be published every five years. Hazardous substances listed under CERCLA must be listed as well as those pesticides under the Federal Insecticide, Fungicide, and Rodenticide Act (FIFRA). At least five contaminants from the list must be considered for regulation based on the best available public health information and on the occurrence database.

In making regulatory decisions, the EPA must use the best available, peer-reviewed science and supporting studies conducted according to scientific practices and using data collected by acceptable methods. For each regulated contaminant, the populations affected must be addressed by estimating public health risks. When any national primary drinking water regulation includes an MCL, the EPA must develop and apply analyses containing

❖ Health risk reduction benefits likely to occur

❖ Health risk reduction benefits likely from reductions in multiple contaminants that can be attributed solely to complying with the MCL

❖ Costs likely to occur from complying with the MCL

❖ Incremental costs and benefits associated with each alternative MCL considered

❖ Target populations and subpopulations and the effects of the contaminant on them

❖ Risks connected to compliance and risks associated with multiple contaminants

❖ Uncertainties in the analyses, degree and nature of the risk, and other factors [7]

The EPA publishes a review of their decisions on tested contaminants when a standard is proposed based on costs and benefits.[8] Any determinants about contaminants that disinfect or contain byproducts of disinfectants for cryptosporidium are published. Stage I and II disinfectants and disinfectant byproducts are listed in the Interim Enhanced Surface Water Treatment Rules.

In its determination of monitoring requirements for public water treatment systems, the EPA reviews contaminants and disseminates the information for others to make any required modifications. Unregulated contaminants are monitored, and the EPA develops a list of no more than 30 contaminants to be monitored by public water systems and included in the occurrence database. Adequate supplies of available water treatment chemicals must be assured. The EPA must conduct a comparative health effects assessment of water treatment chemicals and their byproducts through a university consortium called the National Center for Ground Water Research, which works with the Robert S. Kerr Environmental Research Laboratory.

Contaminant research

All plans, strategic plans and EPA drinking water research must be subject to scientific research review. This scientific research review is further subjected to a method called practical quantification levels (PQLs). PQLs are "the lowest concentration of a contaminant that most laboratories would be able to accurately quantify in a sample of drinking water."[9] The PQLs are reviewed and accepted on the basis of good science. The Science Advisory Board was established under the Environmental Research, Development, and

Demonstration Act of 1978,[10] prior to the proposal of MCL goals and national primary drinking water regulations.[11]

There is a continuing research program to identify those groups at risk from exposure to contaminants in drinking water. Drinking water studies must also include study of estrogen substances, subpopulations at greater risks, biomedical issues, harmful substances in the drinking water, and waterborne disease occurrence. Subjects of study must include women, children, infants, pregnant women, the elderly, individuals with serious illnesses, or others likely to have increased health risk from water contamination. Research results must be reported to the U.S. Congress.

Biomedical research is conducted to provide more accurate health models showing how the human body absorbs, distributes, metabolizes, and eliminates the waterborne contaminants. New approaches are encouraged through the SDWA to study complex mixtures in drinking water to determine the synergism of chemicals (if any) or the adverse effects from combinations of chemicals or biological agents. Toxicological studies must be conducted by the EPA to determine exposure levels from disinfectants and disinfecting byproducts used in water treatment. Dose-response curves are required for pathogens (including cryptosporidium and the Norwalk virus).[12]

The Centers for Disease Control and Prevention and the EPA must develop and perform a joint waterborne disease occurrence study. National health care provider training and public education campaigns must be completed to inform the public about waterborne disease and the symptoms caused by infectious agents, such as microbial contaminants.

New contaminants under EPA consideration for regulation[13]

Contaminants are regularly reviewed as new findings unfold. Radon, arsenic, sulfates, disinfectants and their byproducts, and many other substances are under study. The impacts of and details about these contaminants provide insights into the potential threats to public health, safety, and welfare.

Radon is a radioactive gas that can become a trigger for cancers. Radon is present in groundwater in places, and is common in the Western United States. Waterborne radon can affect people who drink this contaminated water or inhale water vapor containing it. Presently radon is being studied so that the EPA can adopt a national MCLG and a national primary drinking water regulation for radon. The EPA must also publish guidelines for states to develop their own multimedia radon mitigation program.

Arsenic is a naturally occurring contaminant in groundwater which is found in many places. It can poison people causing serious sickness or death. There is a current standard of 50 ug/l—with indication that high levels of arsenic in drinking water can increase internal organ cancers. As a result of controversies over the allowable level of arsenic, new research for risk assessment and risk management for low-level exposure to arsenic is required. A number of federal agencies are combining to fund the research on this chemical, and private funds have also been applied.

Sulfates are also a naturally occurring substance in water. Severe laxation is a threat to young people, but it is not generally serious in adults. The MCL for sulfates is 250 mg/1, based on odor rather than health effects. Studies are presently being performed to obtain a reliable dose-response indicating harm.

Exhibit 15: This worker is testing around a well pad for possible herbicide use. Herbicides can percolate downward to a water table drawn-down area. The railroad indicates an industrial freight loading land use.

Disinfectants and disinfecting byproducts are commonly used to chlorinate water. When it is used as a disinfectant, chlorine may combine with other compounds to form chlorinated organic compounds.[14] All chlorine byproducts and compounds are considered disinfecting byproducts.

Regulating Drinking Water in Public Water Systems

Only public drinking water systems are covered under the SDWA. By definition, these water systems are piped water to serve the public for human consumption. The system must have 25 or more service connections or they must serve at least 25 persons. Public water systems include collection, treatment, storage, and distribution facilities. Irrigation districts in existence prior to 1994 that provide agricultural service through a piped water system with only incidental residential use is not a public water system.

Drinking water is regulated by specifying the contaminants (any physical, chemical, biological, or radiological substance in water) that may have adverse health effects. The EPA issues MCLs that are as close to the minimum contaminant level goal (MCLG) as is feasible. "Feasible" means using the best technology, treatment, and other considerations that are available—taking the cost of meeting those levels into consideration.[15] Health risk reduction must consider costs for treating contaminants and the methods and approaches to measure and value the benefits of reducing drinking water contaminant amounts.

If an MCL is not feasible, the EPA must promote a national primary drinking water regulation for that contaminant that requires using a treatment technique in lieu of establishing a maximum contaminant level. The specification of a particular MCL is based on the likelihood that the contaminant will occur with frequency and at levels of public health concern. Another decision criteria is feasibility defined by the economics of technology needed to reduce those levels. The efficiency and economy in removing the contaminants are criteria in selecting alternative technologies. The major factors in setting MCLs (including carcinogens) are the facility itself and whether the levels or presence of a contaminant can be detected.

Protecting Underground Water[16]

States have primary enforcement responsibility in protecting ground water. Their enforcement programs include issuing administrative orders and taking civil and criminal actions. Well operation permits are required; some areas of a state can be designated as areas where no new underground injection wells may be operated. For example, states can create, with the approval of the EPA, critical aquifer protection areas that contain sole or principal source aquifers. When designated, a comprehensive management plan for ground water in the critical aquifer protection area must be developed and filed.

Underground Injection Control (UIC)

When any liquid is injected into the ground that is listed as—or obviously is—hazardous waste, it is regulated under the Resource Conservation and Recovery Act (RCRA). Nearly 95 percent of the waste disposed is wastewater, according to RCRA records. Because so much of the wastewater is injected underground (especially oil and gas wastes), a lot of regulatory attention is paid to injection. The EPA estimates that about 400,000 injection wells are subject to UIC requirements. There are about six times as many UIC wells than discharges of wastewater that are given permits (under the CWA).[17]

Any situation which could create any contaminated fluid movement into the drinking water source is prohibited. It should be noted that "dissolved solids can only be tasted in drinking water at levels beginning around 1,000 mg/l. Moreover, the secondary drinking water standard for total dissolved solids (TDS) is 500 mg/l, and much of the water consumed in the nation has even lower levels."[18]

Underground sources of drinking water (USDW) are identified by three criteria:

1) They are aquifers or portions of an aquifer that supplies any drinking water system (but not individual household wells)

2) They contain enough groundwater to supply a drinking water system

3) They contain less than 10,000 mg/l total dissolved solids (TDS)

Classification of wells

There are five classes of wells in the UIC program:[19]

Class I: For injections of hazardous, industrial, and municipal disposal wastes below the lowermost drinking water formations (issued for ten-year period).

Class II: For the oil and gas industry, salt water injection wells, liquid hydrocarbons storage wells, natural gas plant wells, and enhanced recovery wells (issued for life).

Class III: For extracting minerals, such as sulfur, uranium, potash, salts (issued for life).

Class IV: For hazardous or radioactive waste into a formation within one-quarter mile from a USDW.

Class V: For any other injection well—geothermal wells, septic system wells from dwellings, drainage wells, air conditioning return flow wells to return aquifer water from a heat pump, cesspools, cooling water return flow wells.

A report is required for Class V wells only if drinking water sources are threatened with contamination.[20] By contrast, Class I wells have closely imposed operating requirements. There are basic construction and operating requirements for Class I, II, and III wells to help eliminate the potential for leaking wells:[21]

❖ Areas around a well must be analyzed to prevent open holes or abandoned wells from facilitating the movement of fluids from the injection zone to the groundwater.

❖ Construction, such as cementing and logging, must be performed to prevent fluids from traveling behind the well casing.

❖ Any leaks of fluid from the well or any boreholes must be stopped immediately.

❖ Financial capabilities of owners or operators must be verified to be certain that the well can be plugged or repaired if it fails.

Exhibit 16: Ground water is a major source of drinking water. The top of this well has had its valving and piping removed, and the owner neglected to cap the well as required by water regulations. Other wells that use the same ground water can be contaminated.

❖ There must be mechanical integrity so that the well does not leak.

❖ There must be monitoring of injection pressures, along with the volume and rate of fluid injected.

❖ Records must be kept, and fluid injections reported in order to be certain about the quantities of leaks, if any.

The state usually issues permits and enforces the UIC regulations. Class I hazardous waste injection wells are under the SWDA and RCRA. The land disposal restriction program under RCRA also makes for very strict construction and operating requirements for those wells.[22]

Hazardous wastes are regulated by the EPA under a series of recommendations for the best available technology (BAT) standards. In many instances, BAT applications for changing liquids to solids or vapors may be approved. The land disposal restriction can be lifted when an owner or operator can prove that no hazardous waste will migrate. Mathematical models that show that no wastes will migrate laterally or vertically for 10,000 years must be included in the BAT application.[23]

Class II wells are oil and gas injection wells. The major wells are saltwater disposal wells and enhanced recovery injection wells. Often the water on top of the oil will be salty and contain high levels of TDS. As an oil field is emptied, the water mixes with the oil and may become salty. Finding places to dispose of this water is difficult. Enhanced recovery wells are those wells in which water is injected or other fluids to push the oil upward out of the well. Again, byproducts of salt water or other kinds of contaminated water can be expected.[24]

Class III wells are used in mining and have stringent operating requirements controlled by the states. Class IV wells may not be used for injection, especially injecting above or into a USDW. In these latter wells, waste injections are particularly prone to leaks. Class V wells include a broad range of potential wastes. No permit is needed for Class V wells unless it could leak into a USDW. Gasoline service stations having Class V wells near them have been particular problems. Leaking oil pits, hydraulic lifts, or steel drums or the washing of the oil-containing floors into drainage pipes have endangered many USDWs. EPA has categorized Class V wells into ten general categories:[25]

1) Beneficial Use Wells—Those wells that improve the quality or flow of aquifers to provide some other benefit

2) Cesspools—Those wells receiving untreated household wastes

3) Drainage Wells—Wells that drain surface and subsurface fluids such as agricultural runoff and storm water

4) Experimental Technology Wells—Any injection well that is not proven to be safe as yet

5) Fluid Return Wells—Wells used to contain spent fluids from the production of geothermal energy for heating or power, extraction of minerals, or from aquaculture

6) Industrial Waste Discharge Wells—Wells used to inject wastewater from industrial, commercial, and service businesses

7) In-situ and Solution Mining Wells—Those wells used to obtain oil and gas from underground formations and bring them to the surface

8) Mine Backfill Wells—Wells that bury slurries of sand, gravel, cement, mill tailings, refuse, or fly ash in underground mines. This backfill prevents subsidence and can control mine fires.

9) Septic Systems—Wells composed of septic tanks and fluid distribution systems such as leaching fields; for household wastes only

10) Sewage Treatment Effluent—Wells used to inject effluent from public or private treatment facilities

Exhibit 17: Streams are sources for drinking water. Stream purity is extremely important. Runoff from fields, indsutrial areas, and accidental releases of contaminants can affect the operations of publicly owned treatment works.

SDWA Enforcement

States have primary enforcement responsibility for public water systems unless the EPA does not approve the state for enforcement responsibility, takes over responsibility from the state, or refuses a state's control in a particular matter. States prepare periodic reports and submit annual reports on violations of national primary drinking water regulations by public water systems for maximum contaminant levels. The reports include treatment requirements, lists of variances and exemptions granted, and requirements for monitoring. The EPA must include the annual state reports in its own annual report. A public water system can be granted an exemption by a state, but the state must first find that: 1) the public water system cannot comply with the MCL or treatment requirement or develop an alternative source of water supply, 2) the system was in operation on the effective date of that contaminant level or treatment method requirement, 3) the granting of the exemption will not increase health risks, and 4) changes will be made to improve the quality of the drinking water.

States which have primary enforcement responsibilities for public water systems must develop a source water assessment program containing the boundaries of the areas; the identities of the contaminants; the sources of the drinking water supplies; the water flow, discharge, and recharge rates; and other reliable information. Public water system operators must be certified according to specific state guidelines. Individual state programs for certification can be developed. Variances may be granted for systems that cannot meet an MCL because of the characteristics of the raw water sources available to the system. Exemptions for only three years may be granted for not meeting an applicable MCL. If an unreasonable risk to public health could occur, an exemption cannot be granted.

EPA and SDWA enforcement

The EPA enforces the SDWA in different ways. Civil actions may be enacted against any person or the United States government and specific governmental agencies. A public water system may be given fines per day of violation, but there are no criminal penalties. Notices of violations are published in periodicals, and news releases are issued to the media. Alternative water supplies are arranged until the violation is corrected.

Owners or operators of (public or private) water systems must give notice to the communities they serve if the system fails to comply with an applicable MCL or treatment technique, fails to perform required monitoring or testing, or fails to comply with a prescribed schedule demanded in its granted variance or exemption. If a contaminant level is exceeded, the EPA requires owners or operators to give notice to all persons served.

Enforcement and funding amendments[26]

The EPA's enforcement duties for violations of drinking water standards were extended under later amendments to the CWA.[27] Fines can be assessed only after public notices of impure water are given and after public comments are received. There are also new funding methods in the amendments which help water works to comply, improve infrastructure, improve water source quality, increase research on the potential adverse health effects of contaminants, and improve system operating procedures.

A State Revolving Fund (SRF) of $9.6 billion was authorized to improve drinking water infrastructure.[28] Over 34 billion in available funding has accumulated and can be used for different state programs.[29] States can receive grants, loans, or letters of credit. To qualify, a state must develop its own program for a water treatment revolving loan fund according to EPA requirements. Each state must have the technical, management, and financial capability to meet the requirements of its program and must already comply with the primary drinking water regulations. A needs survey for the state becomes the basis for the grant awards. All amounts deposited with the state from the SRF must only be used for loans, loan guarantees, or as sources of reserve and security for leveraged loans.[30] Water systems may only use the money to help meet national primary drinking water regulations, install water treatment equipment, or further protect health. The SRF funds can be used to alter the structure of a municipal or other interstate agency in the state, purchase insurance for a bond, or provide security for revenue or general obligation bonds issued by a state.

The state loan fund may be combined with another other revolving funds to avoid administrative costs. Funds cannot be used for monitoring, operating costs, maintenance, land purchases, or other interests. The SRF sets aside 15 percent of the fund for loan assistance to public water systems serving fewer than 10,000 people. A state must submit a report to the EPA every other year, and the EPA must audit the state loan funds.

To receive a water system grant, a state must prepare and submit a plan that describes the intended use of the SRF funds. The plan must be presented for public comment before adoption. This plan is an intended use plan, which describes a yearly list of projects, terms of assistance, size of the communities, criteria for distributing the funds, status of state loan fund, and the goals for the fund. A state must annually publish a list of projects eligible for funds, priorities, and the expected funding schedule. Each loan must be repaid with interest.

Under the SRF, there are provisions for special assistance for disadvantaged communities (the area served by a public water system meeting affordability criteria developed by the state). For these communities, a state can forgive interest and principal. Matching state funds may total 20 percent of the total amount of the grant. Prepayments by the state are required to be placed in escrow in advance of the contributions.

There are also outright grants to states from the EPA. State ground water protection grants ensure coordinated, comprehensive protection of ground water resources. Both innovative protection programs and technical projects must be evaluated in the application for the program to be potentially effective in protecting groundwater. Grants cannot exceed 50 percent of costs, and the state must pay the balance.

Other Water System Funds, Aids, and Programs[31]

A source water assessment program delineates boundaries where public water systems may obtain their drinking water supplies. When a state wishes to permanently modify its contaminant monitoring program, the source water assessment program requires adding a timetable, a statement on the availability of state funds, a list of the contaminants for which monitoring is required, and the origins of the contaminants identified within each delineated area.

The source water petition program is a quality protection partnership between a state and the community water system. It is a voluntary, incentive-based partnership among the waste system operators, interested persons, and the government. The state can provide financial assistance. Only those contaminants that are detected at levels above the MCLs are part of the petitions.

Water capacity is another issue addressed by the CWA. States must prepare capacity development strategies that contain methods and criteria to be used by the states to identify and set priorities for public water systems according to need. Resources are provided to assist public water systems in meeting national primary drinking water regulations. The EPA publishes guidelines to ensure that all new community water systems meet federal standards (national primary drinking water regulations). States must annually compile a list of their community, non-transient, and non-community water systems that have histories of not complying with provisions of the CWA.

Operators of water systems must be certified according to EPA-specified standards. The guidelines consider the current state programs, system complexities, and other factors. Users must receive a consumer confidence report which specifies how the source water is being provided, if regulated contaminants have been detected, the levels of contami-

Exhibit 18: Drilling is performed for new wells of all types and for taking core samples. The drill bit is connected to machinery mounted on a truck. In this photo, cover material and a shovel are shown in the steel drum.

nants, information on compliance with the drinking water regulations, and any required monitoring that is performed according to EPA requirements. A state is allowed to forgo mailing consumer confidence reports to communities which have fewer than 10,000 persons, but in those cases the consumers must be informed by newspaper notices.

Critical aquifer protection area demonstration program [32]

A critical aquifer protection area is one that contains an aquifer designated as a sole or principal source aquifer and has had an area-wide ground water quality protection plan approved under section 208 of the CWA. When an application is approved for this program, the EPA can enter into an agreement with an applicant to establish the demonstration program and grant 50 percent of the costs of implementing the plan. The EPA can also reimburse a successful applicant and recipient of an approved plan up to 50 percent of her or his costs for developing the plan. Total grants cannot exceed $4 million in one year.

State wellhead protection programs [33]

A wellhead protection area is a surface and subsurface area surrounding a water well or a field containing many wells supplying a public water system and through which contaminants can move and taint the ground water well or well field.[34] Each state is required to protect its wellhead areas from contaminants. Criteria are developed for acceptable radii of effect, depth of drawdown of the water table, time or rate of travel in different hydrologic conditions, distance from the well or well field, engineering pump tests and comparable data, field reconnaissance, topographic information, and the geography of the formation. The state must develop and submit a program for approval by the EPA that

❖ Describes assistance programs for financial assistance, controls, education, training, and demonstration projects
❖ Determines the wellhead protection area for each wellhead
❖ Identifies all potential sources of contaminants
❖ Includes contingency plans for locating and providing alternate drinking water supplies
❖ Includes consideration of all potential sources of contaminants within the expected wellhead area of a new water well serving a water supply system
❖ Specifies the duties of state and local government agencies and their water supply systems

Each public entity defines the area boundaries and identifies the potential contaminants. They are required to provide appropriate technical and financial assistance that includes contingency plans to locate alternate drinking water supplies in case of well field contamination. The EPA can make grants to states to develop and implement a state program to comprehensively protect ground water. Every three years, the EPA must evaluate the state ground water protection programs which it funded through grants.

If a state has more than 2,500 active injection wells, the state program must certify to the EPA that drinking water is protected from contaminants from oil and brine injection or surface disposal.

Chronology of the Safe Drinking Water Act (SDWA)

1974, Safe Drinking Water Act of 1974, Pub. L. 93–523, 42 USC 300–300j-26

1977, Safe Drinking Water Act of 1977, Pub. L. 95–190

1986, Safe Drinking Water Act Amendments of 1986, Pub. L.104–182

1996, Safe Drinking Water Act Amendments of 1996, Pub. L. 104–182, 110 Stat. 1613

CHAPTER 11

Oil Spills into Water: Oil Pollution Act (OPA)

Overview

❖ There been many oil spills in ship channels, rivers, lakes, bays, and oceans.

❖ Certain types of oils, such as edible oils, are regulated differently from petrochemical oils.

❖ Vessels having single hulls with no oil leak protection systems are particularly subject to leaks, but double hull vessels can be damaged also.

❖ Double hulls are mandatory for vessels transporting oil.

❖ Under the OPA, those owners or operators responsible for the spills are financially liable.

❖ Many of these spills are so costly that insurance carriers are needed to ensure payments for cleanups.

❖ An oil spill liability trust fund is established.

❖ The federal government holds first strike responsibilities for cleanups of oil spills.

❖ The U.S. Coast Guard evaluates the manning, training, qualifications, and watch-keeping standards.

❖ The National Contingency Plan (NCP) and the National Response System (NRS) require coordination with oil spill responses.

❖ State authority is dominant in oil spill removal.

❖ Vessels and facilities must have approved spill response plans.

Oil Pollution Act Acronyms

CWA—Clean Water Act

EPA—Environmental Protection Agency

NCP—National Contingency Plan

NOAA—National Oceanic and Atmospheric Administration

NRDA—Natural Resource Damage Assessments

NRS—National Response System

OPA—Oil Pollution Act

General

A series of major chemical and oil spills into ocean waters provided legislators with good reasons to develop and pass this federal act.[1] The act establishes oil pollution liability and compensation, enforces strict liability for comprehensive damage, controls oil spills into the water from vessels and industrial facilities, describes the authority of the federal government to direct and manage oil spill clean up operations, and compels vessel and facility operators to file detailed oil spill response plans for private sector clean up and removal. Vessels operators must work actively to prevent oil spills and replace vessels with double-hulled oil tankers and barges. Tanker safety is promoted through many requirements to prevent spills in water. Compensation by owners or operators is required for spills at sea or in ports.

The federal government holds first strike responsibility for cleaning up oil spills from vessels and facilities. There are claim procedures, financial responsibility requirements, and provisions for how the Oil Spill Liability Trust Fund is to be used. A vessel (pleasure craft or cargo ship) that spills oil or a dangerous cargo substance is potentially liable for cleanup costs or criminal charges. Double hulls are only required for vessels that transport oil. Both on- and offshore facilities used for exploration, drilling, production, storage, handling, transfers, processing, or transportation of oil are regulated. Each responsible owner or operator is liable for all removal costs paid by the government. Removal costs under OPA can include the costs by any agency or department of government to avert a release, ensure containment, prevent dispersal, or remove a contaminant. Costs include those actions to protect fish, shellfish, wildlife, property, shorelines, beaches, or other natural resources.

Provisions of OPA

Provisions of OPA state that no funds can be used by the Coast Guard to issue, implement, or enforce a regulation or to establish interpretations or guidelines that do not recognize and provide for environmental effects; fats, oils, and greases; and differences in physical, chemical, biological, and other relevant properties.[2] These sections of OPA are called the Edible Oil Regulatory Reform Act which requires that animal fats, oils, and greases, fish and marine mammal oils, and other oils and greases be considered and controlled differently due to their potential to naturally disperse, degrade, and decompose.

Any foreign country that issues vessel documents must have U.S. Coast Guard evaluation of the manning, training, qualifications, and watch-keeping standards. This provision ensures that the other country's standards are equivalent to those of the United States or international standards. The Coast Guard conducts periodic reviews of each country's manning standards and performs post-casualty reviews of any spills for which the country might be responsible. Many standards are formulated by the Coast Guard that include navigation, cargo handling, and maintenance of tank vessels. Officers and crew members are restricted to working no more than 15 hours in any 24-hour period and no more than 36 hours in any 72-hour period.

Marine casualty reports of significant harm to the environment must be submitted to the U.S. Coast Guard. Tankers weighing over 1,600 gross tons must have a licensed master or mate on the bridge in addition to the pilot. Single hull tankers must be escorted by two tug boats through certain waters in the Northwest.[3] Non-United States and non-Canadian vessels of any type (not just tankers) must retain a Canadian or United States pilot on the Great Lakes.

The Act specifies the thickness of hull plates for particular types of vessels and establishes minimum standards for overfill, tank level, and pressure-monitoring devices. Radio equipment is regulated. Double hulls are specified for tank vessels, and a phase-out schedule for single hull tankers runs until the year 2015. Under the phase-out, the older and larger vessels are retired first. If a vessel is newly constructed and less than 5,000 tons, it must be built with a double containment system that is determined by the Coast Guard to be as effective as a double hull. All single-hulled tank vessels are required to have written bridge procedures, training for sailors, ship charts that contain enhanced shore and bottom surveys, on-board cargo and mooring system surveys, working auto-pilot alarm systems, completed maneuvering tests, and calculated keel clearances. Notice must be given to the harbormaster or the U.S. Coast Guard prior to entering ports.

The Department of Transportation is authorized to make loan guarantees to construct replacement vessels or reconstruct existing vessels according to Coast Goard criteria.[4] The OPA oil spill response system relies on private resources to minimize or remove spills. Immunity from spill liability is given to those helping, rendering care, or giving assistance or advice in response to a spill. Federal authorities must remove or ensure removal of a discharge and prevent the substantial threat from a discharge. Spills or threats in waters or other places where natural resources are affected are also under federal removal authority.

Measuring natural resource damages under OPA

Each government agency develops a plan to repair environmental damages from the spill. The plan must provide for payment of the necessary repairs. The federal government develops and administers the methods for assessing damages. Limits of liability must be adjusted to the consumer price index every three years. The National Oceanic and Atmospheric Administration (NOAA) is the federal agency that prepares and publishes regulations on natural resource damage assessments (NRDA). There are three major components of a damage assessment:

1) Preassessment

2) Restoration planning

3) Restoration implementation

In the first component, preassessment, a preliminary determination is made concerning injury to the environment. The second, restoration planning, identifies a number of restoration alternatives. Methods to evaluate the restoration alternatives are prescribed to help decide on the most appropriate course of action. In restoration implementation, the responsible parties must complete and fund the cleanup.

The Oil Spill Liability Trust Fund pays for cleanup costs and damages. Government and private use of this fund is limited to $1 billion per incident. Private use of the fund can pay for uncompensated removal costs and damages submitted according to claims procedures. Uncompensated claims can draw from this fund.

National Contingency Plan and the National Response System

The National Contingency Plan (NCP) and the National Response System (NRS) require that any cleanups of oil spills be coordinated with the NCP. The NCP is placed under the CWA, which describes methods for containing, dispersing, and removing oil and hazardous substances. The NCP assigns duties among federal departments and agencies, other levels of government, and establishes Coast Guard response teams. A national surveillance and notice system provides a national coordination center and warnings of spills or threats of spills. The NCP requires that federal and state officials work together to calculate the appropriate amount and use of dispersants and other chemicals.[5]

The National Response System under the CWA creates a multilevel governmental hierarchy to respond to spills, and creates the National Response Unit, Coast Guard Strike Teams, Coast Guard District Response Groups, Area Committees, Area Contingency Plans, and vessel and facility response plans.

Local Area Committees are composed of federal, state, and local agencies to prepare contingency plans for worst-case discharges from a source. These plans are federally reviewed and approved. The plans are to be integrated with the procedures of the NRS, other area plans, and vessel and facility response plans. Area plans describe and list all available equipment and personnel available.[6]

Exhibit 19: Rocks near the coast are threatening to ships and can injure their hulls. The scenic beauty, marine wildlife, and recreational potential are protected by the regulations from cargo and bilge spills, oil and gas drilling, and accidents from ship transfers. (Photo: author)

Vessel and facility response plans

Owners and operators of tank vessels and facilities must prepare response plans to remove any oil releases into waters. Their plans must be coordinated and consistent with the NCP and Area Contingency Plans. The person in charge of initiating and ordering spill removals must be identified. The vessel or facility response plans must be periodically updated and must describe training, equipment testing, unannounced drills, and response actions by personnel to decrease or prevent discharge. A vessel response plan must contain these provisions to be approved by the Coast Guard:

❖ Discharge notices and procedures

❖ Detailed descriptions of drills and training

❖ Private finances available to respond to a worst case discharge

❖ Responsible individual and an alternate

❖ Worst-case discharge quantities

A response must be initiated within two hours of discovering a spill, and equipment and manpower must be in place within 12 hours in high-volume port areas; within 24 hours in river, inland, near shore and offshore areas; and within 24 hours plus travel time for spills occurring into the open seas more than 50 miles from shore. Tier 1 resources must arrive at the scene within 12 hours in high-volume port areas or 24 hours in other areas. Tier 2 and 3 resources must be capable of arriving in 24-hour increments thereafter.[7]

Vessels that are 400 feet or more in length must be able to contain and remove on-deck cargo spills of at least 12 barrels. Those vessels under 400 feet in length must be able to contain and remove at least seven barrels. Inland oil barges must handle an on-deck spill of at least one barrel. Vessels carrying oil as secondary cargo must be able to handle a spill of one-half barrel. There are also two different planning standards—one for oil cargo vessels and the other for oil as a secondary cargo on a vessel.

The regulations vary for facilities. If more than 250 barrels of oil are transferred over water, owners or operators must develop an approved response plan. The factors determining which facilities must submit a plan are as follows:

❖ Type of facility

❖ Storage capacity and material stored

❖ Number of tanks, their age, and secondary containment

❖ Proximity to navigable waters and public drinking water supplies

❖ Proximity to sensitive environmental areas, spill history, and likelihood of natural disasters

❖ Number of annual tank barge or tank vessel transfers

❖ Type or quantity of petroleum product transferred each year

❖ Multiple transfer ability

❖ Any other risk factors

Methods for containing and cleaning a worst-case discharge must be stated along with the methods for handling the loss of the entire facility or tank, etc. Onshore pipelines must be designed for worst-case discharges, and the design and engineering must be materials approved.[8]

Chronology of the Oil Pollution Act (OPA)

1990, Oil Pollution Act of 1990, Pub. L. 101–380, 33 USC 2701–2761

1990, Great Lakes Oil Pollution Research and Development Act, Pub. L. 101–646

1995, Edible Oil Regulatory Reform Act, Pub. L. 104–55, 1, 109 Stat. 546, 33 USC 2704–2716

CHAPTER 12

Ocean Dumping: Marine Protection, Research, and Sanctuaries Act (MPRSA)

Overview

❖ MPRSA prohibits ocean dumping of material that can endanger human health or marine animals and their environment.

❖ Dumping of industrial waste or sewage sludge is not allowed.

❖ Most dumping today consists of dredged material—sediments taken from water bottoms to maintain navigation channels.

❖ Permits must be issued prior to ocean dumping.

❖ Decisions on permits are made by U.S. Army Corps of Engineers using EPA criteria.

❖ The EPA recommends the disposal sites for use under the permits.

Marine Protection, Research, and Sanctuaries Act Acronyms

DOC—Department of Commerce

EPA—Environmental Protection Agency

MPRSA—Marine Protection, Research, and Sanctuaries Act

Purpose and Programs

MPRSA protects the marine environment, its ecology, and its economic future.[1] The common name of this act is the Ocean Dumping Act. The act regulates the dumping of waste into the ocean, promotes and maintains research programs, and requires the designation and regulations of marine sanctuaries.

Ocean dumping is regulated twelve miles from shore. No materials can be dumped into ocean waters that could harm public health and welfare, marine environment, ecological systems, or the economic potential of the land or sea. There is a dumping permit program that includes sewage sludge, industrial waste, dredge material. Transporting wastes and dumping into the ocean is prohibited. Wastes and other materials that cannot be dumped include the following:

❖ Biological and laboratory wastes

❖ Excavation debris

❖ Chemicals

❖ Warfare agents

❖ Industrial, municipal, agricultural, and other wastes

❖ Wrecked or discarded equipment

❖ Rocks and sand

❖ Sewage sludge

❖ Munitions

Sewage from vessels or oil is not included, and disposal by pipes is covered under other federal regulations.[2]

A monitoring and research program considers long-range pollution effects, overfishing, and man-induced changes to ocean ecosystems. In order to keep ship channels and river beds to the appropriate depth, dredging of the bottoms must be performed regularly. Disposing of such material is permitted at sea sites designated by the EPA.[3] Other federal agencies must coordinate places of dumping with the EPA.

Exhibit 20: Ocean wave action pulls a shoreline discharge of contaminants (dark area in right foreground) into the deeper waters. A large area can be contaminated through diffusion of concentrated chemical substances. (Photo: author)

The U.S. Department of Commerce (DOC) is responsible for designating National Marine Sanctuaries in consultation with interested federal, state, and local agencies. Sanctuaries can be located anywhere in the marine environments of the Great Lakes, ocean and coastal waters, bays, estuaries, or other submerged lands.[4]

Permits required

For ocean dumping to be approved, owners or operators must apply for a permit and have it issued by the EPA or U.S. Army Corps of Engineers. The EPA can issue permits for ocean dumping (from sea vessels or aircraft) after a few procedures are followed. Notice must be given to the public that they may attend a public hearing.

Fees must be paid to obtain the dumping permit. Additionally, an agreement to comply with the terms of the permit must be signed. Criteria for awarding the permit include these requirements:

❖ The marine environment, ecological systems, economic potential, and human health and welfare will not be endangered.

❖ There must be a need for the proposed dumping.

❖ The effects cannot be harmful to fisheries, shellfish, wildlife, shorelines, or beaches.

❖ Marine ecosystems will not be harmed.

❖ Species and population dynamics will not be harmed

❖ There will be little effect from dumping the volumes and concentrations of the materials.

❖ The locations and methods of disposal must be considered, as well as the land disposal alternatives.

There are different permit categories. Sites may be specified, and time periods and sites may be restricted in the permits. Dredge material disposal sites shall have site management plans which outline baseline assessment of conditions at the site, monitoring, special conditions or practices, quantities of materials to be disposed, biodegradability of the waste, and which state the anticipated use of the site over the long term.[5]

Sewage sludge and industrial wastes

The dumping into the ocean of industrial wastes or sewage sludge may be allowed in emergencies. The EPA must determine that there are no other alternatives, that an emergency does exist which requires the dumping of the waste, and that dumping it elsewhere poses an unacceptable risk to human health.[6]

Radioactive material

The dumping of radioactive material may be permitted with approval of Congress after the applicant submits an acceptable Radioactive Material Disposal Impact Assessment. This assessment must include details of the containers to be disposed, the number to be dumped, structural diagrams of each container, the number of curies in each container, and the exposure levels in rems inside and outside of each container. There are many other requirements for the assessment.[7]

New York Bight Apex

In the waters of the Atlantic Ocean about 18 miles from Long Island are two restricted dumping areas known as the New York Bight Apex and the 106-Mile Ocean Waste Dump Site. Only those who had been approved prior to earlier court orders can apply for a permit to dump in these areas. Prior to the court orders, municipal sludge had been approved for ocean dumping. No disposal or sewage sludge is allowed to be deposited on Staten Island.[8]

Enforcement

An enforcement agreement includes a plan negotiated by the owner or operator that, if adhered to by the owner or operator, will result in the phase-out of ocean dumping and transporting of wastes for ocean dumping. Each state that is a party to a compliance or enforcement agreement must establish a separate Clean Oceans Fund for deposit of all fees and penalties connected with ocean dumping permits and violations. The Coast Guard must perform constant surveillance to deter ocean dumping. The EPA must make annual reports on ocean dumping to Congress.[9]

Research and science

The DOC, in coordination with U.S. Coast Guard, maintains a continuing program of monitoring and research on the effects of dumping material into ocean and coastal waters or the Great Lakes. Regional management plans are to be examined to ensure proper regulation of the disposal of waste materials. In addition, the long-range effects of pollution, overfishing, and man-induced changes to the ocean ecosystem must be addressed.[10] Sewage disposal in the New York Metropolitan Area that is related to landfilling, incineration, ocean dumping, or recycling must be reported to Congress.

A North Pacific Marine Research Institute is established at the Alaska SeaLife Center by the North Pacific Research Board. The emphasis of this institute is research into marine mammals, sea birds, fish, and shellfish populations in the Bering Sea and Gulf of Alaska. Its functions are to conduct research, education, and demo projects on the North Pacific marine ecosystem. Populations located in or near Kenai Fjords National Park and the Alaska Maritime National Wildlife Refuge are included in the research. The institute supports and upgrades the facilitiès and related equipment required at the Alaska SeaLife Center. All research conducted there is provided to National Park Service, U. S. Fish and Wildlife Service; and NOAA—National Oceanic and Atmospheric Administration.[11]

Chronology of the Marine Protection, Research, and Sanctuaries Act (MPRSA)

1972, Marine Protection, Research, and Sanctuaries Act of 1972, 33 USC 1401–1445; 16 USC 1431, 33 USC 1271

1988, Ocean Dumping Ban Act of 1988, Pub. L. 100–688, Title I, 1001, 102 Stat. 4139.

1992, MPRSA Amendments, Marine Mammal Health and Stranding Response Act, Pub. L. 102–587, 106 Stat. 5059

1994, MPRSA Amendments, Marine Mammal Protection Act Amendments of 1994, Pub. L. 103–238

1997, MPRSA Amendments, International Dolphin Conservation Program Act, Pub. L. 105–42, 111 Stat. 1122

2000, MPRSA Amendments, Striped Bass Conservation, Atlantic Coastal Fisheries Management, and Marine Mammal Rescue Assistance Act of 2000, Pub. L. 106–555, 114 Stat. 2765

CHAPTER 13
Ocean Dumping and Ships:
Prevention of Pollution from Ships (PPS)

Overview

❖ Waste discharges from ships are recognized to contaminate shorelines.

❖ Dry bulk cargo residue disposal is regulated on the Great Lakes.

❖ Cruise vessels cannot discharge untreated sewage into waters.

❖ Treated sewage and galley, dishwasher, bath, and laundry wastewater cannot be discharged in ports or while traveling.

❖ Commercial vessels are inspected for compliance to the PPS.

❖ The State of Alaska and the EPA may designate no discharge zones for cruise vessels.

❖ Plastic processor equipment must be installed on ships to compact and weigh down plastic wastes so that they sink.

❖ A public outreach program about plastic pollution is developed.

Prevention of Pollution from Ships Acronyms

EPA—Environmental Protection Agency

FWPCA—Federal Water Pollution Control Act

MARPOL—Protocol of the International Convention for the Prevention of Pollution from Ships (a term derived from "marine pollutant")

PPS—Prevention of Pollution from Ships

Pollution from Ships

The PPS act recognizes that commercial, government, and personal ships are contaminating the waters of the United States.[1] Provisions in the act recognize discharges of dry cargo residues, bulk cargo, treated sewage, gray water, and other effluent can kill ecosystems as well as marine mammals. Therefore, all cruise vessel discharges must be reported. The U.S. Coast Guard enforces the provisions of the PPS, and all inspections of commercial vessels are required to comply with the FWPCA.

There are locations, or zones, that prohibit any discharges. Besides cruise ships, only those ships registered in the U.S. or operated under its authority are subject to the regulations. Other excluded vessels include warships, submersible ships, and U.S. Navy ships—but these ships must comply with the special area requirements by developing technologies and practices for solid waste management aboard their ships. Additionally, Alaskan cruise ships which have over 500 passengers are regulated.

Regulated Items

Plastic processor equipment that will be able to compact and weigh down plastic wastes so that they sink must be installed in ships. Cargo residues in the Great Lakes are studied. Dry bulk cargo residue disposal is regulated to prohibit incidental discharges of nonhazardous and nontoxic dry bulk cargo.[2] Treated and untreated sewage cannot be discharged into waters. Gray water (defined as galley, dishwasher, bath, and laundry wastewater) cannot be released in ports and release is restricted during traveling.

Gray water discharges must satisfy the minimum level of effluent quality:

❖ Not exceed a mean of 20 fecal coliform/100 ml with not more than ten percent of the sample exceeding 40 fecal coliform/100 ml

❖ Concentrations of total residual chlorine may not exceed 10 ug/l

❖ At least five representative samples of discharges must be tested prior to any discharge

Commercial vessels are inspected under the PPS and must comply with the FWPCA. Inspectors can

❖ Review onboard compliance records

❖ Inspect proper operations and functions of discharge abatement and control equipment

❖ Make unannounced inspections of any aspect of cruise vessel operations, equipment, or discharges

❖ Review owner or operator logbooks that detail times, types, volumes, or flow rates and the locations of any dumped sewage or gray water

❖ Review and approve plans for sampling and testing discharges for compliance with the FWPCA in meeting cruise vessel effluent standards

Any ships required to be regulated under the MARPOL Protocol are issued certificates, and any non-complying ships will be detained. The Coast Guard inspects cargo holds and checks for appropriate ship disposal, particularly on covered ships. Civil and criminal penalties are issued for violations. Marine debris data that are developed under the provisions of the Marine Protection, Research, and Sanctuaries Act are to be used as enforcement references.

Public Outreach

A plastic pollution public education program teaches the harmful effects of plastic pollution in bodies of water, the need to reduce it, the need to recycle plastic materials, and the need to reduce the overall quantities of plastic debris in the marine environment. PPS encourages volunteer groups, or "Citizen Pollution Patrols," to assist in monitoring, reporting, cleaning up, and preventing ocean and shoreline pollution.

Chronology of the Prevention of Pollution from Ships (PPS)

1980, Act to Prevent Pollution from Ships, Pub. L. 96–478, 74 Stat. 2297

1987, Marine Plastic Pollution Research and Control Act of 1987, Pub. L. 100–220

1989, Amendments, Pub. L. 100–220

2000, Dry Bulk Cargo Residue Disposal on the Great Lakes; Study and Regulations, Pub. L. 106–554

2000, Certain Alaskan Cruise Ship Operations, Pub. L. 106–554

CHAPTER 14

Ocean and Paints:
Organotin Antifouling Paint Control Act
(OAPCA)

Overview

❖ The OAPCA protects the aquatic environment by controlling antifouling paints that contain tin organotin biocides.

❖ A major target of OAPCA are vessels less than 75 feet in length and coated with organotin antifouling paint.

❖ Each application of antifouling paint containing organotin requires prior certification by the EPA.

❖ Estuaries and near coastal waters are monitored, and there must be quarterly monitoring of waters serving as the home port for any U.S. Navy vessel coated with organotin antifouling paint.

❖ EPA provides states with assistance in monitoring waters.

Organotin Antifouling Paint Control Act Acronyms

EPA—Environmental Protection Agency

NOAA—National Oceanic and Atmospheric Administration

OAPCA—Organotin Antifouling Paint Control Act

Protecting Waters

The purpose of the Organotin Antifouling Paint Control Act is to protect the aquatic environment from the antifouling paint used by certain vessels.[1] The paint contains tin organotin biocides and is used to prevent the buildup of barnacles and other organisms on the hulls of ships. Organotin is very toxic to marine and freshwater organisms at very low levels. The compound mixes with waters to create unreasonable risks to oysters, clams, fish, and other aquatic life.

Particular targets of the OAPCA are vessels less than 75 feet in length which account for the largest amount of organotin releases into aquatic environments. Major concerns are degrading of the paint coating and its release into the waters of the Great Lakes.

Control methods

The U.S. Coast Guard enforces the act and issues civil and criminal penalties for noncompliance. Each application of paint requires that the particular antifouling paint containing organotin be first certified by the EPA. Manufacturers must test the release rate for organotin, and their products must comply with test standards of no more than 4.0 micrograms per square centimeter per day.[2] Alternative antifouling materials research is promoted.

Under NOAA (an agency of the U.S. Department of Commerce), the EPA must monitor estuaries and near coastal waters for organotin and report annually. There must be quarterly monitoring of waters serving as the home port for any U.S. Navy vessel coated with an antifouling paint containing organotin. The U.S. Navy and the EPA specify each department's duties and responsibilities and agrees on a monitoring program. Additionally, the EPA provides states with assistance in monitoring waters. There are civil and criminal penalties for noncompliance.

Chronology of the Organotin Antifouling Paint Control Act (OAPCA)

1988, Organotin Antifouling Paint Control Act of 1988, Pub. L. 100–333

CHAPTER 15

Shore Protection:
Public Vessel Medical Waste Antidumping Act (PVMWADA) and the Shore Protection Act (SPA)

Overview

❖ These acts promote the protection of shores from dumping of municipal, commercial, and medical waste.

❖ PVMWADA prevents the washing ashore of potentially infectious medical wastes from vessels.

❖ SPA controls vessels, vehicles, and facilities from which municipal or commercial waste is loaded onto a vessel.

Public Vessel Medical Waste Act and Shore Protection Act Acronyms

DOT—Department of Transportation

EPA—Environmental Protection Agency

FWPCA—Federal Water Pollution Control Act

MPRSA—Marine Protection, Research, and Sanctuaries Act

SPA—Shore Protection Act

SWDA—Safe Drinking Water Act

Dumping of Medical Waste

This act provides a needed layer of protection from vessels that dispose medical wastes into oceans. The accidental washing ashore of potentially infectious medical wastes from public vessels requires regulation,[1] and past contamination incidents have made such legislation a priority. The PVMWADA recognizes that the public health and welfare of coastal communities are threatened without controls on dumping of medical wastes. Coastal waters are defined as the seas of the United States, the Great Lakes and connecting waters, marine and estuarine waters up to the heads of tidal influence, and the Exclusive Economic Zone, the boundaries of which are determined by the President.

Medical wastes are defined as "potentially infectious medical waste," including isolation wastes, infectious agents, human blood and blood products, pathological wastes, sharps, body parts, contaminated bedding, surgical wastes, and other disposable medical equipment and material that can pose a risk to public health, safety, and welfare or marine environments.

Shore Protection

SPA protects the shores by controlling vessels, vehicles, and facilities from which municipal or commercial waste is loaded onto a vessel.[2] By focusing on receiving facilities where municipal or commercial wastes are unloaded from a vessel, the SPA can address the unique operations affecting shoreline environmental safety.

Vessel permits are required. Applications for a permit must include information about the history of the types of cargo and the type of municipal or commercial waste transported as well as municipal, commercial, medical, or waste of another kind. Municipal or commercial waste is defined for this act as solid waste, waste generated by a vessel during its normal operations, debris from construction, sewage sludge subject to regulation under the MPRSA, and dredge or fill material under the MPRSA.

Permits have five-year limits and are terminated when the vessel is sold. Permits can be denied if the applicant has a record of violations of the SWDA, MPRSA, Rivers and Harbors Appropriation Act, or the FWPCA.

The owners or operators of waste sources must load and unload in such a way that ensures minimizing the deposing of waste in coastal water. Any waste must be secured on a vessel with netting or other means during travel. Offloading from a vessel must be performed safely. When wastes are allowed to be deposited into coastal waters according to the permit, adequate cleanup must be performed. The DOT can revoke a permit for violations and assess fees or civil penalties. There are recommended waste tracking systems for vessels.

Chronology of the Public Vessel Medical Waste Antidumping Act

1988, United States Public Vessel Medical Waste Antidumping Act of 1988, Pub. L. 100–688, 102 Stat. 4152

Chronology of the Shore Protection Act

1988, Shore Protection Act of 1988, Pub. L. 100–688

Section Four

Waste and Tanks

CHAPTER 16

Solid Waste:
Solid Waste Disposal Act (SWDA)

Overview

❖ The Solid Waste Disposal Act (SWDA) contains provisions for solid industrial hazardous and nonhazardous wastes.

❖ The Act includes regulations for state or regional solid waste plans, research and demonstration programs, underground storage tanks, and medical waste tracking.

❖ Solid waste and hazardous waste differences are defined.

❖ Some solid wastes are not hazardous, but it is difficult to predict if they will remain harmless.

❖ Solid wastes can transform into hazardous wastes under certain conditions.

❖ Special site standards are applicable when off-site storage of wastes is needed during the cleanup of sites.

❖ Federal policies promote safety through long-term conversion from landfills and dumps to other methods of treatment, storage, and disposal.

❖ Recycling and reusing can reduce the need for space in land waste storage.

❖ Definitions of many waste terms are provided.

❖ The relationship among waste acts is explained.

❖ Small-town environmental planning for solid wastes is a program that helps cities with populations of 2,500 or fewer comply with the federal regulations.

Solid Waste Disposal Act Acronyms

CAMU—Corrective Action Management Unit

CERCLA—Comprehensive Environmental Response, Compensation, and Liability Act

EPA—Environmental Protection Agency

ISR—Interim Standards Rule

RCRA—Resource Conservation and Recovery Act

SWDA—Solid Waste Disposal Act

TCLP—Toxicity characteristic leaching procedure

TSD—Treatment, storage, and disposal facility

Waste and the Environment

The Solid Waste Disposal Act (SWDA)[1] defines solid waste as follows:

The term 'solid waste' means any garbage, refuse, sludge from a waste treatment plant, water supply treatment plant, or air pollution control facility and other discarded material, including solid, liquid, semisolid, or contained gaseous material resulting from industrial, commercial, mining, and agricultural operations, and from community activities....[2]

Because there are so many kinds, random mixtures, and consistencies of waste that have different treatment, storage, or disposal methods, the federal regulations provide ways to handle them under different kinds of conditions.

Exhibit 21: Discarded materials, or wastes, are dumped in a landfill by a truck (left, center). The dark areas of wastes are hazardous, and the lighter soil will be used to cover those wastes. Strict operational requirements are specified in waste handlers' permits.

Solid waste becomes the general term for all kinds of waste—liquid and solid—and the term itself does not indicate if the waste is hazardous to human health or the environment. As the term is used in the federal regulations, household and solid industrial waste are considered benign and are regulated accordingly. However, some solid waste might be hazardous waste or might become hazardous over time. The chemical composition of a benign solid waste can change, or a waste could mix with another to become harmful. Under the SWDA-RCRA provisions, no clear distinction can be made between treatment, storage, and disposal of benign wastes versus hazardous wastes. While the regulations try to make the distinction, they are not clear. Some state regulations have clarified these differences in support of the intentions of SWDA-RCRA.

❖ Solid Waste Disposal Act

Many people believe that household wastes are not harmful and cannot create any environmental problems other than spreading disease from insects, rodents, or birds feeding on that waste. In the past, many communities filled over their daily waste deposits with dirt to lessen the potential for human and animal infections. Thus, the land areas used for this dumping were called landfills. The dirt covering supposedly made them sanitary by shielding the waste from the insects and animals; therefore, the term "sanitary landfills" became common. For many decades, most communities have disposed of household wastes in sanitary landfills.

Exhibit 22: A top layer of soil has been graded to receive the next load of wastes in a large landfill. Note the sloping of the earth on all sides as a method of waste containment. Under this landfill lies a protective membrane (impermeable layer) and a pipe system to carry away any methane or other gases that might collect.

Municipal and private solid waste storage areas (landfills) are the final resting places for household waste. Even though some household waste may be hazardous, the landfills are operated as if the wastes are not hazardous but might become so. In some parts of the United States, there are few land areas remaining that are geographically suitable for landfills. Also, residential and other land uses have consumed many thousands of acres to accommodate housing needs, leaving the least suitable lands for land-based waste storage areas. For these reasons, as well as the questionable long-term safety of landfills, the EPA promotes alternative methods of treating, storing, and disposing of solid waste.

If a waste storage site is abandoned and leaks hazardous substances, it may be subject to government cleanup and subsequent prosecution of responsible parties.[3] Fines may be assessed, incremental penalties and restrictions imposed, or site permits cancelled. All money collected from fines and penalties for violating the SWDA may be used by the state for projects designed to improve or protect the environment or to defray the costs of environmental protection or enforcement. Not only are planning and management methods suggested to avoid future leaks, but also research and demonstration projects are promoted as a means to find better ways to do things. States are guided to develop statewide and regional waste plans and are given technical advice and grant assistance.

Terms

The federal regulations contain common terms about solid waste:

Disposal is the discharge, deposit, dumping, injection, spilling, leaking, or placing of solid, liquid, or hazardous waste into the land, water, or other media. **Hazardous waste** is a liquid, solid waste, or combination of solid and liquid waste that, because of its quantity, concentration, or characteristics (chemical, physical, or infectious), can harm humans. Waste that may present hazards to health when improperly treated, stored, transported, or disposed is hazardous waste.[4] **Hazardous waste management** is control (using set procedures) of the collection, separation, transportation, treatment, storage, disposal, process, or recovery of hazardous waste.

An **open dump** is one that is not a sanitary landfill and one that is not operating under a government permit for disposing hazardous waste. **Resource recovery** is the extraction of materials or energy from solid waste. **Sludge** is solid, liquid, or semisolid waste generated from a wastewater, water supply, or air pollution facility.

Hazardous waste lists

Lists of hazardous wastes are developed, and numbers are assigned to each waste. One list contains general sources. Another contains specific sources of waste. Yet another lists commercial chemical products such as residues, containers, and other items that must be treated as hazardous wastes when discarded. Not mentioned on any of the three lists (general, specific, or commercial chemical products) are hazardous wastes that are ignitable, corrosive, reactive, or toxic. These are regulated as well.

Exhibit 23: When facilities are abandoned or no longer profitably maintained, the remaining debris can contaminate adjoining property. This site was once used to treat lumber with chemicals.

Exceptions

Even though a number of wastes are regulated, a number of industrial and household wastes are not. The important exceptions to the regulations, controls, and subsequent code provisions of the SWDA are

❖ Household wastes

❖ Agricultural wastes used as fertilizer

❖ Mining spoils returned to the mine

❖ Utility wastes from coal combustion

❖ Oil and gas exploration drilling waste

❖ Ores, coal, and other extracted minerals

❖ Cement kiln dust

❖ Arsenic treated wood wastes

Exhibit 24: A large pile of heat-treated soil has been created by the conveyor belt from the industrial heating machine.

❖ Chromium-bearing wastes

❖ Certain petroleum contaminated debris and media

Waste Policies and Programs

There are different requirements for treating, storing, and disposing solid waste and other kinds of waste in the SWDA-RCRA. The programs vary and include very specific provisions for municipal solid waste (landfills and dumps), hazardous solid and liquid waste, medical waste, and underground storage tanks. Each program within the solid waste regulations targets a federal policy.

Dangers can occur if solid and hazardous wastes are improperly disposed on the land. Open dumping without covers or earthen linings can harm health and pollute drinking water and air. Safe, long-term containment of wastes on the land must be assured. Storage of waste on the land must be minimized (because the more land area consumed, the greater the chance of contamination and creation of dead zones).

EPA and SWDA

The U.S. Environmental Protection Agency (EPA) is the major agency responsible for managing and controlling wastes. EPA develops rules and programs to meet the intent of Congress. The agency promotes partnerships between all levels of government. Some waste programs are delegated to state and local governments. The EPA coordinates with other federal agencies such as the Departments of Energy, Transportation, Commerce, Navy (and Coast Guard), through an Interagency Coordinating Committee. Broadly summarized, the EPA through SWDA-RCRA provides the framework for both technical and financial help for waste planning to state and local governments. The act defines the differences between solid (benign) and hazardous wastes and outlines methods to improve the collection, treatment, and disposal of wastes.

Burning hazardous waste: Kilns and incinerators

Standards are set to control emissions of hazardous air pollutants from incinerators, cement kilns, and lightweight aggregate kilns that burn hazardous wastes.[5] Interim emissions limits or standards are set until a final limit is published in the Federal Register. This temporary adoption of standards is an Interim Standards Rule (ISR).

Small town environmental planning

The SWDA contains a program to assist small communities in planning and financing new and improved facilities for environmental protection. Compliance with federal environmental laws has been difficult for small towns (fewer than 2,500 people). In recognizing this problem, the Small Town Environmental Planning Program was developed. New ways to improve working with the EPA are defined, including the potential to revise the regulations (or develop and implement new ones) to more easily comply. All small town environmental planning is required to address promoting regional waste treatment and regional infrastructure systems. Additionally, the EPA must notify all small communities about applicable federal programs through an Office of the Small Town Ombudsman. Multimedia permits that could benefit small towns are examined.[6]

Exhibit 25: Landfills are constructed according to careful engineering practices and dug to various depths. A synthetic fabric liner is laid completely under the area to be filled. Each joint is properly sealed to prevent leaks. To further protect from leaks, clay cover may be placed over the liner, as shown.

Waste Management, Recycling, or Reusing Wastes

Recycling and reuse of solid wastes are promoted, and new and innovative methods of waste disposal need to be developed in response to the lack of suitable storage places throughout the United States. The government recognizes that millions of tons of usable material are needlessly buried annually when the materials could be used for other purposes. Solid waste is a potential source of fuel, oil, or gas that can be converted into energy in support of our national policy to promote alternative energy sources.

Exhibit 26: A large plastic, bubble-like building is constructed as a staging area to contain the contaminated soil prior to heat treatment.

If different processes can recover usable materials, a manufacturing operation should adopt it. For these programs, the goal is to reduce or eliminate, wherever possible, hazardous waste produced at its source. To reach this goal, a national research and development program targets waste management and conservation; improved organizational productivity; and better transport, recovery, treatment, storage, and disposal methods. When there are no other options and waste must be produced, that waste must be treated, stored, or disposed to minimize danger to the environment.[7]

Off-site management or Corrective Action Management Units (CAMUs) of CAMU waste[8]

Corrective Action Management Units (CAMU) are off-site locations used during on-site waste cleanup and management. There are standards that control the types of wastes that may be managed in a CAMU, the treatment requirements for wastes placed in CAMUs, the design standards that apply to CAMUs, information required to be submitted on CAMU applications, responses to releases from CAMUs, and public participation requirements for CAMU decisions. In addition, the CAMU rules "grandfather" certain categories of CAMUs and create new requirements for those CAMUs used only for treatment or storage (i.e., those in which wastes will not remain after a site closes). The rule grants interim authorization by rule to states currently authorized for the CAMU rule and expedites the authorization process for those states authorized for corrective action but not the CAMU rule.

Physical treatment of wastes is allowed on off-site staging piles. CAMU-eligible wastes include buried tanks containing wastes. EPA Regional Administrators have discretion to choose a leaching test other than the Toxicity Characteristic Leaching Procedure (TCLP) to assess treatment. Off-site placement of hazardous CAMU-eligible waste is allowed in hazardous waste landfills if the landfills are treated to EPA treatment standards.

Exhibit 27: This land area is being prepared for soil cleaning by means of a heating process. Large industrial boilers, or heaters, are used in conjunction with conveyor belts.

Selected target and grant areas

Leaking storage tanks are identified in some of the more recent additional provisions of the SWDA. An aboveground storage tank grant program is established along with an underground storage tank program targeted to Indian tribes. Oil transport leaks in the national Wildlife Refuge System in Alaskan native villages are controlled through the formation of the Denali Commission.

Relationship Among Waste Acts

There is a fine line between handling benign solid wastes and handling hazardous wastes. Given certain conditions, their chemical and biological condition can change. The Solid Waste Disposal Act (SWDA) has been amended with many new provisions that subtly adjust for this potential shift in classification such as adding and renaming the sections as Resource Conservation and Recovery Act (RCRA) and stressing the handling of hazardous wastes in innovative ways.

❖ Solid Waste Disposal Act

SWDA with its RCRA Amendments provides the protective framework for household and industrial solid and liquid wastes, hazardous wastes, medical wastes, and leaking sites or facilities. Under the RCRA amendments to the SWDA, the treatment, storage, and disposal of wastes are controlled to reduce wastes at their sources, promote high technology treatment, and designate safe methods to store those wastes. RCRA applies to all treatment, storage, and disposal (TSD) facilities. To complement RCRA, abandoned and inactive waste sites that leak and are in questionable ownership are protected under the Comprehensive Environmental Response, Compensation, and Liability Act (CERCLA), also known as Superfund.[9]

If there is combined storage of industrial solid and household wastes with hazardous wastes, owners or operators of some landfills are required to comply with the provisions of the hazardous waste regulations. SWDA-RCRA imposes a "cradle-to-grave" system for the EPA and the states to work together to identify hazardous wastes and their constituents; to identify sites and facilities; and to notify the generators of waste, waste transporters, and owners and operators of TSD facilities (or sites) that they must comply with the federal regulations. Each entity within this system—the generators, truckers, and owners/operators of sites and facilities—must obtain the permits for which they help set the standards. All entities are also subject to inspections and enforcement, if necessary.[10]

Exhibit 28: A soundproof wall is constructed to block the noise created by a thermal desorption machine. The hearing of residents living close to this site is protected.

Chronology of the Solid Waste Disposal Act (SWDA)

1965, Solid Waste Disposal Act, Pub. L. 89–272, 90 Stat. 2795

1970, National Materials Policy Act of 1970, Pub. L. 91–512

1976, Resource Recovery and Conservation Act of 1976, (the RCRA Amendment), Pub. L. 94–580, 42 USC 6901 et seq.

1980, Solid Waste Disposal Act Amendments of 1980, Pub. L. 96–482, 42 U.S.C. 6901

1980, Used Oil Recycling Act of 1980, Pub. L. 96–482, 94 Stat. 2334

1984, Hazardous and Solid Waste Amendments of 1984, Pub. L. 98–616, 42 USC 6917 et seq.; SWDA amended entirely as the Resource Conservation and Recovery Act (RCRA), 42 USC 6901, Subtitle D amended by 42 USC 6941–6949a

1988, Medical Waste Tracking Act of 1988, Pub. L. 100–582, 102 Stat. 2950

1991, Federal Agency Recycling and the Council on Federal recycling and Procurement Policy, Executive Order 12780

1992, Federal Facility Compliance Act of 1992, Pub. L. 102–386, 106 Stat. 1505

1993, Federal Acquisition, Recycling, and Waste Prevention, Executive Order 12873

1996, Land Disposal Program Flexibility Act of 1996, Pub. L. 104–119, 1, 110 Stat. 83

CHAPTER 17

Hazardous Waste: Resource Conservation and Recovery Act (RCRA)

Overview

❖ The EPA lists hazardous wastes according to toxicity, persistence, degradability, potential to accumulate in human tissues, flammability, corrosiveness, and other characteristics.

❖ Medical wastes are hazardous wastes that have special provisions and requirements.

❖ Waste minimization (planning, reusing, and recycling) is preferred to increasing the land areas needed to permanently store waste.

❖ Both the EPA and DOT regulate truckers who haul hazardous waste.

❖ Liquid hazardous wastes must be placed in containers prior to disposing in landfills.

❖ Permits are required for owners or operators who generate or handle hazardous solid or liquid wastes.

❖ Permits are required for hazardous waste research, development, and demonstration.

❖ Compliance orders may be issued to enforce the regulations in the act, and civil and criminal penalties may be assessed to owners and operators for different violations.

❖ State and regional solid waste disposal plans are required to be submitted to EPA.

❖ Demonstration facilities and projects are promoted.

Resource Conservation and Recovery Act Acronyms

DOI—U.S. Department of the Interior

DOT—U.S. Department of Transportation

EPA—Environmental Protection Agency

NIOSH—National Institute of Occupational Safety and Health

RCRA—Resource Conservation and Recovery Act

SWDA—Solid Waste Disposal Act

TDI—Toluene diisocyanate

TSDs—Treatment, storage, and disposal facilities

USDA—U.S. Department of Agriculture

USTs—Underground storage tanks

Programs and Requirements

Those persons generating and transporting waste, and owners and operators of treatment, storage, and disposal (TSD) facilities are regulated under SWDA-RCRA.[1] This act prohibits the careless handling and permanent storage of hazardous wastes. It only applies to entities which generate over 275 tons (550,000 pounds) of hazardous waste per year.

Any transporter of hazardous waste must adhere to standards developed by both the EPA and DOT. Records and manifests must be kept. Wastes need to be labeled. Owners or operators of treatment, storage, and disposal facilities are responsible to

❖ Report contaminant spills and releases to the appropriate local, state, and federal agencies

❖ Monitor and inspect equipment and facilities

❖ Use safe methods approved by the EPA

❖ Secure a permit before designing, locating, and constructing facilities

❖ Operate according to safety requirements

❖ Develop contingency plans for emergencies

❖ Maintain the financial ability to perform emergency repairs

Hazardous wastes that are produced, stored, disposed, or treated at a facility are subject to a number of requirements. The facility must have a permit that describes its operating restrictions, some of which may be unique to that facility alone. Open dumping of solid or hazardous waste is not allowed unless it is dumped into a sanitary landfill. Records must be maintained at every facility. Any containers used for hazardous waste must be labeled and designed to safely contain such waste. Manifests must disclose the chemical composition of those wastes, and a permit must be obtained for persons working with them. Summaries must be developed and maintained by the EPA of the total quantities of wastes generated per year for every facility that is issued a permit.

Exhibit 29: A drainage channel (ditch) crosses through a chemical refinery property and catches runoff (rain mixed with spills and natural mixtures of background chemicals and compounds). Pipes and manufacturing lines can be viewed along the side and horizon of the photograph.

In order to reduce the total amount of hazardous wastes generated, each facility owner or operator must develop a method to treat, store, or dispose wastes in ways to reduce the amounts of wastes. This reduction effort is

❖ Resource Conservation and Recovery Act

commonly called waste minimization. Hazardous wastes must be reduced in quantity or volume at their sources, treated with high technology equipment, or securely contained in land disposal areas to minimize present and future risks to the population. In order to meet the act's expectations, there are provisions for each of the following tasks:

❖ Properly storing and managing hazardous wastes

❖ Developing state and regional solid waste plans

❖ Managing resource and recovery

❖ Handling federal responsibilities

❖ Meeting requirements for research, development, demonstration, and information dissemination

❖ Regulating underground storage tanks

❖ Tracking medical wastes

Exhibit 30: This man-built drainage channel is surrounded by pipes, mechanical devices, and storage areas in an apparently random manner.

Owners and operators of TSD facilities have to comply with performance standards, adhere to monitoring requirements, install air emission controls, and perform corrective actions. Land disposal is prohibited unless the hazardous wastes are treated. RCRA permits are issued which specify the operating conditions for each site or facility.

A state can administer the RCRA program as long as it meets the conditions established by the EPA and administers and enforces a program that is consistent with the federal program. Methods must be adopted to compile an inventory of all hazardous waste sites in each state.

Every two years, the EPA compiles a list of all hazardous waste managers in the United States who reported their facilities to be treatment, storage, or disposal facilities.[2] It is not just large waste volume industries and facilities that are regulated. EPA regulates about 200,000 companies producing less than 1,000 kilograms of waste per month. Underground storage tanks (UST) containing petroleum or other hazardous substances are regulated, and landfills containing liquid and other hazardous wastes are regulated. Every industry and business producing hazardous waste is regulated under RCRA.

The SWDA requires that the EPA annually transmit a report containing all activities of the past year to the President and Congress. It must include how the EPA met the objectives of the environmental regulations, opinions about EPA effectiveness, outstanding solid waste problems, and plans for solid waste activities for the next year.[3]

Restrictions on Hazardous Waste Placement

Land disposal of hazardous waste is defined as the placement of waste in a landfill, surface impoundment, waste pile, injection well, land treatment facility, salt dome formation, salt bed formation, or underground mine or cave. There are limitations on storing and disposing hazardous wastes; land disposal of hazardous waste is prohibited because of long-term uncertainties concerning almost any disposal technique.

Exhibit 31: Hazardous waste landfills may be constructed differently depending on the types of waste to be contained. In this landfill, composite liner material is required for safe storage.

Land disposal of hazardous waste is placing waste in a landfill, waste pile, injection well, land treatment facility, reservoir, mine, or cave.[4] There are limitations on storing and disposing hazardous wastes on the land due to population concentrations and land development pressures. Because there are uncertainties about almost any land disposal method, hazardous waste may not be placed in a salt dome formation, salt bed formation, underground mine, or cave. Liquid hazardous waste may not be poured onto landfills. If disposed in a landfill, liquid hazardous waste must first be placed in containers. Solvents and dioxins cannot be injected underground.

Air emissions are controlled at all hazardous waste TSD facilities, such as open tanks, surface impoundments, and landfills. All hazardous waste landfills require double liners prior to receiving any deposits. Ground water must be monitored around the impoundments, waste piles, land treatment units, or landfills. Any location may be prohibited from receiving wastes if it is determined to be unsafe or threatening to the environment.

Domestic sewage transport through a sewer system to a publicly-owned treatment works is controlled. Wastewater lagoons are regulated, as are landfills and surface impoundments. The potential pathways, nature, and magnitude of human exposure to hazardous wastes or constituents from releases must be documented for any sewage transport. Additionally, health assessments must be made by the EPA or the appropriate state agency.

State and Regional Solid Waste Plans

Federal environmental regulations require each state to plan for the disposal of solid waste. Plans must include recovering energy and materials and conserving resources. Funds and technical advice are available to state and regional authorities for comprehensive planning. Guidelines for comprehensive solid waste plans suggest these considerations:

❖ Analyze regional geological, hydrological, climatic and other factors to protect ground and surface waters from leachate contamination and surface runoff

❖ Protect air quality

❖ Improve methods of collecting, storing, processing, and disposing of wastes

❖ Enforce the closing or upgrading open dumps

❖ Provide population density, distribution, and growth information

❖ Describe the type and location of transportation

❖ Develop a profile of industries

❖ List the predicted composition and amount of waste

❖ Examine political, economic, organizational, financial, and managerial problems that could affect solid waste management

❖ Consider alternative types of resource recovery facilities and systems

❖ Search for new and additional markets for recovered material and energy, as well as methods for conserving materials and energy.[5]

Within each state plan, one or more agencies must be designated to implement the plan with both the planning and the implementing agency identified.[6] The state must be divided into regions with boundaries mapped. If a state provides assistance for solid waste management facilities to a city that has a population less than 5,000 (not within a metropolitan area), that city may qualify for federal grants.

Hazardous waste site inventory

There are two site inventory programs: state and federal. Each EPA-approved state must maintain and publish an inventory of each location where hazardous waste has been stored or disposed. The inventory must include the following information:

❖ Location

❖ Amount, nature, and toxicity of the waste

❖ Names and addresses of the owners of the site

❖ Techniques of waste treatment or disposal used at each site

❖ Current site status.[7]

The EPA may carry out the inventory program in a non-approved state.

Underground Storage Tanks (USTs)

If a tank (or combination of tanks and their connections) contains a regulated substance and is at least ten percent under the ground, the tank is subject to the federal programs and controls explained in the next chapter. Some underground tanks are excluded from regulation regardless of their contents:

❖ Farm and residential tanks of 1,100 gallons or more

❖ Tanks used for storing heating oil on the premises

❖ Septic tanks

❖ Pipeline facilities and their gathering lines

❖ Surface impoundments (lagoons, pits, and ponds)

❖ Storm or waste water collector systems

❖ Flow-through process tanks

❖ Liquid traps for oil or gas production

❖ Tanks located above the floor surface in underground areas such as basements, tunnels, or shafts.

Under the SWDA, all owners of USTs must report them to the appropriate state or local agency indicating their size, type, age, location, and uses. Methods to detect the release of a tank's contents and to prevent and stop the leaks are developed. Requirements include

❖ Leak detection methods

❖ Inventory controls

❖ Tank tests

❖ Record keeping

❖ Reports of any leaks and stoppages to government agencies

❖ Closing of tanks to prohibit any more leaks

❖ Methods of maintaining financial responsibility, or the ability to pay to fix leaks from accidents.[8]

New tanks must meet design and construction standards and have release detection equipment. Petroleum storage tanks, such as at gasoline service stations, are the major targets of the UST regulations.

Medical wastes

The EPA, in response to Atlantic Ocean beach pollution in which medical wastes washed ashore, requires a medical waste tracking program. The types of wastes that are tracked include

❖ Infectious agents from laboratories

❖ Pathological wastes such as tissues and cultures

❖ Human blood wastes

❖ Needles, pipettes, broken glass, and scalpel blades

❖ Contaminated animal carcasses and human body parts

❖ Surgical and autopsy wastes

❖ Laboratory research wastes that had been in contact with infectious agents

❖ Dialysis wastes

❖ Discarded medical equipment and parts that were in contact with infectious agents

❖ Biological waste and discarded materials contaminated with blood or excretion

❖ Oher waste materials that could be threatening.[9]

Owners, operators, and persons who store medical wastes are subject to inspections, requests for records, and monitoring by the EPA or other designated public agencies. If there is any violation, a compliance order is issued which assesses a penalty and requires compliance immediately or within a specified time period. The EPA can also begin court action against a person or company. The alleged violator may request a public hearing within 30 days of issue of a compliance order. Both civil and criminal court proceedings can be applied to a violator.[10] State agencies have the same power to enforce federal medical waste rules and regulations.

Identifying and Listing Wastes

The EPA has the responsibility to identify and list hazardous wastes according to toxicity, persistence, degradability, flammability, corrosivity, and for the potential to accumulate in human tissues. Most hazardous wastes fall into one or more of the categories shown in the box below. Note that the list is a dynamic once, and there are regular additions.

Exhibit 32: A core sample of potentially hazardous material (from 15 to 17 feet below grade) is being inspected during this EPA facility visit.

Exhibit 33: A portion of the core sample has visible contamination, as indicated by the circled dark areas.

Categories of hazardous waste

There are different types of hazardous waste that can be grouped into categories. Environmental professionals and advocates use these categories:

bottom ash waste	flue gas emission waste from burning fossil fuels
bromacil	fly ash waste
carbamates	halogenated-dibenzofurans
cement kiln dust	halogenated dioxins
chlorinated aliphatics	inorganic chemical industry wastes
chlorinated aromatics	linuron
chlorinated-dibenzofurans	lithium batteries
chlorinated dioxins	ore and mineral processing waste
coal slurry pipeline effluent	organo-bromines
coke byproducts	paint production wastes
dimethyl hydrazine	refining wastes
dioxin	slag waste
drilling fluids	solvents
dyes and pigments	TDI (toluene diisocyanate)

Enforcement of the SWDA

Inspectors from the EPA or state environmental protection agency must have access to enter a permitted facility at all reasonable times. These inspectors have power to enforce environmental regulations and can inspect, obtain samples, and review records; they can make all records, reports, or other information available to the public.

The EPA can issue a compliance order that assesses a civil penalty for any past or current violation. Compliance is required immediately, within a specified time period, or a civil action may be initiated in U.S. District court. Any of these compliance orders can include suspension or revocation of an operating permit. The EPA or a state can conduct a public hearing and issue subpoenas for attendance and testimony of witnesses. If a violator fails to make corrections within the specified time, the EPA can assess a monetary penalty. Criminal penalties can be imposed in any of these situations:

❖ Hazardous waste is transported without a permit.

❖ Hazardous waste is treated, stored, or disposed without a permit.

❖ Conditions of the permit are knowingly violated.

❖ Material information is knowingly omitted from a permit application.

❖ Wastes are mishandled.

❖ Wastes are transported without a manifest.

❖ Wastes are exported.

❖ Used oil is not identified or listed as a hazardous waste.

Permits for research

One-year permits may be issued for research, development, and demonstration of innovative and experimental hazardous waste treatment technology or processes. Criteria stated in the permit application determine the efficacy and performance capabilities of the process or technology. Any EPA protections may be added as conditions for the permit.[11]

Resource Recovery and Technology

In order to encourage greater commercialization of proven resource recovery technology, the U.S. Department of Commerce has the responsibility to provide specifications for the recovered materials, stimulate markets for these materials, promote the technologies, and provide forums to exchange technical and economic data about resource recovery.[12] Recovered materials can be divided into manufacturing and post-consumer wastes, as shown in the table below for paper waste:

Two categories of paper waste

Manufacturing waste:

❖ Bag, box, and carton manufacturing wastes

❖ Bindery trimming

❖ Butt rolls, mill wrappers, and rejected stock

❖ Envelope cuttings

❖ Fibers recovered from waste water

❖ Finished paper from obsolete inventories

❖ Other waste from converting operations

Post-consumer waste:

❖ Mixed waste paper

❖ Old magazines

❖ Old newspapers

❖ Tabulating cards

❖ Used cordage

❖ Used corrugated boxes

EPA's Role

All federal agencies are required under the SWDA to cooperate with the EPA in administering and enforcing all environmental regulations, rules, and codes. Conversely, the EPA must notify NIOSH and the U.S. Department of Labor of any information that it may have about hazardous waste treatment, storage, and disposal sites; sites planned or in progress of cleanup; hazards to persons working at hazardous waste sites and facilities; and incidents of worker injury or harm at those kinds of sites. The EPA must encourage public participation in developing, revising, and enforcing regulations. If additional training is required by environmental regulations, the EPA may award grants and contracts to another organization to administer that training. Training may be required to develop or carry out a program or to train instructors, supervisory personnel, or other government agencies that may be enforcing a portion of some regulation.

Exhibit 34: A worker is inserting an organic vapor analyzer (a measurement instrument) into an open liquid waste scum ditch. A measurement is taken before they bale or collect the groundwater and send it for tests. These ditches are common in manufacturing facilities and are safely constructed to contain and move the waste material into treatment ponds, lagoons, or other storage areas.

The EPA must perform a number of activities that relate to their environmental protection mission, including research, investigations, experiments, training, demonstrations, surveys, public education programs, and studies. It must conduct research to determine the effects of contamination on human health and the economy, and it must disseminate information about how to operate and finance solid waste management programs. The EPA is also responsible for the following:

❖ Developing methods for resource recovery and conservation systems

❖ Implementing hazardous waste management systems

❖ Marketing recovered resources

❖ Producing fuel from solid waste

❖ Reducing the total amounts of waste materials

❖ Improving collection and disposal methods

❖ Identifying the components of solid waste and their recoverable materials

❖ Identifying low technology and small-scale solid waste identification

❖ Improving the performance of recovered resources from solid waste

❖ Improving land disposal practices

❖ Mitigating any adverse effects on air quality

EPA's teaching role

The EPA also has a teaching mission. It must develop, evaluate, coordinate, and disseminate information about these waste-control activities:[13]

❖ Methods and costs of collecting solid waste

❖ Cost, operation, and maintenance of solid waste management

❖ Amounts and percentages of resources that can be recovered from solid waste using different methods

❖ Methods to reduce the amount of solid waste generated

❖ Existing and emerging technologies to recover energy and materials from solid wastes

❖ Hazardous solid waste resulting from disposal of wastes

❖ Methods of financing appropriate facilities, landfills, or treatment facilities

❖ Available markets to purchase materials or energy recovered from solid waste

❖ Research and development projects for solid waste management

Demonstration facilities, projects

The EPA may contract with public agencies, companies, or persons to construct and operate a working demonstration facility. In addition, the EPA may conduct studies or initiate demonstration projects to recover useful energy and materials from solid waste. The studies and their recommendations can include the following information:

❖ Recovering materials and energy from solid waste

❖ Recommending uses for the wastes

❖ Finding potential markets for the recycled waste

❖ Understanding the impact that distributing waste has on existing markets

❖ Discovering the potential for energy conservation and recovery

❖ Reducing waste during manufacturing

❖ Collecting, separating, and containing waste

Exhibit 35: Samples of potentially hazardous material are prepared for testing. The material has been taken from the completed monitoring well located at the feet of the EPA inspectors.

❖ Using federal procurement to develop market demand for recovered resources

❖ Recommending incentives to accelerate recycling and reclamation of materials from solid wastes

❖ Applying economic incentives

❖ Imposing charges on disposal, packaging, containers, vehicles, etc.

❖ Examining legal constraints and institutional barriers to acquire land for wastes

❖ Consulting with the USDA about agricultural waste management problems and practices

❖ Consulting with the DOI about mining waste management problems and practices

Chronology of the Resource Conservation and Recovery Act (RCRA)

1976, Resource Conservation and Recovery Act (RCRA), Pub. L. 94–580; 7 USC 1010 et seq.; 40 CFR 280 and 281

1984, Hazardous and Solid Waste Act (HSWA), 40 CFR 261, 262, 267, 268, 271, and 272

1984, Standards for Treatment, Storage, and Disposal Facilities (TSDs), 40 CFR 264 and 265

CHAPTER 18

Storage Tanks: Resource Conservation and Recovery Act (RCRA)

Overview

❖ While the EPA regulates underground storage tanks (USTs), some states also have aboveground storage tank regulations.

❖ Owners or operators of tanks containing regulated substances must notify the designated state agency or the EPA with descriptions and characteristics of the tanks.

❖ Leaking tanks must be replaced with nonmetallic tanks or metal tanks which have cathodic protection.

❖ The most common type of leaking underground storage tank has been service station gasoline storage tanks made of steel.

❖ Some tanks are excluded from the tank regulations.

❖ Violators of the UST-RCRA provisions are served with compliance orders, civil actions, and permanent injunctions.

❖ Reports and records of USTs must be submitted.

❖ Tanks, pipes, and connections must meet construction product standards.

❖ Release detection devices must be installed on USTs.

❖ Action plans for cleanups must be developed and submitted to the appropriate regulatory agency when requested.

❖ Procedures must be followed and requirements must be met when USTs are closed.

Resource Conservation and Recovery Act Acronyms

ASTs—Aboveground Storage Tanks

CERCLA—Comprehensive Environmental Response, Compensation, and Liability Act (Superfund)

EPA—Environmental Protection Agency

RCRA—Resource Conservation and Recovery Act

SWDA—Solid Waste Disposal Act

UST—Underground Storage Tank

Tanks and Environmental Protection

Nationwide, there are over two million underground storage tanks and an additional two million aboveground storage tanks. The Resource Conservation and Recovery Act (RCRA), which is part of the Solid Waste Disposal Act (SWDA), establishes regulatory controls on existing and proposed storage tanks. As a result of this environmental control legislation, over $5 billion has been spent to fix or replace leaking USTs. Under many of the provisions and programs of the Clean Air Act, Solid Waste Disposal Act, Toxic Substances Control Act and others, ASTs are accommodated in the federal framework of environmental protection.

The EPA believes that about 75 percent of the USTs can dangerously leak.[1] To date, an emphasis has been placed on the cleanup, repair, or replacement of leaking petroleum tanks more than on tanks containing other potential pollutants.

Current federal regulations require registering all USTs by submitting information to either the EPA or the delegated state agency. There may well be as many as 400,000 UST sites containing about 1.1 million federally regulated UST tanks nationwide. At these sites, there were 341,773 confirmed releases at the tanks, and 292,446 cleanups initiated with 178,297 completed.[2] As many as 220,000 more USTs are not regulated (of which about 25,000 may be holding hazardous substances) and are now required to be registered.[3]

Tanks, locations, problems

Storage tanks can be above or below the ground and located almost anywhere. They are used to hold both harmless or harmful gases or liquids for short- and long-term periods. Some of the most common storage tanks are those below ground that hold gasoline at retail filling stations. In addition to

the service station tanks, there are other substance-containing tanks—for example, tanks holding liquid chemicals at factories that make synthetic fibers, plastic food wraps, or packaging materials contain many kinds of fluids.

Along with their associated piping and electronic control mechanisms, above- and belowground storage tanks can fail and leak liquids into the soils, surface, or ground waters. Owners, op-

Exhibit 36: Note that these aboveground storage tanks have a concrete curbed containment area. The facility owner or operator must plan for potential leaks from the tanks. Liquid materials can be seen under these tanks.

erators, and other private parties must be diligent in their attempts to keep their tank systems intact, safe from both spills and accidental releases of fluids or gases. Nevertheless, no matter how careful these parties are, tanks and their connections can fail. Corrosion of the tank materials, unexpected impacts, or leaky valves can cause problems. For the worst cases, gases or fluids can be released into the air, which may make bystanders seriously ill.

Storage tanks must be designed, engineered, and installed in a manner to avoid serious environmental problems. Pipe systems linked to most ASTs have many connectors, such as valves, right angle joints, pressure reducers, and automatic diverters. If the AST is constructed of a metal that can corrode, it could leak. Tank materials must be non-corrosive, sturdy, and composed of materials that cannot react with their contents. Without environmental controls on tanks, leaks can weak havoc over large land areas.

As a result of changes in the topography of the soils, it is difficult to predict the direction of underground flow once a liquid contaminant penetrates the ground. At times, the soils are not horizontal, nor are they uniform. Different soils, such as gravel or sand, may be located at different angles to each other at different depths. Therefore, if a liquid contaminant moves along a line between these different layers, it may move in different directions than predicted. As a result, water wells, surface water drinking supplies, or other places may be contaminated far from the source of contamination. For all of these reasons, federal environmental protection from leaking tanks is considered important for protecting public health, safety, and welfare.[4]

Controls on USTs

Underground storage tanks contain many different kinds of liquids, gases, and compounds. Any of these substances can be contained in the UST, but controls are focused on those regulated and unregulated substances that could leak into the environment. Regulated substances are dangerous liquids and gases as defined in the Comprehensive Environmental Response, Compensation, and Liability Act (CERCLA, or Superfund) and petroleum products. Those same substances are controlled under RCRA's UST regulations for underground storage tanks.[5] Fuels and petroleum substances are also regulated under RCRA. Even though some of the regulated substances are harmless if safely contained in the proper tank system, they may be harmful if released to the air or water, or if mixed with other substances.

Generally, UST systems are required to have leak detection and inventory control systems. Records must be kept of monitoring, testing, inventory control results, and owner or operator continuing financial responsibility. Corrective actions and cleanups must be promptly performed by owners and operators—and reported. Under some situations, tanks must be closed to prevent future releases of regulated substances. Compensation may be due to an owner/operator whose businesses is harmed by the closure or interruption of use of a UST due to studies and tests as a result of this act.[6]

Responsibilities for Underground Storage Tanks

Owners or operators of all tanks that contain regulated substances must provide notification and documentation to the EPA or its designated state agency. In a sense, notification with the required descriptions is equivalent to registering the tank. Through this notification requirement, the government can closely track compliance with its underground storage tank regulations.

Notification to the EPA is required prior to installation of new USTs. Existing tanks must be modified to meet design and operating standards or be closed. For example, it is common for service stations to replace older or leaking metal tanks with tank systems having synthetic materials. Existing tanks that have leaked and caused environmental problems must be fixed according to stated standards. Both filling and draining of tanks are to be operated in a manner that prevents spills or leaks. Reports based on site investigations must be prepared and submitted to document any releases and their cleanups. Other reports are required to substantiate financial capability to support cleanups of spills, leaks, or potential tank system replacements, if needed.

Exhibit 37: Aboveground storage tanks are common in facilities that process chemicals, such as this one. The tanks and their valves, fittings, and pipes must be engineered to prevent liquids from leaking.

Franchise model for managing USTs

...[Office of Underground Storage Tanks] has adopted the franchise model as its implementation approach in managing the national UST program. The State, as franchisee, operates dependently, under a signed agreement with EPA, to operate the UST program. Regions serve as the field representatives or liaisons between EPA Headquarters and the States to relay ideas, need, and information between the EPA and the States. The States, therefore, run their programs using a management style that is tailored to meet the specific needs and demands of their own regulated community.

The demand for service and support varies in each State, and is affected by such factors as UST population, ground-water usage, weather and climate conditions, and financial conditions of owners and operators. The aim of State program approval is to develop the State-Federal partnership that will allow both parties to focus on preventing leaking USTs from causing further environmental contamination.[7]

Subchapter I of RCRA establishes a federal program for the regulation of USTs. Subtitle I of RCRA also allows the EPA to approve state programs to operate in place of the federal UST requirements if those state programs have standards that are no less stringent than the federal requirements and provide adequate enforcement of compliance with those standards. States with approved UST programs will have primary enforcement responsibility with respect to UST program requirements in their states.[8]

Performance Standards

In order to prevent tanks and pipe connections from failing and leaking, tanks, piping, and spill and overfill prevention equipment must meet certain performance standards. Tanks or pipes may be constructed of metal without corrosion protection only if a corrosion expert determines that the site itself does not contain soils that could cause a release during the tank's operating life. Records must be kept to demonstrate compliance with tank system performance.[9] Spill and overfill prevention equipment must meet these safety measures:

Exhibit 38: Portions of this and other tanks are underground. Not only are there cracks in the concrete containment area, but liquid wastes can be noted floating in the foreground.

❖ The flow into a tank must automatically shut off when it is no more than 95 percent full.

❖ A loud alarm must trigger to alert a transfer operator when the tank is more than 90 percent full, or the flow into the tank must be restricted.

❖ The flow must be restricted 30 minutes prior to overfilling, and a loud alarm must alert the operator one minute before overfilling

❖ The flow into the tank must automatically shut off so that the fittings on top of the tank are not exposed to the liquid substance.[10]

A release of a regulated substance into the environment cannot be made when a transfer hose is detached from a fill pipe. Industry codes of practice must be followed for installing new tanks, pipes, and valves.

Operating requirements

Underground storage tanks must be operated according to a number of requirements. The volume of the tank must be verified prior to filling that it is greater than the volume of the regulated substance to be poured into the tank. Transfers must be monitored constantly so that overfills and spills do not occur.[11] Any overflows or spills that occur during filling must be reported to the appropriate agency. Because so many tank systems are steel or another corrosive metal, corrosion protection methods must ensure that they are continuously maintained to protect any components in contact with the ground. If a cathodic protection system is used, it needs to be inspected by qualified testers and records must be maintained for the tank

Exhibit 39: Hazardous liquids have leached onto the ground at this industrial facility. The plastic chain barrier around the pool of liquids serves as a warning to employees.

system's cathode protection. Tank materials must be compatible with the substances stored in them. Repairs must be performed in a manner that can prevent leaks, releases, or structural failure. If corrosion or damage to pipes and fittings result in a substance release, they must be replaced, not repaired.

Detecting releases of tank system substances

Methods of detecting releases from any portion of the tank system (tank, piping, and valves) must be devised. These methods may include inventories that record the amount of the substance stored in a tank, gauges and monitoring devices for the spaces between the UST system, gas release protection, groundwater purity tests, tight pipe lines, and any other methods.[12] Each method has to detect leaks at a statistical probability of 95 percent accuracy.[13]

After leaks are detected, they must be stopped. Many states and the EPA maintain funds for cleanups of releases. Some states allow owners or operators who have financial problems to borrow from the state fund as needed. The Leaking Underground Storage Trust Fund of the EPA is used to pay for costs of corrective action, enforcement, and cost recovery for instances in which the administrator of the UST program cannot identify a UST system owner or operator.

Tank Systems

Petroleum underground systems

There are different monitoring requirements for tanks that contain petroleum products. If they do not meet the performance standards for new and upgraded UST systems, they must be monitored every 30 days, at a minimum.[14] Monthly inventory control or manual tank gauging and tank tightness testing must be performed. If the tank has a capacity of 550 gallons or less, weekly tank gauging can be used instead of other release detection methods. Underground piping must be monitored also. If a regulated substance is under pressure, there must be an automatic line leak detector installed, annual line tightness testing, or monthly monitoring. If the regulated substance is under suction, then the piping must have line tightness testing conducted at least every three years or have a monthly monitoring method. If the suction piping conforms to design and construction standards, it can be excused from release detection requirements.[15]

Cargo tanks that are used to transport liquid petroleum products that are flammable but not classified as hazardous wastes are allowed to be of any construction and not subject to federal specifications. Both leaded and unleaded gasoline is classified as a marine pollutant when transported by highway.[16]

Hazardous substance underground storage tank systems

These systems have different requirements. Release detection methods must be installed to meet the petroleum underground storage tank system requirements. Additionally, there must be secondary containment systems for both the tanks, piping, and valves. The tank system components must be monitored for a release every 30 days at a minimum. Owners or operators can obtain approvals to use their desired methods of release detection if they desire to do so. Information about acceptable ways to stop leaks, the health risks of the substance, chemical and physical properties of the substance, and the nature and characteristics of the UST site must be submitted.

Exclusions from RCRA

Three tank systems—primary, secondary, and tertiary—are excluded from the tank regulations.

Note: These systems are expected to be regulated in the future. Meanwhile, no one can install deferred UST systems storing regulated substances unless these conditions are met:

Primary exclusions

These tanks could cause environmental problems but are not regulated.

❖ Farm or residential tanks of 1,100 gallons or less to store motor fuel

❖ Heating oil tanks used on premises

❖ Septic tanks

❖ Pipelines regulated under other federal or state acts[18]

❖ Surface impoundments, lagoons, pits, or ponds

❖ Wastewater or storm water collection systems

❖ Processing tanks that are "flow-through"

❖ Gathering lines and liquid traps for oil or gas production

❖ Tanks located on or above the floor of a cave or other underground area

❖ Any pipes connected to tanks in any of the above items[19]

Secondary exclusions

❖ Hazardous wastes or their mixtures that are listed under RCRA Subtitle C

❖ Wastewater treatment tank systems regulated elsewhere under the Clean Water Act

❖ Hydraulic lift tanks, electrical equipment tanks, or other equipment or machinery needed for industrial operations that contain regulated substances

❖ UST systems which have less than 110 gallon capacities

❖ UST systems which contain a minimum (de minimis[20]) concentration of regulated substances under RCRA Subtitle C

❖ Containment systems used for overflow or emergency spill containment that are quickly emptied after being filled

Tertiary exclusions

This category is deferred for consideration for a period of time by the EPA:

❖ Tank systems used for wastewater treatment

❖ Tank systems containing radioactive material regulated elsewhere[21]

❖ Tank systems that are part of emergency generator systems at nuclear power generating facilities[22]

❖ Airport fuel distribution tank systems

❖ Field constructed USTs

State and Federal Enforcement

Even though the EPA has the ability to designate states to implement and enforce RCRA, only 25 states (and Puerto Rico and the District of Columbia) have received EPA approval to administer their own UST programs.

Compliance orders, civil penalties, and criminal penalties are the major enforcement methods that can be used against violators of the UST regulations under RCRA. A **compliance order** is a written summons to perform corrections to any underground storage tank violation within a set time period or the violator can face **civil action** in the United States District Court. The court will then order a temporary or permanent **injunction**. An injunction requires a violator to obey immediately. Presently, each single day of violation after the injunction results in a $25,000 per day civil penalty. A **criminal action** may be initiated for a number of reasons, but **civil penalties** are more common. For example, if an owner or operator of a UST gives false information or fails to give notices to the EPA or state agency, as much as $10,000 per tank may be assessed.

Violators can request a public hearing to challenge the EPA within 30 days after receipt of an EPA order or action.[23] Owners must notify the EPA and submit accurate information or face civil penalties. Additionally, owners or operators can be cited for improper leak detection equipment, poor record keeping, not reporting to the appropriate regulatory agency, not taking actions to correct their tank's problems, improperly closing or sealing tanks, and not demonstrating financial responsibility to properly maintain or repair the tanks. If a petroleum release occurs, the EPA can order owners and operators of USTs to stop the leak and clean up the contamination.

State UST Programs

The RCRA UST programs may be delegated to the states. To qualify for delegation, a state must adopt laws, regulations, and rules to meet or exceed the RCRA UST provisions. The state then becomes the primary permitting authority for USTs, and the EPA passes on its responsibility.[24]

For the states that do not qualify or do not submit for RCRA responsibilities, the designated EPA regional office performs those functions. If a state fails to perform its RCRA duties satisfactorily, EPA may withdraw that state's authorization.

Local governments (cities, townships, or counties) may have stricter regulations than their states, but local intervention to control the environment is uncommon.

UST records

Many reports and records must be submitted to the UST enforcing agency (state or EPA) and kept over long periods. In the first notification to the EPA or state agency, owners and operators must certify that they have complied with proper installation requirements, electronic or cathodic protection, financial responsibility, and release detection. Next, they must report any suspected releases, spills or overflows, and confirmed releases. For any releases in excess of a substance's reportable quantity, reports must be submitted to the National Response Center and the RCRA-responsible agency. Any actions to correct, contain, or stop leaks have to be reported. Those reports must include details of the character of the site at the time of the leak, the removal of the materials flowing out of the leak, results of soil and groundwater cleanups, and action plans to correct the problems if required. Notice must be submitted prior to permanent closing of a tank or a change in service. Submissions must be made that certify an owner or operator's financial capabilities to respond to leaks and other accidents from tank systems.

When a tank system is removed from the ground or removed from service, notice is to include the date of stopping operations; age of the tank on that date; size, type, and location of the tank; and the type and quantity of substances stored in the tank.[25]

If records are to be kept confidential, they have to be submitted separately from the public information. When metal USTs and systems are installed without corrosion protection, notice must be provided to the appropriate

UST regulatory agency. Inspection and testing of cathode protection systems require the submittal of records. UST system repairs must be recorded. Performance claims made by manufacturers of release detection equipment must be maintained along with sampling, testing, and monitoring results. Permanent closing of a tank or change in service of a tank system requires records. If a tank system is closed permanently, closure records can be sent to the agency.

Exhibit 40: Leaks of hazardous liquids from underground tanks may occur above ground through piping systems.

When an owner initiates the construction a new UST system to contain regulated substances, the regulatory agency must be notified and given certification of compliance with UST requirements for installation, cathodic protection, financial responsibility, and release detection. The new tank system must be constructed of non-corrosive materials that cannot fail structurally. It must be designed to prevent a release of any stored substance. Finally, the tank system must be composed of materials compatible with the substances to be stored. Methods used to install the system must be certified to comply with industry codes of practice and national testing laboratories. Installers must comply. Anyone selling a tank to be used as an UST has to notify the purchaser of the many notification requirements. When upgrading an existing USTs, tanks, pipes, and valves must each meet new UST performance standards, tank upgrading specifications, and closure and corrective action requirements.[26]

Leaks and Releases

Leak and release reports

Because so many underground storage tanks, pipes, and valves had been constructed of steel and have been in direct contact with moist soils for a period of time, many have corroded and leaked. Leaks pose particular threats to soils, surface, and groundwater. Any suspected release has to be reported to the state agency or EPA within 24 hours of the event. Some conditions that require reporting are

❖ Adverse monitoring reports from a release detection method

❖ Discovery of spilled or released regulated substances at the tank system site or in the surroundings

❖ Problems with dispensing equipment

❖ Sudden loss of the substance from the UST system or some unexplained reason for water in the UST system.[27]

Release investigation

An investigation of a suspected release is conducted to confirm the problem. A **tightness test** (system test) must be conducted to determine where and whether a leak exists. If no leak is found, then no further investigations are required.

If environmental contamination can be found but with no negatively related system testing results, then additional procedures must be taken. A **site check** is performed to evaluate whether a release has occurred from the UST system. If not, no further investigations are necessary.

If a release is confirmed, an **initial release response** is performed within 24 hours, and immediate action is taken to prevent any more substance being released. Hazards such as fire, explosions, and vapor hazards have to be eliminated at that time. **Initial abatement measures** must be performed following any release confirmation. The substance must be removed from the UST system. A visual inspection must be performed. Contaminated soils have to be cleaned if the substance has been released into the ground. The location of the release has to be determined. Finally, the substance ("free product") must be removed as soon as practical.

Contamination cleanup

If the investigation shows that the substance is present in the soils, air, or water, then it must be removed and reported to the agency. Soil and water in the area of the release (and the entire site) are required to be investigated to determine if any of these conditions exist:

❖ Contaminated soils are touching groundwater or surface water

❖ The substance needs to be recovered

❖ A larger area is in danger of being contaminated

❖ Water wells have been contaminated.

As previously stated, all spills and overfills have to be contained and cleaned up at once. Reports must be submitted within 24 hours if the spills or overfills are petroleum based exceeding 25 gallons, cause a sheen on nearby surface water, and equal or exceed its reportable quantity for that substance.[28]

Cleanup action plans (Corrective action plans)

These plans are developed and submitted to the agency when requested. The plans address methods to clean contaminated soils and groundwater. A schedule and format is established by the regulatory agency, and owners and operators must comply. When the corrective action plan is approved, the plan must be placed in service, and monitored, evaluated, and the results reported according to a set schedule and format. Owners and operators can begin cleanup of soil and groundwater before the action plan is approved, but they must first notify the agency of their intent and comply with any conditions set by the agency.

Closing a UST System

Whether a UST is temporarily or permanently closed, the same requirements apply—release detection, release reports, corrosion protection, investigation, confirmation, and corrective actions. If the UST is empty, release detection is not required. For temporary closings, the vent lines are to be open and functioning, and all other lines and valves are to be secured and capped. If the temporary closing exceeds 12 months, it must be permanently closed. Permanent closings or changes in service require an owner or operator to notify the agency at least 30 days in advance. For permanent closure, tanks must be cleaned, emptied, and then filled with solid material or removed from the ground and the hole backfilled. Records must be kept to indicate complete compliance with the UST requirements of the appropriate agency.

Financial responsibility must be demonstrated to the extent that owners or operators can show ability to pay for cleanups, property damage, or bodily injury to another party that might be caused by operating a UST. The amount of money demonstrated ranges from half a million to two million dollars. To meet these financial requirements, large companies may self-insure. Large company subsidiaries can obtain guaranties, letters of credit, surety bonds, trust agreements, or EPA-approved state assurance funds.[29] Most states have established tank system cleanup funds to help owners and operators pay for cleanups. Records proving financial ability must be maintained and submitted. Updated copies of certification of financial responsibility or other evidence may be required.

Exhibit 41: When tanks are taken out of use, there are many regulatory requirements, such as signs, record keeping, monitoring, and containment.

Chronology of the Resource Conservation and Recovery Act (RCRA)

1976, Resource Conservation and Recovery Act (RCRA), Pub. L. 94–580; 7 USC 1010 et seq.; 40 CFR 280 and 281

1984, Hazardous and Solid Waste Act (HSWA), 40 CFR 261, 262, 267, 268, 271, and 272

1984, Standards for Treatment, Storage, and Disposal Facilities (TSDs), 40 CFR 264 and 265

CHAPTER 19

Federal Compliance:
Federal Facility Compliance Act (FFCA)

Overview

❖ The Federal Facility Compliance Act (FFCA) is an amendment to the Resource Conservation and Recovery Act (RCRA).

❖ The FFCA ensures that all government buildings and facilities comply with the same environmental controls and regulations that apply to individuals, businesses, industries, and local and state governments.

❖ Federally-owned facilities, such as military bases, airports, buildings, and munitions storage areas, can be fined by the U.S. Environmental Protection Agency for violations of any environmental regulations.

❖ All waste and tank control programs apply to every federal site.

❖ Criminal laws apply to federal officials violating the FFCA.

❖ Warships of the U.S. Navy are excluded from the regulations, except when unloading hazardous wastes in ports.

❖ Federally-owned treatment works must comply with the same regulations as publicly-owned treatment works.

Federal Facility Compliance Act Acronyms

CEI—Compliance evaluation inspections

EPA—Environmental Protection Agency

FFCA—Federal Facility Compliance Act

FOTW—Federally-owned treatment works

POTW—Publicly-owned treatment works

RCRA—Resource Conservation and Recovery Act

Federal Facility Compliance Act (FFCA)

This act amends the Resource Conservation and Recovery Act (RCRA) to ensure that federal facilities would not continue to be exempt from violating the same environmental regulations placed on the public.[1] Both the states and the EPA may impose penalties and fines on federal buildings and facilities for violating federal, state, or local laws that regulate solid and hazardous waste. All controls and management of wastes that apply to the public sector must be respected by every federal facility. Areas of concern include public vessels, radioactive mixed wastes, munitions used by the military, and federally-owned wastewater treatment works.[2]

All criminal laws that apply to the waste management business apply to federal officials under FFCA. The EPA must conduct annual Compliance Evaluation Inspections (CEIs) for each federal facility holding a RCRA Treatment, Storage, and Disposal Permit (often called a Part B permit). State agencies are also allowed to independently inspect federal facilities.

U.S. Navy warships are exempted from some FFCA requirements. If they were not exempted, some ships that create hazardous wastes and that must remain at sea over 90 days would violate RCRA's restrictions. When the navy unloads the hazardous wastes at ports, they become regulated according to FFCA. Vessel wastes are also regulated when the waste is stored on any public vessel for more than 90 days after the public vessel is placed in reserve, is otherwise no longer in service, or when the waste is transferred to another public vessel within territorial waters and stored on such vessel or another public vessel for more than 90 days after the date of transfer. (A public vessel is one owned or chartered and operated by the United States.)

Munitions stored at Department of Defense facilities could leak into soils and ground waters. Therefore, munitions must be transported, treated, and stored according to RCRA requirements.

Flows of effluent from domestic sewage and industrial processes are handled at federally-owned and publicly-owned treatment works (FOTWs and POTWs, respectively) and subject to the same requirements, enforcement, and penalties. All federal facilities must pay fees connected to solid and hazardous waste regulatory programs.

The FFCA broadens the EPA's enforcement powers against federal facilities violating RCRA. Methods for calculating penalties are based on the severity of the violation, major, moderate, or minor. The severity is the extent of deviation from the regulatory requirement. Daily penalties may be imposed. Because so many of its provisions apply to RCRA, the FFCA may be considered a part of RCRA rather than a separate act.

FFCA and the Small Town Environmental Planning Program

The EPA assists small communities in planning and financing environmental facilities. Requirements are developed using federal environmental and public health regulations. As part of the SWDA, the Federal Facilities Compliance Act makes the government subject to the same rules as individuals and businesses. By extending downward to other lower levels of government and small towns with populations of fewer than 2,500, even more public agencies are led to compliance.

An Office of the Small Town Ombudsman is created within the EPA as a primary means of providing assistance. Multimedia permits (combination air, water, or waste) are promoted for small towns to adopt as a means to coordinate their environmental and public health activities. By combining the media into a single permit, efficiencies for filing, approving, and managing are promoted. In this way the EPA and the communities in which federal buildings and facilities are located can maintain a more effective ongoing communication which leads to sound practice by both parties. An important function of the Small Town Environmental Planning Program is to notify small communities of current and future regulations. The EPA is to provide the federal agency filters and notification duties to deliver this information in the most efficient manner.[3]

Chronology of the Federal Facility Compliance Act (FFCA)

1992, Federal Facility Compliance Act, Pub. L. 102–386, 106 Stat. 1505

Section Five

Safety

CHAPTER 20

Workplace:
Occupational Safety and Health Act (OSH)

Overview

❖ The OSH Act regulates and inspects workplaces.

❖ The provisions of the OSH Act cover all workers except federal non-postal workers.

❖ Permanent standards are established under the National Institute of Occupational Safety and Health (NIOSH) within the U.S. Department of Health and Human Services.

❖ Employers must keep records of employees and hazard communication documents such as MSDSs for chemical substances in the workplace.

❖ While there are concerns for indoor air in office buildings, there are many other health and safety issues in manufacturing facilities, such as dust and dirt, machinery safety, and aromatic chemicals.

❖ Other federal agencies have responsibilities that overlap with the OSH Act.

Occupational Safety and Health Act Acronyms

DOL—Department of Labor

EPA—Environmental Protection Agency

ETS—Emergency temporary standard

FAA—Federal Aviation Administration

HAZCOM—Hazard communication

MSDS—Material safety data sheets

NIOSH—National Institute for Occupational Safety and Health

OSH Act—Occupational Safety and Health Act

OSHA—Occupational Safety and Health Administration

OSHRC—Occupational Safety and Health Review Commission

The Occupational Safety and Health Act (OSH)

The OSH Act ensures that workers suffer no harm to their health from job exposure. Employers must adhere to OSH unless they have fewer than ten employees or they are federal or state government agencies covered under other regulations. The primary agency administering OSH is the Occupational Safety and Health Administration (OSHA), a division of the U.S. Department of Labor (DOL). OSHA is an enforcement agency that has both health- and labor-protecting functions. State and federal inspectors enforce its regulations while at the same time providing education about worker safety. Even though many environmental, health, and safety concerns overlap between two federal agencies—EPA and OSHA—each of the agencies regulates different things about asbestos, vinyl chloride, cancer-causing agents (carcinogens), warning labels, and other items.

Exhibit 42: Labeling of substances stored in drums and other containers is important to workers.

Workers' Rights

Workers have the right to refuse to work if there may be risk of serious injury or death.[1] Workers are protected if they complain to government officials about unsafe work conditions.[2] There is an independent panel of judges as part of the Occupational Health and Safety Review Commission that handles disagreements between labor and management. Under the OSH Act, workers who complain and are fired can have their jobs restored or lost pay reimbursed.[3]

Federal employees (with the exception of postal workers)[4] are not directly covered by the OSH Act. Responsibility for providing safe and healthy working conditions is designated to the head of each public agency.[5] State government employees are excluded from protections from the OSH Act although most all states have similar programs that cover their employees.

OSH Standards

Regulating threats to health in the workplace is a major concern. Some threats can be can be sudden and catastrophic and others slow and cumulative. For the slow and cumulative threats, OSHA may require health standards that require medical surveillance, record taking, monitoring, medical examinations, and workplace air sampling. By contrast, regulations for those safety threats that could bring immediate and violent harm are more stringent. By applying OSHA standards and regulations, injuries such as burns, electrical shock, cuts, broken bones, loss of limbs, loss of eyesight, or risk of death are minimized.

The affiliated National Institute for Occupational Safety and Health (NIOSH) within the U.S. Department of Health and Human Services develops standards for on-the-job safety and health. OSHA Standards are established for a wide scope of worker issues on the job. For example, standards may be developed to ensure safety in any of the following areas:

❖ Means of egress
❖ Powered platforms, man lifts, and vehicle work platforms
❖ Ventilation, noise
❖ Hazardous materials (gas, flammable mixtures, radiation)
❖ Protective equipment (masks, respirators)
❖ Sanitation, labor camps, and safety color codes for hazards
❖ Available and accessible medical and first aid
❖ Fire protection
❖ Gas and compressed air equipment and devices
❖ Materials handling and storage machinery
❖ Guarding of machinery (portable power tools and equipment)
❖ Welding, cutting, and brazing
❖ Pulp and paper production
❖ Textiles, laundry equipment
❖ Telecommunications equipment
❖ Electrical devices
❖ Commercial diving
❖ Control of toxic and hazardous substances (air contaminants, asbestos, benzene, lead, vinyl chloride, and others)
❖ Record keeping[6]

Permanent standards

To date, only a short list of permanent standards have been enacted with ranges of safety:[7]

❖ 1,2-dibromo-3-chloropropane
❖ 2-acetylaminofluorene
❖ 3,3'-dichlorolenzidine
❖ 4-aminodiphyenyl
❖ 4-dimethylaminozaobenzene
❖ 4-Nitrobiphenyl
❖ Acrylonitrile
❖ Alpha-nephthylamine
❖ Asbestos
❖ Benzene
❖ Benzidine
❖ Beta-propiolactone
❖ Beta-naphthylamine
❖ Bis-chloromethyl ether
❖ Carcinogens
❖ Coke oven emissions
❖ Cotton dust
❖ Ethyleneimine
❖ Ethylene oxide
❖ Field Sanitation
❖ Inorganic arsenic
❖ Lead
❖ Methyl chloromethyl ether
❖ N-nitrosodimethylamine
❖ Vinyl chloride

Because there are many workplace hazards, three different types of standards are used: consensus, permanent, and emergency temporary standards.

Consensus standards are those developed prior to 1973 by other federal agencies, industries, and private groups. These standards listed of about 400 toxic chemicals and their maximum allowed air concentrations. The concentrations are listed as thresholds, established limits below which a worker is assumed to be safe. Since the consensus standards were not based on firm scientific evidence but accepted without question from industry standards and guidelines, no testing had been performed to provide positively sound data on which to base those standards.

NIOSH may establish permanent standards using the results of a tragedy or accident, court action, new scientific studies, or by adopting the conclusions in a "criteria" document. Crite-

Exhibit 43: The mix of wastes, materials, and trash on this vehicle would violate many provisions of the Occupational Health and Safety Act.

ria documents compile all of the scientific reports on a chemical (epidemiological and animal studies) and are submitted to OSHA for adoption as a standard. Standards include antidotes, labels, medical monitoring, suggested exposure limits, and other details. Emergency temporary standards may be imposed as needed if questions arise about worker safety.

Other Federal Agencies that Regulate Occupational Safety

Other federal agencies have duties and responsibilities that overlap with OSHA's. Ten federal regions of OSHA have the same boundaries as the EPA regions. Each region contains from four to nine area offices, district offices, or field stations.

According to the OSH Act, memoranda of understanding have been signed between a number of agencies and OSHA. For example, the U.S. Department of Transportation's Federal Aviation Administration (FAA) and Federal Railroad Administration promote rules for the safety of work crews, maintenance personnel, and travelers. In addition, if the EPA lists a toxic substance, such as a pesticide, OSHA may control its use by workers in the fields. The Occupational Safety and Health Review Commission (OSHRC) maintains a review process wherein failures to challenge a citation automatically requires the

OSHRC to uphold that citation. NIOSH (U.S. Department of Health and Human Services) holds the training and research functions for the OSH Act. NIOSH reports to the Center for Disease Control. There is a NIOSH priority system to produce criteria documents based on severity of response needed, population at risk, current standard, and advice from other federal agencies and professional groups.

Other standards

Establishing an emergency temporary standard (ETS) is an approach for times when the normal rulemaking process would be too slow. If an on-the-job catastrophe occurs, it could trigger an ETS. For example, a new chemical or biological mixture may cause hospitalization of a few workers on an assembly line. While the hazard is investigated, an emergency temporary standard might be used to continue the manufacturing process in a modified manner. These ETSs are effective for six months beginning with publication in the Federal Register.[8] Another standard, the General Duty Clause, covers situations for which no other standards exist. Inspectors are given the authority to cite violations for any unsafe conditions.[9]

When a company complains that the standards are unrealistic, it can seek a temporary or permanent variance. A temporary variance is one that employers may apply when they cannot meet the standard for these or other reasons:

❖ Professional or technical personnel are not available

❖ Technical materials or equipment are not available

❖ Changes to the building(s) or facility cannot be completed in time

Temporary variances may be issued for less than a year, with no more than two six-month renewals. In order for the temporary variance to be granted, owners or operators must prove that they are taking every step to provide worker safety and that they have an effective compliance program that can meet the standard quickly. A permanent variance can be granted to those employers with evidence demonstrating that "conditions, practices, means, methods, operations, or processes used or proposed to be used" they can provide as safe a workplace as meeting the standard.[10]

Inspecting the workplace

Compliance with the OSH Act is typically handled by inspections. OSHA performs about 50,000 inspections annually, with about the same amount performed by similar state agencies. Random inspections are common, and high priority is given to inspecting high hazard occupations. Inspectors usually obtain voluntary entry to facilities but when refused, a search warrant is obtained from a federal district court. If a hazard is discovered, citations are issued according to severity. The four types of violations are willful, serious, repeated, or nonserious.[11]

Exhibit 44: This worker can easily read the hazard warning labels on the chemical drums in this loading area.

One thing inspectors will be looking for is records. Records such as accident reports, monitoring, medical records of employees, and hazard communication must be kept. Employees and their legal or union representatives are required to be given access to all facility records within 15 working days of their request.

The OSH Act requires that OSHA encourage state job and health safety programs. If there are any state enforcement gaps, then the federal enforcement can apply. State plans for occupational health and safety must be reviewed by OSHA to ensure compliance with federal intent and provisions. The DOL, through state personnel, provides owners or operators with information about complying with OSHA standards independent of any enforcement activity.[12] There are typically more state health and safety agencies inspecting workplaces than there are OSHA inspectors. Also, small employers as well as larger ones may request OSHA consultation on site. At that time, the OSHA inspectors educate employers about how to comply.

Hazard communication

OSHA developed the hazard communication (HAZCOM) regulation to give workers the right to know about any hazardous chemicals in the work place.[13] Each employer must assess the toxicity of the chemicals it produces and uses. They must notify persons who purchase the products by providing them with Material Safety Data Sheets (MSDSs). Trade secrets are protected even though a worker is given the right to be free of exposure to any harmful chemicals. The method of protecting the trade secrets is the signing of a need-to-know statement and the identity of the chemical substance must be disclosed to a treating nurse or physician who determines that a medical necessity exists.

❖ Occupational Safety and Health Act

All chemicals are to be labeled, and training and education about the chemicals must be provided. (New Jersey has the stiffest label law in the country where industries must label all of its chemical substances—hazardous or not—and supply the information to community groups, workers, and health officials.) Chemical manufacturers must evaluate all the chemicals they sell for the potential to be exposed to workers.

Hazardous chemical lists

The following four lists are lists of hazardous chemical substances:

❖ International Agency for Research on Cancer Monograph

❖ Annual Report on Carcinogens (National Toxicology Program)

❖ OSHA's Subpart Z list in 29 CFR 1910

❖ Threshold Limit Values for Chemical Substances and Physical Agents in the Work Environment (American Conference of Governmental Industrial Hygienists)

Chronology of the Occupational Safety and Health Act (OSHA)

1970, OSHA Amendment, Pub. L. 91–596, 91st Congress, S. 2193, 29 USC 651 et seq.

1990, OSHA Amendment, Pub. L. 101–552, Section 3101.

CHAPTER 21

Chemicals:
Toxic Substances Control Act

Overview

❖ TSCA controls toxic chemical and biological substances before they are sold.

❖ All manufacturers of such substances must notify and give information to the EPA prior to start of manufacture.

❖ Periodic updates and reports must be submitted and approved by the EPA. 179

❖ Exemptions may be granted for some substances.

❖ Testing of any substance may be ordered by the EPA for many reasons.

❖ Manufacturing and other facilities are inspected.

❖ Strict penalties can be assessed and conditions for penalty reductions are clearly stated.

Toxic Substances Control Act Acronyms

CAIR—Comprehensive assessment information rule

CBI—Confidential business information

CERCLA—Comprehensive Environmental Response, Compensation, and Liability Act

EPA—Environmental Protection Agency

FDCA—Federal Food, Drug, and Cosmetic Act

FIFRA—Federal Insecticide, Fungicide, and Rodenticide Act

ITC—Intragency Testing Committee

LVE—Low volume exemption

MCAN—Microbial commercial activity notice

OPA—Oil Pollution Act

PAIR—Preliminary assessment information rule

PCB—Polychlorinated biphenyls

PMN—Premanufacture notice

RCRA—Resource Conservation and Recovery Act

SNUR—Significant New Use Rule

TSCA—Toxic Substances Control Act

Toxic Substances Are Regulated

Many chemicals and mixtures are dangerous when manufactured, used, or disposed. Because so many substances are constantly produced, federal regulations must be put in place to protect interstate commerce.

Toxic substances are harmful chemicals or biological agents. The Toxic Substances Control Act (TSCA) identifies and controls toxic substances both before they are sold and also after approval for sale.[1] By contrast, other federal regulations (such as RCRA, CERCLA, and OPA) control toxic chemical and biological substances after they have been released to the environment.

Chemical substances are substances of a molecular identity that includes combinations which result from a chemical reaction or an occurrence in nature. Any element or uncombined radical is considered a chemical substance regulated under TSCA. Some exclusions from the classification as a chemical substance are made for commercial food, food additives, drugs, and cosmetics; commercial pesticides; tobacco products; nuclear source materials and byproducts; and pistols, firearms, revolvers, shells, and cartridges. TSCA also excludes chemical substances of small quantities manufactured for research or development; pesticides; articles having no change in chemical composition after manufacture; impurities; and byproducts without a specified commercial purpose that are produced when another chemical substance or mixture is manufactured. Intermediate chemicals that are partially or totally consumed in the chemical reaction process are excluded.[2]

There are four major sections within this environmental regulation:

1) Controlling toxic substances

2) Responding to asbestos hazard emergencies

3) Eliminating or reducing indoor radon

4) Reducing exposures to lead

Controlling the toxic substances is, by far, one of the most difficult tasks in regulating the environment.

Regulatory requirements

TSCA requires a number of procedures, tests, record keeping, and other actions to be followed and enforced by EPA. Rules may be developed to enforce TSCA after considering and publishing statements about human exposure, environmental exposure, and the benefits and consequences of using such a substance.

First, suspected dangerous chemicals must be identified and tested. Manufacturing, processing, or distributing them is restricted beyond their intended use or in amounts in excess of recommended quantities or concentrations.

Next, the EPA requires review, tests, and substantiation of safety for new chemical substances before their introduction to the environment.[3] Also, the manufacture, use, distribution, or disposal of existing chemical substances can be limited or prohibited. Warning labels and application instructions are specified by the EPA.

Finally, the EPA can require record keeping and reporting for new chemical substances and can require export notices or import certificates. Commercial uses may be restricted for certain methods of applying, disposing, manufacturing, processing, and controlling quality in manufacturing the regulated substance. The effects on the environment and the magnitude of exposure are considered in relation to the benefits of each substance and the availability of substitutes. If importers ship any chemical substance or mixture into the United States, they must certify to the U.S. Bureau of Customs that the shipment is or is not subject to TSCA.

Under TSCA, manufacturers and processors have the responsibility to test chemical and biological substances. They must develop safety and environmental data when the chemical or biological substance could present unreasonable risks of injury, or when substantial

Exhibit 45: Treatment lagoons, such as this one, are used for the treatment of biological wastes. Note the murky nature of the liquid.

quantities of the chemical or biological substances are produced with the possibility for substantial human or environmental exposure. An Intragency Testing Committee (ITC) makes recommendations to the EPA about those substances and mixtures that should have priority consideration.

Any potential immediate or unreasonable risk from a hazardous substance may be mitigated through the TSCA regulations. Companies or persons involved with TSCA-listed chemicals are carefully regulated. Anyone manufacturing substances or mixtures of chemicals must submit tests and data to the EPA. A premanufacture notice (PMN) must be prepared and submitted before any unlisted chemical substance is manufactured. Polychlorinated biphenyls (PCBs) are prohibited from manufacture. Records of chemical substances must be maintained, and reports on the substances have to be submitted to the EPA. Companies must certify that they comply with TSCA if chemical substances are imported. If a company extracts a chemical from another substance or mixture, that company is defined as a manufacturer and is subject all of the provisions of TSCA.[4] Likewise, if a company or person prepares a chemical substance or mixture for distribution in commerce or merely distributes it, the company or person is considered a processor and subject to TSCA.

TSCA, FIFRA, and the FDCA

Other federal regulations relate to TSCA. FIFRA states that chemicals must meet TSCA pesticide exclusions to be classified as a pesticide, fungicide, or insecticide. The Federal Food, Drug, and Cosmetic Act (FDCA) covers substances excluded from TSCA such as foods, food additives, drugs, devices, or cosmetics. If the EPA adopts a test rule for a chemical, state or local governments cannot adopt a different one. TSCA governs state and local actions.

Exemptions to TSCA regulations

Several exceptions from regulation under TSCA are described below:

Test market exemption: This exemption may be granted by the EPA if no unreasonable risk to human health or the environment can be determined. By requesting a test market exemption, a company can spend some time collecting data and demonstrating the product's safety.

Research and development exemption: This exemption may be granted when small quantities of new chemicals are used solely for research and development under qualified technical supervision.

Low volume exemption (LVE): This may be granted during a 30-day review. Low-release, low-exposure chemicals are exempted if the volumes do not exceed 10,000 kilograms per year. For the LVE exemption, there can be no dermal exposure, no inhalation exposure, and no drinking water exposure.

Polymer exemption: This is given if no unreasonable risk of injury to health or the environment is present. Polymer exemptions do not require an application, but an annual report must be submitted to EPA which indicates the number of new polymers that were manufactured or imported for the first time during the previous year.

Polaroid exemption: This exemption allows the Polaroid Corporation to be exempted for any new chemical substances used for instant photographic and peel apart film.

Exemptions are also made for the following substances:

❖ New chemicals imported in articles that contain fluids or particles not intended to be removed from the article and that have no separate commercial purpose

❖ Impurities byproducts, nonisolated intermediates, and chemicals formed incidentally when exposed to the environment or to other chemicals

❖ Chemicals formed during the manufacture of an article are exempted from the regulations, such as those chemicals formed from using adhesives, curable plastic, inks, drying oils, rubber molding compounds, or metal finishing compounds[5]

Chemical Reviews

The EPA continuously updates and maintains the inventory database of new chemicals that have cleared TSCA PMN review. Every four years, reports are required for all chemical substances listed on the TSCA Inventory except for polymers, microorganisms, naturally occurring substances, and inorganic substances.[6] As a result of this requirement, the TSCA inventory has become very large (about five volumes of listed substances). A registry number is assigned for each chemical substance. New chemical reviews are made to determine if the chemical substance complies with the PMN requirements prior to manufacturing. Under PMN, the EPA has to determine the risks from manufacturing, processing, distributing, using, and disposing the new substance based on information supplied by the PMN.

Over 20,000 new chemical substances have been reviewed through the PMN process. There are four types of PMN:

❖ Standard: for a single chemical substance
❖ Consolidated: for two or more chemical substances which have similar molecular structures and use patterns
❖ Joint: for use when two companies must submit data together
❖ Exemption: for low volumes, low release, low exposure or test marketed substances.

A significant new use (SNUR) is a chemical substance that can result in increased production volume, different or greater exposure, different disposal method, or different manufacturing site.

Tests, triggers, and rules

Two situations that demand testing are called the risk trigger and the exposure trigger. The term risk trigger means that the EPA has made a determination that a chemical or biological agent may present an unreasonable risk (both in toxicity and exposure). An exposure trigger is when a chemical substance is produced in substantial quantities, is reasonably expected to be released into the environment in substantial quantities, or when there is insufficient data or experience to predict the environmental effects and testing is needed to develop data on the substance.[7] The amount of substantial production or substantial release is considered one million pounds total per year. Substantial human exposure is based upon a general population of 100,000 people, consumers at 10,000 people, and workers at 1,000 workers.

If tests are required, a test rule is developed for the chemical substance, and the applicant must perform that test or combination of tests. Test rules are formalized and placed in EPA records for review by those submitting applications to the EPA. Applicants must follow those instructions, submit a PMN, maintain records, document or certify compliance with TSCA requirements, and submit reports to the EPA. If a chemical substance is questioned for any reason, decisions on allowing it to be listed may be accepted based on the test rule adopted for that chemical substance. If a significant risk is uncovered by the test data, a finding must be published and communicated to the public. Reporting and record keeping requirements are more rigorous for certain substances. Details concerning the manufacturing process, health, and environmental exposure may be required to be submitted to EPA for some listed chemicals. Thirty days after a chemical is placed on the ITC Priority Testing List, that chemical is added to the Preliminary Assessment Information Rule (PAIR) list. More detailed information is needed for some chemical substances, which are subject to the Comprehensive Assessment Information Rule (CAIR). Records of significant adverse reactions that substantially impair normal human activities or causes lasting or permanent damage to the environment or health must be kept along with allegations of any problems submitted by employees or others.

There are only six chemical-specific regulations. They govern the following substances:

❖ Asbestos

❖ Chloroflourocarbon

❖ Dioxins

❖ Hexavalent chromium

❖ Metalworking fluids

❖ Polychlorinated biphenyls (PCBs).

Requirements for these problem substances are precise and carefully crafted.[8]

Facility Inspections

The EPA carries out a six-step process in inspecting a facility for the handling or manufacturing of a chemical or biological substance that is not listed in TSCA.

Exhibit 46: EPA inspectors look for labeling, methods of storing, handling of unlisted chemical or biological substances, and conformity to previous facility reports and requirements.

❖ *Pre-inspection Preparation*

The EPA regional office delivers written notice in advance of a visit. The notice usually discusses the EPA's procedures and intent and allows for the party to make a declaration of confidential business information (CBI).

❖ *Notification and Entry*

This step can be performed with or without a search warrant if a company gives permission.

❖ *Opening Conference*

The conference is usually conducted with facility officials to explain the inspection purpose, scope, and procedures.

❖ *Sampling and Documentation*

The inspector reviews records and may take samples.

❖ *Closing Conference*

EPA presents an itemized receipt of all samples, records, and documents taken to the facility manager. At that time, the inspector may discuss observed deviations and problems or may offer suggestions based on preliminary findings.

❖ *Report Preparation and Follow-up*

This step includes the inspection report or final audit report. The regional EPA office then decides whether it should enforce TSCA through civil or criminal prosecution or if it should take other actions.[9]

Violations and penalties

Under the EPA self-policing policy, there are nine conditions which a facility owner or operator may satisfy in order to relieve penalties for violations of TSCA. All nine conditions must be satisfied to achieve full penalty reduction.

1) Systematic discovery: A company must discover violations through due diligence or an environmental audit;

2) Voluntary disclosure: Not required by an order or permit condition;

3) Prompt disclosure: Violations must be reported within ten days of discovering them;

4) Independent discovery: A company must discover and disclose before a government inspection occurs

5) Correction and remediation: Violations must be certified as corrected within 60 days

6) Prevent recurrence: Steps must be taken to prevent it happening again;

7) No repeat violations: No similar or identical violations can have occurred at the same place within the previous three years, nor can it fit into a pattern of company violations

8) Other violations excluded: No serious harm or present endanger ment could have occurred, nor could the violations fit into the same kinds of violations that have resulted in penalties

9) Cooperation: Company must cooperate with the EPA in its investigations of violations and related compliance issues.[10]

Chemical Programs

Biotechnology

The EPA has placed the regulation of biotechnology under the broad authorities of TSCA. There are PMN requirements for new microorganisms and reporting requirements for all microorganisms. Only informal guidance from the EPA is available at this time.[11] The EPA had proposed that a PMN for new microorganisms using a microbial commercial activity notice (MCAN) be required. Certain microorganisms that do not present unreasonable risk are to be exempted from the MCAN requirement. Presently, more research and development are necessary to further refine the MCAN and PMN requirements for regulating biotechnology.

Indoor radon abatement

The EPA works with other federal agencies to develop model construction standards and architectural design protocols for controlling radon levels in new buildings.[12] These standards are provided along with other radon information (mitigation studies, public information materials, and area surveys of radon levels) to the States as technical assistance. The EPA also operates a voluntary proficiency program to rate effectiveness of radon measurement and monitoring, and of private firms and consultants that offer architecture, design, engineering, measurement, and other mitigation services. The EPA publishes the findings of radon mitigation methods for different structures and geographic areas. Cooperative projects are developed between the EPA Radon Action Program and the states' radon programs.

The extent of radon contamination in school buildings is a major concern, and studies identify and map high-risk school areas. Information is provided to the states about these schools and risks. Radon in federal buildings is required to be measured by each federal agency. High-risk federal buildings are identified and listed along with geology data, high radon levels in housing and other structures surrounding the federal buildings, and information about the physical characteristics of the federal buildings. Research is conducted into different measurement methods, design protocols for different building types, and comparison of levels of radon exposure.

❖ Toxic Substances Control Act

Lead exposure reduction

For decades, lead was a common ingredient of paint and other coatings.[13] When it is intact, lead surfaces do not present significant dangers. As the paint or coating deteriorates over time, however, the chips and soluble particles become a health hazard and a hazard to soils, air, and waterborne media.[14] Lead-based paint is paint or other surface coatings that contains lead in excess of 1.0 milligrams per centimeter squared or 0.5 percent by weight, or any other level established by HUD (or other public agencies).

Deteriorated paint is any interior or exterior paint that is peeling, chipping, chalking, cracking, damaged, or deteriorated. A lead-based paint hazard is any condition that causes exposure to lead from paint that is deteriorated or present in accessible surfaces, friction surfaces, or impact surfaces. Lead-contaminated dust is surface dust in residential dwelling units containing an area in excess of levels determined by the EPA which could hurt pregnant women or young children. Lead-contaminated soil is soil on residential property containing lead.

Anyone engaged in removing lead-based paint must be properly trained in an accredited program, and contractors must be certified. Training programs for workers, supervisors, inspectors and planners are based on minimum standards that include accrediting the training providers, curricula requirements, hours of training, hands-on training, and training program quality control.

Chronology of the Toxic Substances Control Act (TSCA)

1976, Toxic Substances Control Act of 1976, Pub. L. 99–519, 15 USC 2601 et seq.

1977, TSCA Amendment, 15 USC 2601–2671

1978, Federal Pesticide Act of 1978, Pub. L. 95–396, USC 136 et seq.

1986, Asbestos Hazard Emergency Response Act of 1986, Pub. L. 99–519, 106 Stat. 3924

1988, Federal Insecticide, Fungicide, and Rodenticide Act Amendments of 1988, Pub. L. 100–532

1991, FIFRA Amendment, Pub. L. 102–237

1992, Lead-based Paint Exposure Reduction Act, Pub. L. 102–550, 1021(c) Stat. 3924

1976, Toxic Substances Control Act of 1976, Pub. L. 99–519, 15 USC 2601 et seq.

1977, TSCA Amendment, 15 USC 2601–2671

CHAPTER 22

Pesticides:
Federal Insecticide, Fungicide, and Rodenticide Act (FIFRA)

Overview

❖ Pesticides, herbicides, insecticides, fungicides, and rodenticides must be registered with federal government prior to manufacture and distribution for sale.

❖ The EPA is responsible for developing and maintaining labeling requirements for these substances.

❖ The EPA coordinates and works with the Food and Drug Administration (FDA) of the U.S. Department of Agriculture (USDA) and the Occupational Safety and Health Administration (OSHA) to protect the public from lingering residues and worker exposures.

❖ In order to ensure product safety, all contractors and applicators must be certified.

❖ Labels must show ingredients and safety warnings.

❖ Carriers of disease are eradicated according to special means.

❖ Experimental use permits may be issued.

❖ Scientific review of products may be required.

❖ Records must be kept.

❖ States can enforce FIFRA, but any differences between federal and state data must be minimized, reduced, or eliminated.

❖ Onsite inspections are performed and penalties may be assessed.

Federal Insecticide, Fungicide, and Rodenticide Act Acronyms

BACT—Best available control technology

EPA—Environmental Protection Agency

FDA—Food and Drug Administration

FIFRA—Federal Insecticide, Fungicide, and Rodenticide Act

FQPA—Food Quality Protection Act

OSH—Occupational Safety and Health Act (or OSH Act)

OSHA—Occupational Safety and Health Administration

USDA—U.S. Department of Agriculture

FIFRA Regulations

Controlling the use of pesticides, insecticides, and rodenticides is important for protecting the environment. Since there are so many insects, bacteria, fungi, and other pests, the use of insecticides and fungicides may be warranted for many situations but potentially harmful. Many ingredients in these products and mixtures may be safe in certain doses but harmful to agricultural crops, people, animals, fish, or vegetation in other doses.

Before any pesticide regulations are decided or published, the EPA must solicit opinions from the U.S. Department of Agriculture and the U.S. Department of Health and Human Services.[1] Persons who manufacture, prepare, compound, propagate or process any pesticide or device or active ingredient used in producing a pesticide must comply. Under the registration procedure, an applicant may be required to submit methods for the safe storage and disposal of excess quantities of the pesticide, labeling procedures, and how it will be transported, stored, and disposed. Both domestic and foreign producers of fungicides, insecticides, and pesticides are subject to the provisions of FIFRA.[2]

Containers must be designed for safe storage and disposal—they must be capable of removing the pesticides and rinsing them. The design and construction of the container must properly seal and otherwise meet EPA requirements. Potential splashes and leaks from poor container design are prohibited. Safe refill and reuse of the containers are required. The ability for safe pesticide residue removal is required. Splash and leakage from the containers must be avoided. Safe pesticide residue removal is also required.

Each state may be federally authorized to conduct a program to certify the contractors or applicators of pesticides as long as the state's program conforms with FIFRA.[3] Certified applicators of pesticides must keep records of all applications although states do not register the pesticides. Registration is granted by the EPA if a pesticide can perform its intended function without harmful effects on the environment and can be used in a common manner; that is, repeatable, without unreasonable adverse effects.[4]

Pesticides that are identical or very similar to another registered product are called me-too pesticides and are expeditiously approved. Tests must be performed and documented by the applicant prior to submittal for registration. Trade secrets are protected at all times. Each establishment producing a pesticide must be registered with the EPA and given an establishment number. Records must be maintained about the pesticides and methods of manufacture produced there. Establishments can be inspected at any time, and warrants to enter may be issued. At any time, the EPA can stop the sale or use of a pesticide—remove it from manufacture, distribution, or seize it from its owner(s) for container or any violation of registration requirements.

❖ Federal Insecticde, Fugicide, and Rodenticide Act

A balancing test (considering costs and benefits) may be used to decide to allow the continued use of a chemical known to produce cancer in laboratory animals. The EPA can stop the sale, use, or remove and seize pesticides that are not registered. It may do the same for pesticides that are adulterated, misbranded, or mislabeled. Misbranded pesticides can be removed from sale when pesticide claims are unsupported by the registration information.[5] Coloring or discoloring may be required for identifying a pesticide or insecticide. Special storage, disposal, and transportation are required, and certain pesticides or insecticides may be recalled or confiscated at any time if the registration specifically requires such handling. Container design must properly seal and otherwise meet EPA requirements. Violators of FIFRA are subject to civil and criminal prosecution.

The active ingredient in a pesticide is a major concern and is investigated for safety. Chemical research is performed on both the active and inactive ingredients for their potential harmful effects on food. In particular, the research must disclose the risks for anti-microbial pesticides—including new anti-microbial active ingredients, end-use products, and substantially similar or identical anti-microbial pesticides.

Definitions

Insecticides control or kill insects. Fungicides protect vegetation against diseases or insects. Rodenticides control or kill mice, rats, or other rodents. Pesticides are any substances that prevent, destroy, repel, or decrease the numbers of any pest (including insects), or are plant regulators, defoliants, or desiccants. Pests are insects, rodents, worms, fungus, weeds, plants, virus, bacteria, microorganisms, and other animal life.

Definitions of "Active Ingredient"

❖ An *ingredient* which will prevent, destroy, repel or mitigate any pest

❖ If a *plant regulator*, it will accelerate or retard or change their rate of growth for ornamental or crop plants

❖ If a *defoliant*, it is an ingredient that can cause leaves or foliage to drop

❖ If a *desiccant*, it is an ingredient which will artificially accelerate the dying of plant tissue

❖ If a *nitrogen stabilizer*, it is an ingredient that will prevent nitrification, denitrivication, ammonia volatilization, or decrease production through action affecting soil bacteria

Pesticide Registration and Risk

Pesticides are registered to reduce health risks, to reduce risks to nontarget organisms, or to reduce the potential for contaminating water or other natural resources. They can be classified for general use, restricted use, or both general and restricted use. Directions for kinds of use must be printed on the directions, packaging, and labels.

Registered pesticides are given an exclusive use period. There may be a need to rush a pesticide to market in response to an environmental or ecological threat. In that case, there may be expedited registration, but public comments must be solicited in the process.

There are both major and minor allowable uses of a pesticide. If there is a minor use of a pesticide—that is, not the primary focus for the pesticide— and the exclusive use period expires, the pesticide can be used for that minor use without applying for a new registration. The term minor use of a pesticide means that either the total U.S. acreage for the crop is less than 300,000 acres, or there is insufficient economic incentive to support initial registration and continuing re-registration of a pesticide. A registration may be suspended, but a notice of suspension must first be issued. A registration may be canceled if the registrant fails to submit information within the time period or if the registrant does not commit to support a specific minor use. After a pesticide has been registered, the registrant must report any additional factual information about adverse effects on the environment.[6]

Risks

If there is a concern about the active ingredient in a pesticide, the active ingredient is investigated for safety. Residue chemistry for the pesticide and its effect on food is a concern. Risks must be noted for anti-microbial pesticides which includes new anti-microbial active ingredients, end-use products, and substantially similar or identical anti-microbial pesticides.

Pesticide Management

Integrated pest management is defined as a sustainable approach incorporating biological, cultural, physical, and chemical tools to minimize environmental and health risks.[7] The EPA and the USDA must conduct research into integrated pest management and initiate a detailed national monitoring plan.

A scientific advisory panel must comment on the environmental impact from the final form of any regulations. The panel must then evaluate and recommend operating guidelines to improve scientific studies leading to decisions about pesticides and insecticides. A science review board assists in those reviews to support this advisory panel. The FDA and OSHA are consulted for information about pesticide residues and disinfectants. The EPA delegates the primary enforcement responsibility of pesticide or insecticide use violations to the states.

The panel's comment on a pesticide or insecticide may include an agricultural impact statement assessing the effects on production and prices of agricultural commodities, retail food prices, or other agricultural factors.

A pesticide or insecticide may be suspended from use. In FIFRA, suspension means an immediate ban on a pesticide. In contrast, cancellation only initiates administrative proceedings for a pesticide but does not stop its use. The EPA is required to work with other public agencies to periodically revise a national plan for monitoring pesticides. The plan must include monitoring humans and animals, pesticide pollution, incidental exposures, and sources of contamination.

Registration procedures

Before any pesticide is manufactured, distributed or imported, it has to be approved by the EPA. Approval for a pesticide or its component chemicals or compounds is called registration. Registration is followed by labeling. Labels list the contents and warnings and are the primary control device. In order to have the fungicide, insecticide, or pesticide registered, the manufacturer must submit the necessary paperwork which includes laboratory tests and many other details. An approved label constitutes proper registration.

At this point, some comment may be in order. Labeling as a primary regulatory device is questionable, according to some authors.[8] Yet, federal policy is full of notification and open record requirements for chemicals, biological agents, and chemical substances.[9] Also, warnings are important to many people who read labels. Therefore, registration of a pesticide or insecticide with restrictive labeling seems very sound.

Experimental use permits

Experimental use permits for pesticides may be issued. If a pesticide could leave any residue on or in food or feed, the EPA can establish a temporary tolerance level for the residue of that pesticide before issuing an experimental use permit. Also, EPA can allow any state to issue an experimental use permit to any public or private agricultural research agency or educational institution.

The EPA can submit information to an advisory panel to review scientific information. Any Administrative Law judge can refer scientific materials to a Committee of the National Academy of Sciences about the relevance of the science presented in public hearings.

Other environmental regulations

Other federal regulations control fungicides, insecticides, and pesticides. The Food Quality Protection Act, (FQPA), affected pesticide and insecticide regulation in recent years. Now, any pesticide traces on food are unsafe unless a maximum safe level for consumption is specified for that substance and that trace or residue is below that level. The EPA, FDA, and USDA monitor pesticide residues in food.[10] The USDA must collect data of statewide or regional significance on the use of pesticides to control pests and diseases of major crops and crops of dietary significance, including fruits and vegetables.

The Clean Air Act requires that hazardous pollutants be listed. Many such pollutants are fungicides, insecticides, and pesticides. The Federal Water Pollution Control Act requires that pesticide manufacturers apply for discharge permits prior to releasing contaminants into any body of water and that they use the best available control technology (BACT). Soil contamination from fungicide, insecticide, and pesticide runoff or discharge into waters is a concern of the water regulations. The Solid Waste Disposal Act requires special storage, treatment, and disposal methods for pesticides. The Occupational Health and Safety Act protects farm workers and other pesticide and insecticide operators from harm. The U.S. Department of the Interior and the National Oceanic and Atmospheric Administration (U.S. Department of Commerce) monitor pesticides in water, air, and fish. Finally, the U.S. Department of Transportation regulates the transportation of pesticides and insecticides.[11]

Chronology of the Federal Insecticide, Fungicide, and Rodenticide Act (FIFRA)

1947, Federal Insecticide, Fungicide, and Rodenticide Act, 7 USC 136 et seq.

1972, Federal Environmental Pesticide Control Act of 1972, Pub. L. 92–516

1973, FIFRA Amendments, Pub. L. 93–205

1975, FIFRA Amendments, Pub. L. 94–140

1978, Federal Pesticide Act of 1978, Pub. L. 95–396

1988, FIFRA Amendments, Pub. L. 100–532

1991, FIFRA Amendments, Pub. L. 102–237

1996, Food Quality Protection Act of 1996, Pub. L. 104–170, 110 Stat. 1489

CHAPTER 23

Land:
Surface Mining Control
and Reclamation Act (SMCRA)

Overview

❖ The mining of any kind of minerals must be performed according to the provisions of this act.

❖ Both surface mining and underground mining can harm the environment.

❖ Large open pits resulting from scraping coal from the surface can contaminate water supplies, denude the landscape, and accelerate runoff during rains.

❖ Mines create public hazards that could be avoided through mining land regulation.

❖ The Bureau of Land Management (BLM) of the Department of Interior (DOI) is primarily responsible for administering SMCRA.

❖ Both abandoned and existing mines are regulated.

❖ Open tunnels and caves must be filled, waste piles must be removed or covered in a natural manner, and vegetation must be planted to make the surface-mined land appear as natural as possible.

❖ Mining research is promoted through state mining and mineral resources research institutes.

❖ The Abandoned Mine Reclamation Fund to reclaim abandoned mines is administered by the DOI.

❖ Each state that has coal mines must prepare and submit a State Reclamation Plan.

❖ An owner or operator cannot engage in surface mining without a permit.

❖ Site reclamation plans must be part of every permit application.

Surface Mining Control and Reclamation Act Acronyms

BLM—Bureau of Land Management

DOE—Department of Energy

DOI—Department of the Interior

EPA—Environmental Protection Agency

NAE—National Academy of Engineering

NAS—National Academy of Sciences

NSF—National Science Foundation

SMCRA—Surface Mining Control and Reclamation Act

USDA—U.S. Department of Agriculture

USGS—U.S. Geological Survey

Purpose and Programs

Coal is mined from the surface and below the ground. Both mining methods have the potential for harming the environment. Underground coal mining can result in land subsidence if performed improperly. Surface coal mining can scar the landscape and destroy or diminish the usefulness of the land for commercial, industrial, residential, recreational, agricultural, or forestry uses. Landslides or erosion resulting from poor mining practices can contribute to floods, pollute waters, or destroy fish and wildlife habitats. The natural beauty in an area can be destroyed or create diminished property values due to the decreased esthetic quality of the mined land. Other programs to conserve soil, water, and other natural resources can be ruined by poor surface mining practices.[1]

Still, energy needs are placing new pressures to increase coal production. As a result, there is an urgent need to establish standards that minimize environmental damage. SMCRA sets those standards.[2]

Surface mining methods to reclaim the land have been advanced by new concepts, techniques, and successful demonstration projects. State, local, and federal governmental controls can now draw upon those innovations to decrease the overall problems that could occur if left unchecked. Because there are unique local geographic characteristics, SMCRA promotes state responsibility for mining regulations. The Bureau of Land Management (BLM) for each state provides the authority the state needs to develop its own version of SMCRA.

Surface mining of other minerals have controls based on coal surface mining. SMCRA establishes a program that protects the land from the adverse visual and physical effects from surface coal mining. Rights of nearby landowners are protected by requiring that the surface areas of mines are reclaimed to appear as close to adjacent and contiguous areas as possible. Sheet runoff of rains is not allowed onto adjacent lands, nor can existing surface waters be so diverted. Unannounced site inspections are performed monthly.[3]

Problems from the past

When SMCRA was passed, there were a number of surface coal mines that had not been reclaimed but were abandoned by mining companies. Not only were they huge visual scars on the landscape, but they also damaged adjacent parcels with their runoff of chemical substances. Underground mines would often deposit waste materials near the mouths of entry tunnels or caves or on mountainsides.

SMCRA has provisions to reclaim these abandoned areas. Additionally, safe subsurface mining is promoted in the act by encouraging new underground extraction methods. There are now requirements for research, experiments, and demonstration projects for extracting, processing, developing, and producing minerals and for the training of mineral engineers and scientists. The U.S. Department of Interior (DOI) Office of Surface Mining Reclamation and Enforcement is assigned these program responsibilities.

Land Reclamation and Acquisition

Funds for land reclamation

Abandoned mines may be reclaimed through a trust fund (Abandoned Mine Reclamation Fund) administered by the DOI. State abandoned mine funds are stimulated from this federal fund. In the SMCRA, the trust fund grows with reclamation fees, penalties, and civil actions that can be taken to recover fees.

A series of priorities set for spending from the fund begin with protecting public health, safety, welfare, and property from the physical and esthetic dangers of surface mining.[4] Lands and water that are eligible for reclamation or drainage trust fund moneys include lands that had been mined for coal, waste banks, coal processing, or other coal mining. Funds can be used for reclaiming and restoring land and water resources damaged by past coal mining practices; filling holes and sealing tunnels, shafts, and entryways; performing studies, research, and demonstration projects; awarding state grants; and other purposes.[5]

The SMCRA requires that voids, tunnels, shafts, and entryways be filled to avoid hazards to public health and safety. Federal or state funds may be used to fill and seal these areas if mine owners or operators are delinquent or cannot be located. Mine waste piles can be used to fill voids and seal tunnels.

State coal mine reclamation programs

Each state that has coal mines must submit a State Reclamation Plan and a list of annual projects. The state reclamation plan must contain information about the relationship between the reclaimed land and the area around it, the criteria for ranking and identifying the projects proposed for funding, and state capability to perform the work. Tribal lands qualify for funds from the Indian Lands Coal Mine Reclamation Program.

Agreements must be secured from landowners to control and prevent erosion and damages from sediments from the unreclaimed mined lands. Conservation and development of soil and water resources affected by coal mining must be included in the state plan to receive federal approval. The USDA must review and comment on conservation and development plans. If a coal mine has removed or disturbed a water bearing stratum and the water rights or water supply to a tenant or landowner have been adversely affected, the plan can propose methods to enhance the water quality or quantity through joint action with other affected landowners.[6]

Requirements for land acquisition

States can acquire any land adversely affected by past mining practices if it can determine that the land will serve recreational, historic, conservation, or reclamation purposes or provide open space benefits. Permanent facilities such as a water treatment plant or a relocated stream channel can be constructed. If such sites are not acquired by the state, the coal waste disposal sites must be converted to public ownership in order to have a responsible party to meet emergency situations and prevent recurrences of contamination.

Exhibit 47: Lands scarred by surface mining must be returned to normal conditions. Where surface drainage must be accommodated, waterways, ditches, or ponds must be engineered to respect the surrounding environment.

Permit Program

No owner or operator can engage in surface coal mining without first receiving a permit. Permits cannot exceed five years.[7] Each applicant for a permit must include a reclamation plan for the site. The reclamation plan has to include provisions for public agency inspections, insurance certificates, and blasting plans. The DOI requires that all abandoned coal waste sites be reclaimed and that permits be issued for onsite reprocessing of abandoned coal waste.

Inspections of sites must be performed in developing site-specific permits. States may assume exclusive jurisdiction over the SMCRA provisions and issue the permits as long as the state meets all SMCRA requirements. There must be adequate state staff to administer and enforce the necessary programs. A performance bond or other kind of financial insurance of the applicant's ability to perform must be submitted after the permit is approved.

Each reclamation plan submitted as a part of a permit application must include the sufficient detail to indicate that reclamation can be accomplished. Boundaries of lands for surface coal mining have to be indicated, along with phasing, timing, etc. The condition of the land prior to any mining that is covered by the permit has to be submitted in the reclamation plan. The description of conditions must include the following details:

❖ Existing land uses
❖ Ability of the land to support a variety of uses considering soil and foundation characteristics prior to any mining
❖ Topography and vegetative cover
❖ Productivity of the land prior to mining
❖ Use of land after reclamation including capacity of the reclaimed land to support different uses
❖ Post-mining land use and how it will be achieved
❖ Engineering techniques to be used in mining and reclamation and a description of the major equipment to be used
❖ Water drainage plan
❖ Backfilling plan
❖ Timetable
❖ Consistency of surface mining and compatibility with surrounding land uses
❖ Steps that will be taken to comply with air and water pollution regulations
❖ Ownership of contiguous land parcels

Performance standards for environmental protection

Permits will only be issued to those applicants who can meet performance standards for environmental protection. These standards include the responsibility to perform the actions shown in the Land Reclamation Performance Standards box below.

There are additional requirements to restore the land to its original contours. There are steep slope surface coal mining standards. Permit variances may be granted which may not require restoring the land to its original contours. The variance depends upon meeting local government requirements for land use planning.

Land reclamation performance standards:

❖ Ensure maximum conservation of the solid fuel (or coal) resource

❖ Restore the land to a condition capable of supporting any mining, or a higher or better use

❖ Backfill, compact, ensure stability, prevent leaching of toxic materials, slope the land, and grade to the approximate original contour of the land with all high walls, spoil piles, and depressions eliminated

❖ Stabilize and protect all surface areas including spoil piles

❖ Remove the topsoil from the land in a separate layer and replace it on the backfill area

❖ Restore the topsoil or the best available subsoil which is best able to support vegetation

❖ For all farm land, perform special soil placement

❖ Create, if authorized in the permit, impoundments of water on mining sites only when it is demonstrated that the size of the impoundment is adequate for its intended purpose and that the dam is stable and safe

❖ Conduct any boring operations to recover the mineral reserves remaining after the operation and reclamation are complete

❖ Minimize the disturbances to the prevailing hydrology at the mine site and offsite areas

❖ Stabilize all waste piles

❖ No surface coal mining with 500 feet of active or abandoned underground mines

❖ Ensure that all debris, toxic materials, or flammable materials are treated or buried and compacted

❖ Assume the responsibility for successful re-vegetation

❖ Protect offsite areas from slides

Surface Requirements for Underground Coal Mining

According the SMCRA, there are distinct differences in the regulations for underground and surface mining. Each permit for underground coal mining requires the owner or operator to assume the following responsibilities:

❖ Prevent subsidence and material damage, maximize mine stability, and maintain the value and future use of surface lands

❖ Seal all entryways, drifts, shafts, tunnels, or other openings between the surface and the underground mine when no longer needed

❖ Fill or seal exploratory holes no longer necessary for mining

❖ Stabilize all surface waste piles

❖ Ensure that all new coal mine waste piles (mine wastes, tailing, coal processing wastes, or other liquid and solid wastes) are designed, located, constructed, operated, maintained, enlarged, modified, removed, or abandoned according to specific standards and criteria

❖ Regrade areas and establish a vegetative cover

❖ Protect offsite areas from damages

❖ Eliminate fire hazards and health hazards

❖ Maintain water balance (hydrology) at the mine site and off-site areas

❖ Use existing roads as much as possible for site access

❖ Use the best technology available to minimize disturbances and impacts on fish, wildlife, and the environment

❖ Locate openings for all new drift mines and working acid or iron-producing coal seams in a manner that prevents gravity discharge of water from the mine

❖ Any underground coal mining operations in urbanized areas must be suspended to minimize the chance of any subsidence

Inspections of surface coal mining and reclamation

In order to administrate approved state programs or enforce federal SMCRA administration, inspectors have the right to enter any mining or reclamation operation. Records and reports must be made available to the inspectors, and monitoring system records must be maintained. The federal or state permit authority specifies the particular monitoring sites to be used to record the quantity and quality of surface drainage, potential zone of influence, record level, amount, and samples of ground water and aquifers potentially affected by the mining. Also, records of rainfall must be kept for all well logs, bore hole data, and monitoring sites. Inspections must be held once a month at a minimum, must occur without prior notice, and must include the filing of inspection reports for the mine. Each owner/operator must maintain a conspicuous sign at the entrances to the surface coal mining and reclamation operations with the name, address, and phone number of the owner or operator and the permit number.

Notice of any violations may be issued by the site inspector, and penalties may be assessed. Any willful violations of SMCRA may result in imprisonment. Corporations are subject to the same civil penalties, fines, and imprisonment as individuals.[8]

Designation of land unsuitable for noncoal mining

Federal land areas may be reviewed, if requested by a state to determine if they are unsuitable for the mining of minerals or materials other than coal. Criteria submitted must include urban or suburban character, land use, mineral estate in the public domain, and the impact on land for alternative land uses.[9]

Mining Research

SMCRA established state mining and mineral resources research institutes. The DOE, U.S. Bureau of Mines, together with the National Academy of Engineering can designate 13 universities as coal research laboratories. Research at these laboratories is supported with federal and state funds, and fellowships are awarded for coal mining studies.

States that participate could receive federal funds for mining research university projects. These funds are to be used for demonstrations and experiments of basic, theoretical, and practical mining and mineral resource research.[10]

A center for cataloging all current and projected scientific research in mining and mineral resources was created at the DOI. A Committee on Mining and Mineral Resources Research is composed of members from the DOI, U.S. Geological Survey (USGS), National Science Foundation (NSF), National Academy of Sciences (NAS), National Academy of Engineering (NAE), and others. One important duty of the committee is to develop a national research plan.

Chronology of the Surface Mining Control and Reclamation Act (SMCRA)

1977, Surface Mining Control and Reclamation Act of 1977, Pub. L. 95–89, 30 USC 1201 et seq.

1988, Mining and Mineral Resources Research Institute Amendments of 1988, Pub. L. 100–483, 102 Stat. 2341

1990, Abandoned Mine Reclamation Act of 1990, Pub. L. 101–508, 104 Stat. 1388–289.

CHAPTER 24
Nuclear Safety:
Atomic Energy Act (AEA)

Overview

❖ The Nuclear Regulatory Commission (NRC) of the U.S. Department of Energy is the primary agency regulating radioactive materials.

❖ Similar to other federal acts, the AEA mandates federal and state cooperation in controlling atomic energy emissions.

❖ Because radioactive materials are hazardous to health and the environment, sources of radioactive materials, byproducts, special nuclear materials, and radioactive wastes require substantial regulation for safe disposal.

❖ Not only can soil and water become irradiated, but also the soil and water can transfer its radioactivity to people, animals, and plants.

❖ Long-term impacts of storage and disposal are considered.

❖ Scientific research is promoted through demonstration projects.

❖ Safety in processing, possessing, transferring, storing, and disposing of radioactive materials is promoted through licensing each activity.

Atomic Energy Act Acronyms

AEA—Atomic Energy Act

DOE—Department of Energy

EPA—Environmental Protection Agency

NRC—Nuclear Regulatory Commission

Purpose and Programs

There have been changes in responsibilities under the AEA.[1] The Atomic Energy Commission has been abolished and all duties of the commission under the AEA have been transferred to the Nuclear Regulatory Commission and the Administrator of the Energy Research and Development Administration of the U.S. Department of Energy (DOE). Controlling radiation hazards and dealing with the byproducts and sources of radioactive and special nuclear materials are other purposes of the AEA.

The Act develops radiation standards for the application of controls by federal agencies and the states. Agreements with the states are considered (when submitted) for byproducts, sources, and special nuclear materials of a critical mass.[2] States can also have agreements with the NRC to regulate th disposal of low-level radioactive waste.

The AEA requires federal cooperation with states for many reasons, th most important of which is public safety from radioactive emissions. Eve though states have more legislative powers under the Constitution than th federal government, using atomic energy requires expensive technology an highly trained researchers, operators, and security personnel. Some state have smaller budgets but also may have low populations and vast land area that allow safe, long-term storage of radioactive wastes; the AEA encourage states to cooperate with the federal government for technical, financial, an logistical support.

Safe use of radioactive materials, storage, and disposal facilities requir plans with important components or sections. The use of the land surround ing an area is critical. Designating the use of the land is a local government power unless the site is located within a federally owned area. The transpor tation routes and their design are another component of a plan. For example, the roads need to be designed to avoid hazardous curves and high densities of population. Long-term storage is yet another plan element that requires engi neering for safety and expansion of storage capacity.

In addition to developing comprehensive plans and coordinating with state and local governments for the use, storage, and disposal of high-level atomic energy (or fully radioactive, not partially spent or used), different pro visions must be made for low-level radioactive waste disposal as well.

Protecting public health is a major objective of the NRC in disposing byproduct materials. Safety in processing, possessing, transferring, and dis posing of radiation hazards are reasons for regulations. Ownership and cus tody of certain byproduct material and disposal sites requires obtaining a license. Licensing allows for adherence to decontamination, decommission ing, and reclamation standards for sites where ores are processed for source material content and where such byproduct material is deposited.[3]

Regional low-level radioactive waste disposal sites

To accommodate diverse public and private sector needs, the AEA re quires that regional agreements, or compacts, be negotiated between states for disposing low-level radioactive wastes. The AEA spells out the responsi bilities of DOE, licensing procedures for facilities, alternative disposal meth ods, and health and environmental standards for uranium mill tailings.

Agencies, regulatory controls, and demonstration projects

In all of these regulatory activities, the responsibilities for administra tion fall upon the Nuclear Regulatory Commission (NRC) of the DOE. The DOE licenses facilities and approves transport and handling procedures of al kinds. They license facilities that use radioactive materials, and they research and approve new and alternative disposal methods. Additionally, in cooperation with other federal government agencies, the DOE develops and promotes health and environmental standards for uranium mill tailings.

The NRC, not the states, regulates the construction and operation of any uranium enrichment facility, the export or import of any nuclear material, the disposal into the ocean or sea of nuclear waste materials, and the disposal of any nuclear material and the licensing of that disposal. Radiation standards are developed for each material that can protect the environment and people against radiation hazards.

The EPA coordinates its radioactive materials programs with the NRC; National Academy of Sciences (NAS); and experts in biology, medicine, and health physics. Inspections are performed by the NRC as deemed appropriate, anywhere and at any time. Agreements between the federal and state agencies can be suspended if the NRC or the EPA determines that there are dangers, or if a state has failed to take necessary steps to contain or eliminate the cause of danger in a timely manner.[4]

States must comply with all health and environmental protection standards. They must follow NRC procedures for licensing, rulemaking, and license impact analysis. Each license application must include an assessment of the radiological and non-radiological impacts to public health. It must include impacts on waterways and groundwater resulting from the operations proposed in the license application. Alternatives need to be considered, such as alternative sites and engineering methods. Long-term impacts must be considered in the license application, including decommissioning, decontamination, and reclamation impacts in relation to the granting of such a license.

The armed services must dispose of weapons in a safe manner, and the NRC must approve plans for permanent disposal of waste from atomic energy defense activities.

Model and demonstration project

At the Western New York Service Center in West Valley, New York, the DOE has established a high-level radioactive waste management demonstration project. The purpose of the project is to demonstrate methods to solidify high-level radioactive waste for later disposal.[5] Components must include the design and test use of shipping containers and the methods to transport solidified wastes to another permanent disposal federal repository. Public hearings for comments about the facility are required. Detailed engineering and cost estimates are required.

Regional disposal compacts

A regional disposal facility is to be established by each state or group of states to store low-level radioactive waste. Any waste owned or generated by the federal government and disposed of at a regional disposal facility or non-federal disposal facility is subject to the same conditions, regulations, requirements, fees, taxes, and surcharges imposed by those regional agencies to others.

The regional disposal facility compacts follow:

❖ Texas Low-Level Radioactive Waste Disposal Compact Consent Act (TX, ME, and VT)

❖ Appalachian States Low-Level Radioactive Waste Disposal Compact Consent Act (PA, VA, WV)

❖ Central Interstate Low-Level Radioactive Waste Compact (AR, IA, KS, LA, MN, MI, NE, ND, OK)

❖ Central Midwest Interstate Low-Level Radioactive Waste Compact Consent Act (IL, KY)

❖ Northwest Interstate Compact on Low-Level Radioactive Waste Management (AK, HI, ID, MT, OR, UT, WA, WY)

❖ Southeast Interstate Low-Level Radioactive Waste Compact Consent Act (AL, FL, GA, MS, NC, SC, TN, VA)

❖ Midwest Interstate Low-Level Radioactive Waste Compact Consent Act (IA, IN, MI, MN, MO, OH, WI)

❖ Rocky Mountain Low-Level Radioactive Waste Compact Consent Act (AZ, CO, NV, NM, UT, WY)

❖ Northeast Interstate Low-Level Radioactive Waste Compact Consent Act (CT, NJ, DE, MD)

❖ Southwestern Low-Level Radioactive Waste Compact Consent Act (AZ, CA)[6]

The DOE has responsibilities for financial and technical assistance and annually reports to Congress about low-level waste disposal siting and licensing activities within each compact region. Byproduct materials cannot be transferred, transported, or received in different interstate locations except under stated conditions of these compacts, agreements, and established areas.[7]

Chronology of the Atomic Energy Act (AEA)

1954, Atomic Energy Act of 1954, 42 USC 2014, 2012–2021d, 2022, 2111,2113, and 2114

1978, Atomic Energy Act Amendment, Pub. L. 95–604

1982, Nuclear Waste Policy Act of 1982 (NWPA), 42 USC 10101–10270

1983, Nuclear Waste Policy Act of 1982, Pub. L. 97–425

1986, Omnibus Low-Level Radioactive Waste Interstate Compact Consent Act, Pub. L. 99–240, 99 Stat. 1859

1987, Nuclear Waste Policy Amendments Act of 1987, Pub. L. 101–202

1988, Amendments, Pub. L. 100–408

1988, Appalachian States Low-Level Radioactive Waste Compact Consent Act, Pub. L. 100-319, 102 Stat. 471

1994, Central Midwest Interstate Low-Level Radioactive Waste Compact Amendments Consent Act of 1994, Pub. L. 103–439, 108 Stat. 4607

1998, Texas Low-Level Radioactive Waste Policy Act, Pub. L. 105–236, 112 Stat. 1542

Section Six

Responding to Contaminant Releases

CHAPTER 25

Public Notice and Spill Planning: Emergency Planning and Community Right-to-Know Act (EPCRA)

Overview

❖ States must establish local government chemical emergency spill response programs.

❖ These programs require state and local emergency response committees and committed spill cleanup teams.

❖ Public announcements of accidental spills must be made immediately.

❖ A list of extremely hazardous substances and their health threat thresholds is published.

❖ Methods of prompt cleanup must be in place.

❖ Local emergency planning committees must prepare emergency response plans outlining the ways in which they intend to respond to spills.

❖ Reports about existing chemical or biological substances contained in buildings and facilities must be filed and available to the public.

❖ Any amount of toxic chemical release must be recorded in permanent public records.

Emergency Planning and Community Right-to-Know Act Acronyms

EPA—Environmental Protection Agency

EPCRA—Emergency Planning and Community Right-to-Know Act

LEPC—Local emergency planning committee

LFD—Local fire department

MSDSs—Material safety data sheets

OSHA—Occupational Safety and Health Administration

PBT—Lead and lead compound chemicals

POTWs—Publicly-owned treatment works

RQ—Reportable quantity

SERC—State emergency response commission

Emergency Responses and Public Communication

EPCRA requires that states develop, prepare, and establish local chemical emergency programs and communicate information about those hazardous chemicals located within their communities to the public.[1] Those chemicals may be potentially air- or waterborne or may reach the environment through soils, foods, or even direct human contact. This act requires that the potential for risks from accidental chemical spills be disclosed to everyone. There are civil, administrative, and criminal penalties for not complying with EPCRA.

There are four major components to EPCRA for responding to potentially dangerous releases of chemicals:

1) Plans that are capable of quick execution must be developed.

2) Both chemical and biological substance releases (and emergency releases) must be promptly advertised.

3) Public reports containing information about existing chemicals in buildings and facilities (recognizing that the community has a "right-to-know") must be filed.

4) Any amount of toxic chemical releases are required to be recorded in permanent records.

Each of these four components has special reporting requirements.

Required record keeping

Under EPCRA, minimum threshold quantities are established by the EPA for reporting the kinds and amounts of hazardous chemicals at a facility. Material safety data sheets (MSDSs) report the quantities and names of chemicals stored on site or used for any industrial activities. They must be prepared and submitted to the government from each owner or operator of a facility storing a federally listed hazardous material. The MSDSs are required under the Occupational Safety and Health Administration's (OSHA) hazard communication standard regulations, described in the previous chapter of this book. MSDSs must be submitted to the state emergency response commission (SERC), the local emergency planning committee (LEPC), and the local fire department (LFD) that has jurisdiction over the facility.

Exhibit 48: Emergency response or cleanup teams must promptly arrive at the scene of the spill. This crew is wearing clean suits to protect them from the dangers of the hazardous material.

Under EPCRA, owners or operators of certain manufacturing facilities must submit annual reports on the amounts of EPA-listed toxic chemicals that are released from their facilities. All releases to the air, water, or soils must be reported. Discharges from publicly-owned treatment works (POTWs) and transfers to offsite locations for treatment, storage, or disposal are also required to be reported.

Exhibit 49: Suspected dangerous contaminant levels have required the donning of white suits and the use of water level and contaminant measuring devices on this industrial site.

Most states require an owner or operator to submit a Tier II form, but a few require a Tier I. These reports must be submitted regardless of whether the chemical or biological release is accidental, intentional, or routine. Lead and lead compounds are classified as PBT chemicals and require a very low reporting threshold of 100 pounds.

In order to avoid violations or prosecution, any facility subject to these reporting requirements, or any others, must develop written information, management programs, plans, and implementation methods. Annual reports of releases (EPCRA Section 313 release reports) of toxic chemicals must be submitted to the appropriate agencies of local, state, and federal government.

Spill emergency plans

The governor of each state designates a State Emergency Response Commission (SERC) and appoints a local emergency planning committee (LEPC). The SERC must designate emergency planning districts within each state to prepare and implement emergency plans. The LEPC must develop and specify methods for cleaning spills, protecting residents, and distributing information about the spills. The owner or operator of a facility that produces, uses, or stores a hazardous chemical must notify the SERC and the LEPC immediately whenever a listed hazardous substance

Exhibit 50: Pools of different sizes may be used to treat hazardous materials to make them safe for long-term storage or disposal. The edges, or retainers, of these ponds require construction that is resistant to bleed-out of the materials undergoing treatment.

Exhibit 51: This worker is inspecting a monitoring well to ensure that no leaks occur into groundwater.

is released in excess of the reportable quantity (RQ).[2]

Emergency plans must be comprehensive and must specify the kinds of facilities subject to EPCRA requirements within an emergency planning district and identify the safest routes for the transportation of hazardous substances. The plans must contain the methods and procedures to respond to all kinds of releases. The area or population likely to be affected by a release must be defined. A community emergency coordinator, such as a fire department or cleanup company under contract to the community, must be designated. There must be procedures stated in the emergency plans to provide reliable and timely notice of a chemical release to the public. Emergency equipment, storage sites, staging areas, or facilities to be used in cleanups must be designated. Evacuation plans (including precautionary evacuations), training programs, and schedules for medical and cleanup personnel must be included in the spill emergency plan. Finally, methods for initiation of the plan must be clearly stated and a proposed schedule outlined.

Exhibit 52: This image shows the railroad tracks contiguous to a liquid chlorine supply line and a strategically placed monitoring well.

❖ Emergency Planning and Community Right-to-Know Act

Public notice

EPCRA assumes that, given knowledge, people may be able to make decisions for themselves about how best to take care of themselves. When a chemical or biological accident occurs, the public must be notified. Information must be distributed so that residents in states, towns, and cities can understand the potential chemical hazards around them. Release notices must be submitted to the LEPC and must include:

Exhibit 53: This instrument is used on a regular basis to measure collections of materials and waters in monitoring wells.

❖ The chemical name or substance

❖ Whether the substance is listed by the EPA

❖ An estimate of the quantity released

❖ The time and duration of the release

❖ Any anticipated acute or chronic health risks

❖ What precautions to take (such as evacuations, barrier construction, etc.)

❖ The name and telephone number of a contact person(s)[3]

As soon as possible after a release of a chemical or other substance, there must be follow-up emergency notice given, actions taken to avoid any threats or health risks, and medical advice given as appropriate. The toxic chemical threshold amount for reporting is 10,000 pounds of the toxic chemical used in a facility per year. If a toxic chemical is manufactured or processed at a facility, the threshold amount for reporting is 25,000 pounds per year.[4]

Medical needs for chemical information

If information about a chemical is requested by a health professional for diagnosis or treatment, a medical emergency, or the knowledge that the chemical could provide in diagnosis or treatment, then the owner or operator must promptly provide the information. A written request is required.[5] A confidentiality agreement may be required to be signed by health professionals that the information may only be used for diagnosis or treatment, and that they will not disclose the information.

Exhibit 54: Two adjacent montiring wells are placed close to processing equipment.

Chronology of the Emergency Planning and Community Right-to-Know Act (EPCRA)

1986, Emergency Planning and Community Right-to-Know Act, Pub. L. 99–499, 42 USC 11001–11050

1990, Pollution Prevention Act, Pub. L. 101–508, 42 USC 13101–13109

2000, Chemical Safety Information, Site Security and Fuels Regulatory Relief Act, Pub. L. 106–40

Hazardous Waste Spill Cleanup: Comprehensive Response, Compensation, and Liability Act (CERCLA)/Superfund

Overview

❖ Superfund and CERCLA are two names commonly used to refer to this act.

❖ The word Superfund is sometimes used to describe the actual trust fund (created from a tax on the chemical and petroleum industries) that is used to pay for hazardous waste spill cleanups.

❖ When responsible persons cannot be identified to pay for a spill, Superfund provides funds.

❖ There are many more sites needing cleanup than there are funds available to pay the costs.

❖ For sites leaking hazardous wastes, funds are allocated by a ranking system.

❖ Waters of the United States are protected by requiring all facility owners and operators to demonstrate the financial ability to clean up their own spills.

❖ Sites must be cleaned completely and modified to prevent leaks.

❖ Engineering requirements for preliminary site designation are strict.

❖ Hazardous substances are listed in other federal acts, such as TSCA, SWDA, RCRA, CWA, and CAA.

❖ Compliance orders may be issued to those parties responsible for leaks.

❖ Civil and criminal penalties may be issued also.

❖ Brownfields, or previously contaminated sites, are to be cleaned and financial assistance for reuse is made available.

❖ Small businesses are given exceptions from waste site cleanup costs under certain conditions.

Comprehensive Response, Compensation, and Liability Act Acronyms

ARARs—Applicable or relevant and appropriate requirements

ATSDR—Agency for Toxic Substances and Disease Registry

CAA—Clean Air Act

CCL—Construction completion list

CERCLA—Comprehensive Emergency Response, Compensation, and Liability Act

CERCLIS—Comprehensive Emergency Response, Compensation, and Liability Information System

CWA—Clean Water Act

EPA—Environmental Protection Agency

HRS—Hazard ranking system

NCP—National contingency plan

NPL—National Priorities List

PA—Preliminary assessment

PRP—Potentially responsible party

RCRA—Resource Conservation and Recovery Act

RD—Remedial design

RI/FS—Remedial investigation/Feasibility study

ROD—Record of decision

SWDA—Solid Waste Disposal Act

TSCA—Toxic Substances Control Act

Superfund Scope

The Comprehensive Emergency Response, Compensation, and Liability Act is called both CERCLA and the Superfund.[1] CERCLA is a program that attempts to minimize contamination from releases of hazardous substances. It provides for compensation for cleanups of hazardous waste spills until responsible parties are identified and payment can be arranged. The program became commonly known as Superfund because the available funds appear to be so great and the provision for such emergencies seems so innovative.

The act protects the public and the environment from abandoned and leaking hazardous waste sites not otherwise controlled under existing laws. Short-term and long-term remedial removals are funded under the Superfund. The Superfund is funded by a combination of taxes on petroleum and chemical industries, general tax revenues, and a specially-levied environmental tax on corporations. Because of the high costs of planning, designing, engineering, contracting, and implementing remediation programs, these funds are sufficient to pay for cleaning only a limited number of hazardous substance spills.

The EPA can recover its cleanup costs from private parties, and it can obtain judicial orders to require liable parties to reduce any dangers to health or the environment.

Exhibit 55: This transporter of hazardous materials uses a truck that can securely seal and contain wastes. After hauling, the operator safely cleans the containment area.

CERCLA is retroactive; costs may be assessed to previous owners, a series of owners, or officers of defunct companies even when the vessel, site, or facility is 50 or more years old. When the EPA can do so, it may require a potentially responsible party (PRP) to undertake and pay for the cleanup without committing any moneys from the Superfund.[2]

Hazardous substances

Under CERCLA, the EPA may conduct a cleanup of a hazardous substance and later recoup costs from a PRP, or it may compel the PRPs to clean up the site themselves.

A long list of hazardous substances is provided in CERCLA.[3] Any pollutant or contaminant that is released to the environment or poses a substantial threat of being released to the environment is covered under CERCLA. But according to the act, the EPA is entitled to recover its cleanup costs from private parties only if the release is a hazardous substance. Although petroleum is included under RCRA as a hazardous substance, it is excluded in CERCLA as a hazardous substance; therefore, the provisions of CERCLA do not apply to cleanups of petroleum alone, but petroleum additives, such as gasoline additives, are covered under CERCLA. Natural and synthetic gas and liquids or their mixtures are also not included.

The number of substances of concern in CERCLA is very large and includes those substances listed in the Toxic Substances Control Act, Solid Waste Disposal Act, Resource Conservation and Recovery Act, the Clean Water Act, Clean Air Act, and any other substances that may be found to be dangerous to health or the environment.

Useful CERCLA definitions

The phrase "protecting the environment" can be confusing. In some federal acts, environment is not defined, and some of the programs do not require strict definition of the components of the environment. For hazardous substances, the environment is defined as

> ...the navigable waters, the waters of the contiguous zone, and the ocean waters of which the natural resources are under the exclusive management authority of the United States...and any other surface water, ground water, drinking water supply, land surface or subsurface strata, or ambient air within the United States or under the jurisdiction of the United States.[4]

By contrast, natural resource is defined as

> land, fish, wildlife, biota, air, water, ground water, drinking water supplies, and other such resources belonging to, managed by, held in trust by, appertaining to, or otherwise controlled by the United States, state or local government, any foreign government, Indian tribe.[5]

Yet another definition of importance is that of owner or operator. Anyone owning, operating or chartering a vessel is subject to CERCLA. An owner/operator may be defined as anyone owning or operating an onshore facility, building, or site, or anyone who holds title or control of that site, which was conveyed—through bankruptcy, foreclosure, tax delinquency, abandonment, or similar means—to a unit of state or local government. In determining the PRPs, actions of previous owners or operators are balanced against factors for each PRP that include the following:

❖ Volume of hazardous substance contributed

❖ Toxicity contributed

❖ Time during which each party was involved at the site

❖ Care exercised in handling

❖ Cooperation by the parties with government officials to prevent harm to the public or environment

The definition for owner/operator does not include a person who did not participate in the management but who holds ownership only to protect his securing interest in the vessel or facility. If a lender does not participate in management, he or she is excluded from cleanup liability. If a lender did not participate in management prior to foreclosure and tries to sell, release to another, or otherwise divest the person of the vessel or facility at the earliest practical time (taking into account market conditions and legal requirements), he or she is considered liable. There are a number of definitions of participation in management, but generally, lenders that are partial owners are exempt from financial responsibility for cleanup unless they had decision-making control over the environmental compliance of the facility, site, or vessel, or unless they exercised control comparable to a daily manager with respect to compliance and operational functions. If a party only monitors or inspects a facility, he or she is not participating in management. Also, merely providing financial or other advice or counsel to prevent a decrease in the economic value of a vessel or facility is not participating in management.

Exhibit 56: Superfund sites may not look different from any other site. This drainage area may contain contaminants that need to be tested for toxicity. The toxicity levels could determine whether this site is listed on the National Priority List.

Releases of contaminants

Contaminated material can be difficult to contain. A release of a contaminant may be defined as any discharging, dumping, emitting, emptying, escaping, injecting, leaching, leaking, pouring, pumping, spilling, or disposing of a substance into the environment (including abandoning or discarding barrels, containers, and other closed containers holding any hazardous substance, pollutant, or contaminant). Release of a contaminant does not apply to those releases that only expose persons located entirely within their workplace. Also, releases of contaminants are not defined as emissions from engine exhausts of motor vehicles, rolling stock, aircraft, vessels, or pipeline pumping station engines, or sources, byproducts, or special nuclear materials from a nuclear accident.

Responding to a spill

To respond to a spill means to take remedial action. Responsible parties must be aware of the EPA guidelines for reportable quantities. The definitions for reportable quantities of hazardous substances can be changed by the EPA at any time.[6] As soon as a person in charge of a vessel or an offshore or onshore facility has knowledge of any release of a hazardous substance, notice must be given to the National Response Center established under the Clean Water Act.[7] If the National Response Center is not notified, criminal prosecution can result. At every facility, vessel, and site, records must identify the location and condition of the facility and the characteristics, quantity, origin, and condition of any hazardous substances contained or deposited in the facility. These records must be kept for 50 years.[8]

Removal action

Any action that could reduce the threat of a spill is a removal action. For example, the EPA can remove a hazardous substance, provide alternate water supplies if needed, clean spills from containers, or erect fences around hazardous waste sites. More actions are usually needed after the removal if an immediate risk exists. The removal could be part of a broader set of remedial actions to be taken, and more actions could be necessary.

Parties Responsible for Spills

CERCLA applies to every past owner or operator of a vessel or facility. Anyone who, at the time of disposal of any hazardous substances, owned or operated a vessel or facility, can be a responsible party. Anyone who agreed to dispose of or treat the wastes or anyone accepting any hazardous substances for transport to another place can be a responsible party. In any of these instances, all costs for removal or remedial action may be levied against a responsible party or parities. There may be damages assessed for injury to or destruction of natural resources, costs for any health assessment or health effects study needed, or any other related costs for responding to the leak.[9]

CERCLA requires that financial responsibility be demonstrated by owners or operators of vessels that carry hazardous substances or cargo. Bonds, insurance, guarantees, surety bonds, or self-insurance are allowable evidence of financial responsibility. If a vessel owner or operator is not financially responsible, that vessel may not enter the waters of the United States.[10]

Financial responsibility for facilities must be initially established by the owner or operator, recorded at the EPA, and amounts adjusted as necessary to meet changes in the facility. States can impose any additional liability or requirements for the accidental or known releases of hazardous substances.

Before the federal or state governments adopt any plan or proposal for cleanup, public notice must be given and time for written and oral comments allotted.[11] The final plan must be published and made available to the public before adoption.

Responsible party settlements under Superfund

Some responsible parties at a leaking hazardous waste site may want to settle the matter by taking action or paying for a cleanup. Others may wish to delay the inevitable. Concerned parties may quickly respond to the spills when notified and take all necessary actions at their own expense. In other cases, the parties may be willing but unable to pay for anything but their own part of the cleanup. Partial cleanup may not work, so Superfund moneys may need to be allocated as part of these kinds of settlements.

> ...at every multiparty CERCLA site there are parties that wish to settle with EPA and those that cannot or do not. At the same time, there may be a vast quantity of wastes at the site that came from these defunct or bankrupt companies. Waste from these defunct or bankrupt companies have traditionally been referred to as a site's "orphan share." Thus, at most sites, those parties that settle will ordinarily account for less than 100 percent of the volume of hazardous substances at the site. In fact, it is not uncommon for many settlements to involve settlers whose cumulative volume of waste represents less than 50 percent of that present at the site.[12]

De minimis settlements

De minimis settlements are those in which the amount of the hazardous substance deposited at a site by a party is minimal compared with the amount deposited at the same site by other parties. PRPs who deposited relatively small quantities of hazardous substances at a multiparty site may receive offers of a settlement having finality by the EPA. Furthermore, an owner of the property may not have conducted the handling, generating, or disposal of hazardous substances at the facility; may not have contributed to releases; or may not have even known when acquiring the facility that it had been used for hazardous substances.[13]

National Priorities List

Even though most EPA actions under CERCLA relate to hazardous substance dangers, the program requires that the EPA develop nationwide criteria for assigning priorities for releases or threats of releases. The EPA develops the criteria based on risks to public health, welfare, and the environment. In applying this risk criteria, the EPA scores and ranks different sites on its Comprehensive Emergency Response, Compensation, and Liability Information System (CERCLIS) for possible listing on its National Priorities List (NPL).[14] If a site is listed on the NPL, it is merely an annual listing that needs further investigation. Liability is not assigned to responsible parties through the act of listing. The NPL designation does not require the EPA to take action.

There are two sections to the NPL, The General Superfund Section, and the Federal Facilities Section. The Federal Facilities Section of the NPL lists sites that are the responsibility of federal agencies other than the EPA.[15] After collecting site information, the EPA conducts a preliminary assessment (PA) to determine the extent of the leaks. If further site investigations need to be performed, the site may be investigated further and scored to determine its potential to be added to the NPL. The NPL is part of the National Contingency Plan (NCP), the major guide for CERCLA responses and actions. A hazard ranking system includes the following criteria:

❖ Quantity, toxicity, and concentration of hazardous substance in the waste

❖ Potential for or extent of the release into the environment

❖ Degree of risk to the public and the environment

A site may be added to the NPL if it scores high on the Hazard Ranking System (HRS). Systematizing and scoring considers these pathways to harming the environment: ground water, surface water, soils, and air. Each avenue is considered during the ranking process. The EPA policy is that a score of 28.5 or greater (on a scale of 0 to 100) on the HRS makes a site eligible for the NPL. Each state can designate a single site as its top priority, regardless of its HRS score.[16] Even if a site does not score high enough to be included on the HRS, it may still be listed on the NPL if it meets all of these conditions:

Exhibit 57: This landfill contains many different kinds of leaking, hazardous wastes. Changes in site ownership over the years or decades make it difficult to find a responsible party. Using Superfund money for making the site safe ensures quick and long-term protectiion of public health, safety, and welfare.

❖ The Agency for Toxic Substances and Disease Registry (ATSDR) issues a health advisory

❖ The EPA believes there is a significant public health threat

❖ The EPA anticipates that it will be more cost effective to respond immediately to the release than to wait.[17]

The EPA can remove sites from the NPL when it determines that no further response is necessary under Superfund. The NPL has a construction completion list (CCL) developed by EPA to communicate the successful completion of site cleanups. The NPL contained 1,238 final sites in 2002—1,079 in the General Superfund Section and 159 in the Federal Facilities Section. These numbers include 62 sites proposed and awaiting final agency action in 2002—56 in the General Superfund Section and six in the Federal Facilities Section.[18]

Removal or remediation?

The EPA can remove or remediate hazardous wastes. Removal means that wastes are taken from the site. Remediation means that dangerous waste sites are modified, treated, or redesigned to safely contain the wastes. Remedial actions are usually long-term, permanent cleanups. After a cleanup, the EPA recovers its costs from potentially responsible parties (PRPs), or compels PRPs to perform the cleanup themselves after administrative or judicial proceedings. In any remedial action, timing and coordination are major concerns. Swift actions made in a competent and cost-sensitive manner are desired.

After a site is identified on the NPL, the remedial action process requires a Remedial Investigation/Feasibility Study (RI/FS), after which the EPA chooses the best alternative. During the RI, the amount and composition of hazardous substance are determined and site areas needing attention are pinpointed. The RI provides the EPA with good information that can be used successfully in developing the FS. The FS produces a range of alternatives for consideration. A site cleanup can be total or partial, depending on the RI/FS findings. Clearly, the RI/FS process can take a long time.

Applicable or relevant and appropriate requirements and records of decisions

Any remedy that leaves hazardous materials on a site must meet all applicable or relevant and appropriate requirements (ARARs). ARARs are any criteria, limitations, requirements, or standards under any federal environmental program, act, or law, or under any state law stricter than a federal one. The ARARs include the following information:

❖ Purpose of the remediation

❖ Medium of contamination

❖ Regulated substances

❖ Action planned to be taken

❖ Land use

❖ Structure size and type

❖ Potential site use in the future[19]

To select a remedy, ARARs are applied to provisions in the NCP that require consideration of cost effective remedies. Other considerations are just as important, however. CERCLA suggests that remedies consider these factors:

❖ Cost

❖ Ability to carry out the selected alternative

❖ Short- and long-term effectiveness

❖ Reductions in toxicity, movement, or volume during treatments

❖ Public acceptance

Acceptance of the remedial method by the state and the residents living around the site is a very important criterion. If there is strong public opposition to a particular method, it may be abandoned in favor of another.

After completing the RI/FS, a Record of Decision (ROD) is issued by the EPA. The ROD states the facts, site determinations, remedy, applicable ARARs and how they were obtained or why they were waived, and establishes the cost-effectiveness and permanence of the remedy. Public comments about the chosen remedy must be included in the ROD. When the ROD is issued, EPA develops a remedial design (RD) for the site, facility, or vessel. Responding to spills with government action and using the emergency funds allows for swift cleanup when the public is endangered.

Remedial Action and the National Contingency Plan

When there is a release or substantial threat of release of a hazardous substance, the EPA or another federal agency may be engaged to remove the threat or cleanup the release. These actions are long-term and permanent cleanups. Sometimes a remedial action could take a number of years to complete and require a number of steps. At any time, special powers may be exercised under Presidential or EPA orders. For some sites, an RI/FS (remedial investigation or feasibility study) does not need to be performed unless the President orders it. Public health threats are the major reason to seek immediate Presidential action. The President will not order the removal of a hazardous substance in the following situations:

❖ The release or its threat is from a naturally-occurring substance in its unaltered form

❖ The substance has altered solely through naturally-occurring processes or phenomena

❖ The substance has been released from a location where it is naturally found

❖ The substance has been released from parts of a structure within residential, business, or community structures

❖ The substance has been released into drinking water supplies due to deterioration of the system through ordinary use

Investigations, monitoring, coordination, or other actions may be ordered at any time when an illness, disease, or complaints can be attributed to a hazardous substance. The President may promptly notify the appropriate federal and state natural resource trustees of the potential damages to natural resources from releases and have them proceed with planning or cleanup or other remedial actions.

Selecting a remedial action

A state may be granted a credit against the share of the cleanup costs for a facility listed on the NPL. Under the National Contingency Plan, amounts expended for remedial action may be covered according to agreements with the President. If state expenditures are required for a remedial action, or if the total expenses exceed ten percent of all costs, prior approval must be secured from EPA. In order to better choose the remedial action, the APA can enter a facility, site, or vessel and obtain information (or documentation) at any time from any owner or operator. Requested information can include the quantity and nature of the substance released, extent of the release or threatened release, and information about the ability of a person to perform an cleanup. Samples may be requested and obtained from any location for any suspected hazardous substance.

Compliance orders

When danger from a leak occurs, the EPA or Attorney General's office may enforce or require actions to reduce that danger. Fines may be levied or criminal prosecution pursued. An order may be issued that directs owners or operators to comply with the regulations. If an owner or operator interferes with the entry or inspection by the APA, the courts must direct the owner/operator to allow access. If information or documents are requested, the courts can mandate availability or possession, unless the request is found to be arbitrary and capricious or an abuse of discretion. High-cost civil penalties may be imposed on anyone who interferes with inspector entries or access to records.

Information disclosure

All information obtained under a compliance order is considered confidential unless the President (or the state) deems it proprietary. It may not be protected or confidential if the site's substance under question has a trade name, common name, generic class, or category of hazardous substance. Other breeches of protection may be ordered due to boiling points, melting points, flash points, specific gravities, vapor densities, solubility in water, or vapor pressures at 20 degrees Celsius. Other triggers for disclosure by owners or operators are when the substance poses a hazard to health and the environment; potential routes of human exposure are a problem; the location of the leak is dangerous; or any groundwater monitoring, hydrogeological, or geological data discloses threats.

Agency for Toxic Substances and Disease Registry (ATSDR)

CERCLA establishes the Agency for Toxic Substances and Disease Registry (ATSDR) within the U.S. Public Health Service.[20] The ATSDR cooperates with the states to develop a national registry of diseases and illnesses related to toxic substance exposures and keeps records of affected persons. It performs field tests and studies sites suspected of contaminating persons living nearby. Another list designates areas closed to public use or restricted because of contamination. A major function of the ATSDR is preparing a priority list of hazardous substances commonly found at sites on the National Priorities List (NPL).

This agency supports all of the environmental protection programs of other agencies in important ways. Toxicological profiles (evaluation of the potential harm of different substances) are developed for the health effects from human exposure according to the EPA and ATSDR. The ATSDR reports directly to the Surgeon General of the United States. This agency coordinates and cooperates with EPA and all other related agencies and departments of the federal government with regard to public health. The ATSDR also provides medical care and testing to exposed people, conducts periodic surveys, determines relationships between exposure to toxic substances and illnesses, takes tissue samples, and performs epidemiological studies. When people are exposed, they are eligible to be admitted to hospitals and other facilities and services operated or sponsored by the Public Health Service. The ATSDR maintains a library of information, materials, research, and studies on the health effects of toxic substances. Three categories, or levels of intensity, are used: acute, subacute, and chronic health effects.

Exhibit 58: A large multi-family housing complex has had its land areas contaminated. Typical earth moving equipment is used to excavate and transport the dirt for washing.

National Contingency Plan (NCP)

Functions of the Agency for Toxic Substances and Disease Registry (ATSDR) are spelled out:

❖ Establish and maintain inventory of literature, research, and studies

❖ Cooperate with the states to establish and maintain a national register of serious diseases and illnesses and a national registry of persons exposed to toxic substances

❖ Establish and maintain a complete listing of areas closed to the public or otherwise restricted in use because of toxic substance contamination

❖ In cases of public health emergencies from exposure to toxic substances, provide medical care and testing to exposed individuals (tissue samples, chromosomal testing, epidemiological studies, or any other assistance appropriate under the circumstances)

❖ Conduct periodic survey and screening programs to determine relationships between exposure to toxic substances and illness

❖ Prepare a list, in order of priority, of at least 100 hazards substances most commonly found on the NPL that pose the greatest potential threat to human health

❖ After completing the list of 100 hazardous substances, list another 100 within 24 months

❖ Prepare toxicological profiles on each hazardous substance

❖ Ascertain the levels of significant human exposure for the substance and the associated acute, subacute, and chronic health effects

The NCP is developed and disseminated annually to set priorities for contaminant releases. The plan lists sites in order of priority for cleanup. Because funds are limited, the most dangerous sites are cleaned first. The NCP contains procedures and standards to respond to problems, such as the following:

❖ Locate and investigate potentially leaking sites

❖ Determine which sites get cleaned and in what order

❖ Evaluate remedies

❖ Determine the scope of remedies

❖ Decide roles for federal, state, and local governments or private parties

❖ Provide equipment and supplies for cleanups

❖ Decide cost-saving and effective ways to respond to spills and perform cleanups[21]

A hazard ranking system consists of a scoring method for sites to determine if they should be placed on the National Priorities List (NPL). The EPA scores prospective sites according to this system. Higher scores mean higher priority for cleanup.

Demonstration programs for innovative treatments

Exhibit 59: Prior to deciding about cleanup, partial ditches or other exploratory excavations may be dug and their materials tested.

The EPA is required to research, evaluate, test, develop, and demonstrate different technologies for treating hazardous wastes. Contracts may be negotiated with private and public sectors to learn better ways of neutralizing the dangers from hazardous wastes. Plans, sites, and required supervision of the project or program must be submitted and approved by the EPA. The information developed from the approved demonstrations must be disseminated as a part of the funding requirements.

Brownfields Revitalization and Environmental Restoration

A brownfield site is real property, the expansion, redevelopment, or reuse of which may be complicated by the presence or potential presence of a hazardous substance pollutant or contaminant. Brownfield sites may contain petroleum or petroleum products; controlled substances; mine-scarred land; land slated for a CERCLA removal action; a listed NPL site; a site subject to an order or consent decree; a site subject to a corrective action permit or order; land disposal units with a closure notification, plan, or permit; a site subject to the jurisdiction, custody, or control of federal government; land having PCB contamination subject to remediation under TSCA; or a site which has received assistance for a leaking underground storage tank.

Owners of contiguous property are exempt from cleanup liability if their land is contaminated solely by a release from contiguous or similarly situated property owned by another—if the first owner did not cause or contribute to the release; is not affiliated with the potentially liable person; exercises appropriate care with respect to the release; provides full cooperation, assistance and access to persons authorized to respond and restore the site; complies with all land use controls; complies with all information requests; provides all required legal notices; conducts all appropriate inquiries at the time of purchase; and did not know or have reason to know about the contamination at the time of occurrence.[22]

Grant money is available for site identification, assessment, and brownfield remediation. Loans and NCP cleanups are also available. State response programs are funded by the EPA to survey and inventory brownfield sites, provide oversight and enforcement authorities, provide meaningful public participation, develop mechanisms for approval of a cleanup plan, and certify that the response is complete. If a state is cleaning a site under its program or pursuing a cleanup, then the NPL listing may be deferred by EPA.

Small business liability relief and Brownfields Revitalization Act

This expansion of the EPA brownfield program provides additional funds to evaluate and clean brownfield properties. The Act exempts small business contributors of hazardous substances and exempts household, small business, and nonprofit generators of municipal solid waste from liability for Superfund response costs at national priority list sites. The program allows expedited settlements for those persons who have a limited ability to pay. Another exception to the program is the owner, operator, or lessee of residential property to a nonprofit organization or business that employed no more than 100 people during the preceding year at the location from which the municipal solid waste was generated. There are conditional expedited settlements for persons who can't pay response costs and still maintain basic business operations.

Chronology of the Comprehensive Emergency Response, Compensation, and Liability Act (CERCRA) or Superfund

1980, Comprehensive Emergency Response, Compensation, and Liability Act of 1980 (CERCRA), Superfund, 26 USC 4611–4682; Pub. L. 96–510, 94 Stat. 2797

1983, CERCLA Amendments, 42 USC 9601–9657; Pub. L. 98–802, 97 Stat. 485

1986, Superfund Amendments and Reauthorization Act (SARA), Pub. L. 99–499, 100 Stat. 1613

1992, Community Environmental Response Facilitation Act, Pub. L. 102–426

1996, Asset Conservation, Lender Liability, and Deposit Insurance Protection Act of 1996, Pub. L. 104–208, 2501, 110 Stat. 3009–462

2002, Small Business Liability Relief and Brownfields Revitalization Act, Pub. L. 107–118

CHAPTER 27

Asbestos in Buildings: Asbestos Hazard Emergency Response Act (AHERA)

Overview

❖ Airborne asbestos is a recognized health hazard.

❖ Asbestos is required to be contained or removed if found to unsafe.

❖ All contractors that remove or contain asbestos in buildings must be accredited by their state.

❖ Removal management plans must be developed after an inspection and the plans submitted to, and approved by, the state.

❖ Any removed asbestos must be safely transported in sealed containers.

Asbestos Hazard Emergency Response Act Acronyms

ACM—Asbestos containing material

AHERA—Asbestos Hazard Emergency Response Act

DLA-DRMS—Department of Defense Logistics Agency, Defense Reutilization and Marketing Service

EPA—Environmental Protection Agency

MARAD—U.S. Department of Transportation Maritime Administration

NIOSH—National Institute for Occupational Safety and Health

OSHA—Occupational Safety and Health Administration

PACMs—Presumed asbestos-containing materials

TSCA—Toxic Substances Control Act

Regulating for Asbestos

Prior to the 1980s, asbestos was used in many building products. It was used to insulate pipes and structural members, soundproof ceilings, provide finished floor surfaces (floor tiles) or wall boards, and was mixed with compatible building materials such as vinyl. Asbestos has the ability to insulate items from temperature changes and, as a result, was used as a fireproof coating in most large office buildings, schools, institutional buildings, and some residential buildings. Recognition of the need to regulate or ban the product arose as information about the horrors of asbestosis, a lung disease, become known to the public. In this disease, airborne asbestos fibers become embedded in the lungs, which causes extreme breathing difficulties. In the worst cases, the embedded fibers cause the lung tissue to become rigid and immovable and results in death.[1]

AHERA regulates asbestos, which is defined as asbestiform varieties of chrysotile (serpentine), crocidolite (riebeckite), amosite (cummingtonite-grunerite), anthophylllite, tremolite, or actinolite. All asbestos-containing material (ACM) is regulated; any material containing more than one percent asbestos by weight is included. Friable asbestos-containing material means any ACM applied on ceilings, walls, structural members, piping, or any other part of a building which, when dry, may crumble, pulverize, or be reduced to powder by hand pressure. Non-friable asbestos-containing material is similarly regulated in the act if it becomes damaged or dry and then crumbles, pulverizes, or reduces to powder by hand pressure. Each of these kinds of ACMs are commonly found in ceilings and walls, in floor-

Exhibit 60: A protective membrane may be used as a barrier over asbestos-laden soils. Clean soil is placed on top.

ing materials, and covering structural members, piping, and ducts as insulating material. Over time, the asbestos materials can decompose into the air, turning to dust or powder.

Asbestos program highlights

This program is a subchapter within the Toxic Substances Control Act (TSCA).[2] It is not a stand-alone, separately-titled act but is delineated in the provisions and sections of TSCA. AHERA is a program resulting from a congressional finding that easily-crumbled (friable), asbestos-containing material (ACM) in school buildings is unsafe and should be contained or removed.[3] Likewise, all public buildings are to be assessed, inspected, and monitored to either contain or remove the ACM. Nonprofit elementary and secondary schools and public and commercial buildings are regulated. The regulations do not apply to any residential apartment building of fewer than ten dwelling units.

Quick facts by the EPA[4]

❖ Removal is often not the best course of action to reduce asbestos exposure. An improper removal can create a dangerous situation where none previously existed.

❖ The EPA requires removal only to prevent significant public exposure to asbestos, such as during a building renovation or demolition.

❖ The EPA recommends in-place management whenever asbestos is discovered. Instead of removal, a management plan can be used to ensure that fiber releases are controlled when ACM materials are not damaged significantly and are not likely to be damaged or disturbed.

Asbestos Removal

Contractor accreditation

The very act of removing asbestos can release fibers into the air, making it risky to remove the material without enclosing the work area to prevent the airborne release from being inhaled by unprotected workers or building inhabitants. A method of accrediting or qualifying contractors for safe asbestos removal is required by AHERA; the EPA delegates accreditation responsibilities to the states for implementation. Contractors must be certified and can obtain their registration only by completing special courses approved by an EPA-sanctioned state agency. Only accredited persons may inspect buildings, design removal plans, conduct responses, and physically remove or contain asbestos. The EPA approves all training courses for personal and contractor accreditation.

Safety, training, and education programs for workers who are or will be engaged in asbestos-related contracting can be given training grants. States are authorized to develop asbestos management plans and training programs for contractors. They must meet or exceed EPA standards.

Removal management plans

An inspection must be performed on a building or facility and action taken if friable ACM is found. After the contractor removes or contains the material, periodic and long-term re-inspections of any remaining ACM must be performed.

Since the required asbestos removal always includes an inspection, the results of that inspection must be transmitted by the contractor to the approved state agency in the form of an asbestos management plan. The management plan includes many handling details, such as notifying building occupants and protecting them during any removal. Removal plans must be implemented by obtaining state agency approval of the management plan.

Emergency procedures must be established and placed in effect to respond to any sudden or accidental releases during removal. The on-site air must be constantly monitored. Safe waste transportation and disposal must be performed, and worker safety must be promoted at all times. Contractors and workers must be protected during the removal process. Removal containers must be used to prevent scattering the ACM fibers into the air.

Response actions are methods taken to protect health and the environment from ACM. In addition to a general response action, there are four response actions for damaged asbestos, significantly damaged asbestos, potentially damaged asbestos, and potentially significantly damaged asbestos.

Exposure Monitoring Programs for Employees

AHERA implements an exposure-monitoring program to inform employees of exposure-monitoring results. At multi-employer worksites, other onsite employers must be notified by employers about regulated areas and the types of work performed with ACMs and/or presumed asbestos-containing materials (PACMs).

Requirements pertaining to regulated areas must be communicated, as must be the measures to which employers are required to protect their employees from asbestos exposure. Other provisions include

❖ Evaluating and certifying alternative control methods for Class I and Class II asbestos work

❖ Sending a copy of the evaluation and certification for Class I work to the OSHA national office

❖ Informing laundry personnel of the requirement to prevent release of airborne asbestos above the time-weighted average and excursion limit

❖ Notifying employers and building/facility owners or designated personnel and employees regarding the presence, location, and quantity of ACMs and/or PACMs

❖ Using information, data, and analyses to demonstrate that the PACM does not contain asbestos

❖ Posting signs in mechanical rooms or other areas that employees may enter and which may contain ACMs and PACMs, informing them of the identity and location of these materials and of work practices that prevent disturbing the materials

❖ Posting warning signs that demarcate regulated areas

❖ Affixing warning labels to asbestos-containing products and to containers holding such products

❖ Developing specific information and training programs for employees

Exhibit 61: In addition to using the material as a structural member in fireproofing, asbestos has been used to pave sidewalks in residential areas.

❖ Asbestos Hazard Emergency Response Act

❖ Providing medical surveillance for employees potentially exposed to ACMs and/or PACMs, including administering an employee medical questionnaire, providing information to the examining physician, and providing the physician's written opinion to the employee

❖ Maintaining records of objective data used for exposure determinations, employee exposure monitoring, medical surveillance records, training records, the record (i.e., information, data, and analyses) used to demonstrate that the PACM does not contain asbestos, and notifications made and received by building/facility owners regarding the content of ACMs and PACMs

❖ Making specified records (e.g., exposure monitoring and medical surveillance records) available to designated parties

❖ Transferring exposure-monitoring and medical-surveillance records to the National Institute for Occupational Safety and Health (NIOSH) on cessation of the business

These paperwork requirements permit employers, employees and their designated representatives, OSHA, and other specified parties to determine the effectiveness of an employer's asbestos control program. Accordingly, the requirements ensure that employees exposed to asbestos receive all of the protection afforded by the Standard.

Asbestos in Shipyards

There is concern about the release of ACMs when old ships are broken, dismantled, or destroyed. Coordination among the Navy, DLA-DRMS, MARAD, EPA, and OSHA for shipbreaking operations is promoted through AHERA. Scheduling and national reporting systems are required and covered by inter-agency Memoranda of Agreement (MOAs) when inspecting Navy and MARAD shipbreaking operations of vessels. OSHA is required to be involved in the breaking of Navy and MARAD vessels under contract. A system must be met for all OSHA shipbreaking inspections, not just those involving Navy and MARAD vessels. Federal guidance is available to any State Consultation Programs providing assistance to employers engaged in shipbreaking operations.[5]

Chronology of the Asbestos Hazard Emergency Response Act (AHERA)

1976, Toxic Substances Control Act, Pub. L. 94–469,

1986, Asbestos Hazard Emergency Response Act (AHERA), amended by TSCA, Pub. L. 99–519

Section Seven

Nature and Natural Resources

CHAPTER 28

Extinction:
Marine Mammal Protection Act (MMPA)

Overview

❖ MMPA relies upon the National Oceanic and Atmospheric Administration (NOAA), the Department of the Interior (DOI), the EPA, and the Department of Commerce (DOC) as primary federal agencies with responsibilities to prevent mammal extinction.

❖ Humane treatment of marine mammals is the focus of the MMPA.

❖ Marine mammals are defined as any mammal adapted to the marine environments, such as seals, sea otters, walruses, polar bears, and dolphins.

❖ Commercial taking of whales is prohibited and unlawful.

❖ The Act depends on cooperative research, planning, field observation, and coordination with commercial fishermen, other countries, and the U.S. Coast Guard.

❖ Marine research is performed to investigate all kinds of threats to the populations and habitats of marine animals and polar bears.

Marine Mammal Protection Act Acronyms

DOC—Department of Commerce

DOI—Department of the Interior

EPA—Environmental Protection Agency

ESA—Endangered Species Act

MMPA—Marine Mammal Protection Act

NOAA—National Oceanic and Atmospheric Administration

Purpose and Focus

The purpose of this Act is to address the potential extinction and depletion, as a result of human activities, of certain species of marine mammals, which are defined as any mammal adapted to the marine environments, such as seals, sea otters, walruses, polar bears, and dolphins.[1] There is a goal of zero mortality rate for all marine mammals. The DOC or a state may determine at any time that a species or population stock is below its optimum sustainable population or that a species or population stock is an endangered species or a threatened species under the ESA. Marine mammals are not to be diminished beyond the point that they "cease to be a significant functioning element in the ecosystem of which they are a part."[2] Stocks of diminished species are to be replenished and their habitats protected. These habitats may include rookeries, mating grounds, and significant areas for each species of marine mammal. Still, the MMPA recognizes the present lack of understanding about the dynamics of ecology and population which affect breeding. It proposes international research for mammal protection that respects the importance and significance of the mammals themselves.

NOAA is the federal agency responsible for protecting marine mammals. A Marine Mammal Commission is appointed as the overseer, and the U.S. Coast Guard helps enforce the environmental regulations developed from the Act.[3]

Studies of marine mammals and protections

The MMPA provides for maintaining and promoting the maximum productivity and reproduction of marine mammal populations and species.[4] The Act requires studies of mammal epidemics, international fishing entrapment of dolphins, and threats to other species of marine mammals. Since feeding can result in behavior change, feeding studies are also mandated under the Act. Marine Mammal Research Grants may be granted for yellowfin tuna, the Gulf of Maine ecosystem protection, and the Bering Sea ecosystem protection. The Pacific Coast Task Force and the Gulf of Maine Task Force are established.

Fish stocks are identified and grouped according to geographic, scientific, technical, recreational, and economic characteristics in order to promote conservation. Commercial fisheries comply by developing a research program, reducing the level of marine mammals taken in commercial fishing operations, and reducing the level of marine mammals taken in tuna fishing. Incidental takings must be monitored via a program developed by the DOC.

Using driftnets and other reckless tuna fishing is prohibited when marine mammals could be harmed,[5] but there is a "good Samaritan" exception to this regulation. When there is a potential to injure either a mammal or an entire species, the mammal may be removed as long as the removal is reported to NOAA within 48 hours. Humane treatment of mammals is required at all times. Humane means that the method of taking involves the least possible degree of pain and suffering practicable to the mammal. Beyond this exception, no marine mammal may be taken from its habitat on the high seas or in waters or lands of the United States. Pregnant or nursing mammals may not be imported, nor may they be taken or removed from their habitats in a manner deemed inhumane by NOAA.[6] No whales of any species may be taken or removed by commercial whaling.

The ecosystem for marine mammals is protected in the Gulf of Maine and the Bering Sea. There fishing gear research and development is encouraged to avoid harming any marine mammals. Also, the DOI and the State of Alaska must consult with Russia about cooperative research and management programs to protect polar bears in Alaska and Russia.[7] Cooperative agreements may be developed with Alaska Native organizations to conserve marine mammals. If the Secretary of the Interior determines that a species or stock should be designated as depleted (or no longer so designated), a conservation plan must be prepared and public notice must be given along with an opportunity for public comment.[8]

Science and conservation research

Both the Department of Commerce and the Department of Interior must form regional scientific review groups to examine population estimates and to determine a population's status. These groups must include experts in marine mammal biology and ecology, population dynamics and modeling, and commercial fishing technology and practices. A Pacific Coast Task Force and a Gulf of Maine Task Force shall perform scientific investigations to determine under what conditions California sea lions and Pacific harbor seals have a significant negative impact on the recovery of salmon fishery stocks. Unusual marine mammal mortality events must be researched, a National Maine Mammal Tissue Bank established, and tissue analyses initiated. Consultations and studies are to be performed for North Pacific fur seals.

Permits are required prior to any taking or importing any marine mammal. Driftnets and purse seine nets (usually a mile wide and 100 feet deep) have been used in the eastern tropical Pacific ocean. Their use requires the exporting nation to provide proper documents to the United States. Tuna and tuna products are banned unless their harvesting is performed in compliance with the Inter-American Tropical Tuna Commission (International Dolphin Conservation Program) and documentary evidence is provided to appropriate federal agencies. There is a labeling requirement for tuna products that state "dolphin safe."[9] Permits may be issued for taking or importing any marine mammal for purposes of scientific research, pubic display, or enhancing the survival or recovery of a species or stock.[10]

Chronology of the Marine Mammal Protection Act (MMPA)

1972, Marine Mammal Protection Act of 1972, Pub. L. 92–522;16 USC 1361–1407; 86 Stat. 1027

1976, MMPA Amendment, Pub. L. 94–265; 90 Stat. 360

1978, MMPA Amendment, Pub. L. 95–426; 92 Stat. 985

1981, MMPA Amendment, Pub. L. 97–58; 95 Stat. 979

1984, MMPA Amendment, Pub. L. 98–364; 98 Stat. 440

1986, MMPA Amendment, Pub. L. 99–659; 100 Stat. 3706

1988, Marine Mammal Protection Act Amendments of 1988, Pub. L. 100–711; 102 Stat. 4755

1990, MMPA Amendment, Pub. L. 101–627; 100 Stat. 4465

1992, Marine Mammal Health and Stranding Response Act, Pub. L. 102–587, 3001, 106 Stat. 5059

1994, Marine Mammal Protection Act Amendments of 1994, Pub. L. 103–238, U.S.C. 1386 et seq..

1997, International Dolphin Conservation Program Act. Pub. L. 105–42, 111, Stat. 1122 U.S.C. 962 et seq.

2000, Striped Bass Conservation, Atlantic Coastal Fisheries Management, and Marine Mammal Rescue Assistance Act of 2000.

CHAPTER 29
Shoreline:
Coastal Zone Management Act (CZMA)

Overview

❖ The Coastal Zone Management Act (CZMA) is also named the Coastal Zone Protection Act (CZPA).

❖ The CZMA/CZPA protects land and water along the shorelines of the 29 coastal states.

❖ The Act includes provisions of both the CZMA and the Clean Water Act (CWA).

❖ A major concern is plant and animal poisoning from water polluted by contaminants that deplete its oxygen.

❖ The basic purpose of the CZMA is to preserve coastal zones.

❖ The CZMA targets the control of nonpoint pollution from agriculture, silviculture, urban runoff, marinas, and other sources.

Coastal Zone Management Act Acronyms

CEQ—Council on Environmental Quality

CWA—Clean Water Act

CZPA—Coastal Zone Protection Act

CZMA—Coastal Zone Management Act

DHHS—Department of Health and Human Services

DOA—Department of Agriculture

DOD—Department of Defense (U.S. Navy)

DOI—Department of the Interior

EPA—Environmental Protection Agency

FDA—Food and Drug Administration

NASA—National Aeronautical and Space Administration

NCRRDI—National Coastal Resources Research and Development Institute

NERRS—National Estuarine Research Reserve System

NOAA—National Oceanic and Atmospheric Administration

NSF—National Science Foundation

Areas and zones

The basic purpose of the CZMA is to preserve coastal zones.[1] A coastal zone is the waters and the adjacent shore lands which are influenced by each other and include islands, transitional and inter tidal areas, salt marshes, wetlands, and beaches. The zone extends into the Great Lakes waters to the international boundary between the U.S. and Canada seaward to the outer limit of state title and ownership under the Submerged Lands Acts of 1917 and 1953.

The act applies to shorelines and coasts of the United States extending from the Northwest corner of Washington state along the Pacific Ocean to southern California, the Gulf Coast from Texas to Florida, and from southern Florida northward along the Atlantic Ocean to northern Maine.[2] The CZMA also includes the coasts of Alaska, the Hawaiian Islands, and the island territories. Additionally, the Great Lakes have vast coastal areas that are quite important to environmental stability. These various coastal zones contain a wide variety of esthetic, ecological, commercial, natural, and recreational resources that need to be protected. All of those coastal waters, lands, and their adjacent shore lands comprise the coastal zone.[3]

Exhibit 62: Shore lands can be damaged by human development, discharge of contaminants into waters, unexpected erosion or sand deposits, or other environmental changes. Public beach access and shoreline management are regulated by provisions of the Coastal Zone Management Act. (Photo: author)

Issues

CZMA assumes that, without care, the coast will degrade. Increasingly, these lands and waters have been stressed by population growth, building development, mineral extraction, transportation and navigation, waste disposal, and fish harvesting. Over time, there has been loss of wildlife, fish, marine mammals, wetlands, and shoreline. Habitats in the coastal zone are sensitive, fragile, and vulnerable. Global warming may well cause a rising of shorelines. Land use and water use conflicts need to be mitigated through regulation.

Coastal populations have increased 60 percent since 1960; almost half the population of the United States lives in coastal areas. Marine resources contribute to the nation's economic stability. Urban waterfronts and ports—densely populated and highly developed with buildings or facilities used for urban residential, recreational, commercial, shipping or industrial purposes—are prevalent. These waterfronts are becoming highly congested as the population and water uses increase. There is a clear link between coastal water quality and land use activities along the shore. Another issue is nonpoint source pollution that is degrading coastal waters. Global warming could result in significant global sea level rise by 2050.

For all of these reasons, the federal, state, and local governments are required by the CZMA to develop urbanized land and water use coastal programs. Grants are available to help states develop programs to be approved by NOAA that are consistent with the CZMA. Mediation may be necessary to settle conflicts between diverse interests.[4]

Programs and management

To accomplish all of these policies, goals, and objectives requires collecting, analyzing, and diffusing information and research results and providing the means for technical assistance for land use controls on the coastal areas.[5] Changing circumstances can affect the coast; therefore, federal and state cooperation is expected to provide expeditious, strong, and effective ways to avoid environmental problems.

State programs that modify federally approved programs for coastal zones may be approved for changing conditions.[6] The CZMA can support efforts to manage nonpoint source programs, identify land uses and critical coastal areas, monitor improvements, provide technical assistance, improve public participation and administrative coordination, and modify state coastal zone boundaries.[7] Federal and state programs must be consistent with one another.

Grants may be awarded by the EPA to any eligible coastal state to preserve or restore lands and waters for shellfish, redevelop deteriorating and underutilized urban waterfronts and ports, and provide access to public beaches and waters. A Coastal Zone Management Fund, a fund available to improve coastal areas, may be used to manage land and water areas, promote demonstration projects, award emergency grants, develop or confer awards of excellence in coastal zone management, develop special programs, or apply the public trust doctrine to implement state management programs. The EPA provides technical assistance and necessary research to help states implement their coastal zone management plans.[8]

Under the CZMA, a National Estuarine Research Reserve System is created. Priorities for coordinated research are identified, common research principles are developed, uniform methods of research are promoted, performance standards are created, and sources of funds are identified for estuarine research.[9] An advisory council of specialists in ocean and coastal resources is established with representatives from academic institutions in every coastal region. The CZMA also establishes a continuing, active interagency task force composed of representatives from the EPA, CEQ, DOA, DOI, DOD (U.S. Navy), DHHS, NSF, NASA, FDA, Office of Science and Technology Policy, and other federal agencies that may be designated by the President.

All coastal states are required to have coastal zone management programs in place and a clearly outlined planning process, and all state programs must be approved by the DOC. The coastal management plan and program must be coordinated with local, area-wide, and interstate plans.

Each state program must identify land uses that may cause or contribute to degrading coastal waters; identify critical coastal areas; have measures of management; provide technical and other assistance to local governments and the public; provide opportunities for public participation in all aspects of the program; and coordinate its state agencies and local officials responsible for land use programs and permits, water quality permits and enforcement, habitat protection, and public health and safety.

Coastal area hazards

Hypoxia is a condition in which plant or animal tissues are starved of oxygen. The CZMA refers to *histoxic hypoxia*, a type of hypoxia in which the lack of oxygen is from a poison that can keep cells from using oxygen. Hypoxia can lead to necrosis (tissue death).

Harmful algal blooms cause hypoxia and are threatening to many coastal areas.[10] According to NOAA, 53 percent of estuaries experience hypoxia for at least part of the year. Seven thousand square miles of the Gulf of Mexico near Louisiana and Texas is threatened by this damaging biological growth. There has also been a recent outbreak of the harmful microbe pfiesteria piscicida in coastal waters. These kinds of microbes reproduce explosively and are increasing in coastal zones. Other harmful algal blooms include the well-known dead zones, red tides in the Gulf and Southeast, brown tides in New York and Texas; ciguatera fish poisoning in Hawaii, Florida, Puerto Rico, and the Virgin Islands; and shellfish poisonings in the Gulf of Maine, Gulf of Alaska, and Pacific Northwest. Different kinds of pollution cause these blooms, including excessive nutrients and the transfer of harmful species through ship ballast water and ocean currents. Management plans must be developed by each state.

Research system and institute

In support of state programs, the federal government has created a National Estuarine Research Reserve System (NERRS) and a National Coastal Resources Research and Development Institute (NCRRDI). The NERRS system establishes research guidelines that include ways to

❖ Identify and establish priorities for coastal management issues

❖ Establish common research principles and objectives

❖ Identify uniform research methods

❖ Establish performance standards

❖ Consider adding sources of funds for estuarine research

❖ Promote and coordinate estuarine research

❖ Fund a financial assistance component

❖ Evaluate system performance

The National Coastal Resources Research and Development Institute is administered by the Oregon State Marine Science Center to develop policies under a Board of Governors composed of representatives from Oregon, Alaska, Washington, California, and Hawaii.

Chronology of the Coastal Zone Management Act (CZMA)

1972, Coastal Zone Management Act (CZMA) of 1972, 16 USC 1451–1465

1976, Coastal Zone Management Act Amendments of 1976, 16 USC 1452

1980, Coastal Zone Management Improvement Act of 1980, 16 USC 1453(17), 16 USC 1452(3)

1986, Coastal Zone Management Reauthorization Act of 1985, Pub. L. 99–272, 100 Stat. 124

1990, Coastal Zone Act Reauthorization Amendments of 1990 (CZARA), 16 USC 1455(b)

1996, Coastal Zone Protection Act of 1996, Pub. L. 104–150, 110 Stat. 1380

CHAPTER 30
Coastal Ecosystem:
National Coastal Zone Monitoring Act (NCZMA)

Overview

❖ The National Coastal Zone Monitoring Act establishes a national program to consistently monitor coastal ecosystems.

❖ Long-term water quality evaluations and monitoring methods are developed to achieve effective remedial programs.

❖ There are uniform indicators for coastal ecosystem quality.

❖ State programs are coordinated with an emphasis on designing land use plans to protect shorelines.

❖ Under the Federal Water Pollution Control Act (FWPCA), certain water pollution control programs are coordinated to protect coastal waters from contamination.

National Coastal Zone Monitoring Act Acronyms

CZMA—Coastal Zone Management Act

EPA—Environmental Protection Agency

FWPCA—Federal Water Pollution Control Act

NCZMA—National Coastal Zone Monitoring Act

USDA—U.S. Department of Agriculture

Water Quality

The EPA develops a comprehensive coastal water quality monitoring program that is long term and scientifically based.[1] Its purpose is to measure the environmental quality of coastal ecosystems. Program headquarters are located at the Environmental Research Laboratory in Narragansett, Rhode Island.

Elements of the program are identifying, analyzing, and evaluating ambient water quality according to FWPCA; measuring and recording environmental quality including contaminant levels in sediments; identifying and recording the health and quality of living coastal resources; identifying sources of degradation; appraising the impact of programs and management strategies; assessing accumulation of floatables along coastal shorelines; analyzing expected short- and long-term trends in environmental quality; and developing intensive coastal water quality monitoring programs.

State and federal permitting authorities ensure that all coastal zone monitoring conforms to FWPCA. The NCZMA establishes baseline data for monitoring bays, particularly the Massachusetts and Cape Cod Bays. The allowable quantities of bacteria, qualities of indigenous species, and swimming safety are established. Besides the EPA, all other federal agencies are committed to the NCZMA through separate Memoranda of Understandings.

Comprehensive national program

The comprehensive national program for consistent monitoring of coastal ecosystems has a number of functions. It establishes long-term water quality assessment and monitoring programs as a basis for developing effective remedial programs. A system is created to review and evaluate the scientific means available to monitor the environmental quality of coastal ecosystems. Uniform indicators of coastal ecosystem quality are developed.

The EPA provides periodic reports to Congress on coastal ecosystems and disseminates information that can protect coastal ecosystems. The EPA also provides state programs that comply with the CZMA with the information necessary to design land use plans and coastal zone regulations to protect shorelines, beaches, bays, and other waters. The NCZMA provides information to help design and implement effective coastal water pollution controls required by the FWPCA.

A comprehensive implementation strategy is developed along with the National Academy of Sciences, U.S. Fish and Wildlife Service, Director of the Minerals Management Service, Coast Guard, Navy, USDA, states, and heads of all relevant federal or regional agencies.

Chronology of the National Coastal Zone Monitoring Act (NCZMA)

1948, Federal Water Pollution Control Act, Pub. L. 92–500

1972, Coastal Zone Management Act of 1972, Pub. L. 89–454, 92–583, 92–500.

2000, Estuary Restoration Act of 2000, or Estuaries and Clean Waters Act of 2000, Pub. L. 106–457, 114 Stat. 1957

CHAPTER 31

Estuaries:
Estuary Restoration Act (ERA)

Overview

- ❖ The Estuary Restoration Act (ERA) develops a national estuary habitat restoration strategy for partnering public agencies.

- ❖ The ERA provides federal assistance for projects that restore estuary habitats and healthy ecosystems.

- ❖ It applies technology and programs of the National Estuarine Research Reserve System to enhance monitoring and research.

- ❖ The ERA has a goal to restore one million acres of estuaries by 2010.

Estuary Restoration Act Acronyms

CZMA—Coastal Zone Management Act

DOC—Department of Commerce

DOI—Department of the Interior

EPA—Environmental Protection Agency

ERA—Estuary Restoration Act

NERRS—National Estuarine Research Reserve System

NOAA—National Oceanic and Atmospheric Administration

The Estuary Restoration Act

An estuary is a part of a river or stream or other body of water that has an undamaged connection with the open sea; it is a place where sea water is measurably diluted with fresh water derived from land drainage or surface water flows. The ERA includes oceans, gulfs, bays, and the Great Lakes and has a number of important purposes:[1]

- ❖ To restore estuary habitats

- ❖ To develop a national estuary habitat restoration strategy for partnerships among public agencies

- ❖ To provide federal financial and technical assistance for estuary restoration projects

❖ To develop and enhance monitoring and research by using technology and programs associated with the National Estuarine Research Reserve System (NERRS)

Strategies

The goal of ERA is to restore one million acres of estuaries by 2010. Elements of the strategy include encouraging the creation of public-private partnerships to implement the improvements or restoration plans. Another strategy is to ensure equitable geographic distribution of projects.[2]

The U.S. Army Corps of Engineers is the major public agency involved with estuary safety, improvement, and reclamation. The DOC and DOI may carry out a long-term estuary evaluation project to assess and monitor both the Mississippi River south of Vicksburg, Mississippi, and also the Gulf of Mexico; they may also enter into a management agreement with a university-based consortium.

The Estuary Habitat Restoration Council solicits, reviews, and evaluates project proposals and makes recommendations. It develops and transmits to Congress a national strategy to restore estuary habitats. The council reviews strategies for effectiveness, provides advice on developing a comprehensive database, develops monitoring standards, and prepares required reports. Council members include representatives from the EPA, NOAA, DOA, DOI, and the U.S. Army Corps of Engineers.[3]

Estuary habitat restoration

Estuary habitat restorations include these items:

❖ Reestablishing chemical, physical, hydrologic, and biological features and components associated with an estuary

❖ Cleanup of pollution for the benefit of estuary habitats

❖ Control of nonnative and invasive species

❖ Reintroducing native species to the estuary through planting or promoting natural succession

❖ Constructing reefs to promote fish and shellfish production

❖ Providing estuary habitats for living resources

An estuary habitat restoration plan must comply with the CZMA.

Dredged material disposal sites are mapped for restoration projects. There are required Memoranda of Agreement and Memoranda of Understanding with other agencies. Bioremediation technology is studied to examine the efficacy of bioremediation products to reduce low-level petroleum hydrocarbon contamination from boat bilges; to reduce low-level petroleum hydrocarbon contamination from stormwater discharges; and to reduce low-level petroleum hydrocarbon contamination from nonpoint petroleum hydrocarbon discharges.[4]

Chronology of the Estuary Restoration Act (ESA)

1948, National Estuary Program (33 USCA 1330) in Federal Water
  Pollution Act, 33 USCA 1251–1387.

1972, National Coastal Monitoring, 33 USCA 2801–2805.

1972, Coastal Zone Management Act, 16 USCA 1451 et seq.

2000, Estuaries and Clean Waters Act, 33 USCA 2901.

CHAPTER **32**
Species Protection: Endangered Species Act (ESA)

Overview

❖ Many species are endangered.

❖ The act is managed by both the Department of the Interior (DOI) and the Department of Commerce (DOC).

❖ A list of endangered species is published and updated every five years.

❖ Recovery plans must be developed for listed endangered species.

❖ Monitoring of species is required, and civil and criminal penalties can be imposed on violators of the ESA.

Endangered Species Act Acronyms

DOC—Department of Commerce

DOI—Department of the Interior

EPA—Environmental Protection Agency

ESA—Endangered Species Act

Purpose and Programs: Habitats and Ecosystems

The ESA determines and designates species that are endangered or threatened with extinction. Conserving habitats and ecosystems are the major purposes of the ESA.[1] Increases in population have led to extinction of different species of fish, wildlife, and plants in the United States. Some other species have been so depleted in number that they are threatened with extinction.

Critical habitats for endangered species are protected also. A critical habitat is defined as that specific area within the larger geographical area occupied by the species (at the time it was originally listed or added to the ESA) where there are physical or biological features essential to conserving the species, which may require protection or special management considerations. Land acquisition is authorized, if necessary, to protect animal and fish habitats.[2]

Endangered species

An endangered species is any species in danger of extinction throughout all or a significant portion of its living area (other than a species of the Class Insecta determined by the DOI). Endangered species are defined as those threatened with destruction of their habitat or range, subject to disease or predators, or affected adversely by natural or man-made factors.[3] Any species that resembles an endangered or threatened species may be similarly treated as an endangered species.

No person in the U.S. is allowed to import any endangered species; take any from the high seas; possess, sell, deliver, carry, transport, or ship them; deliver, receive, carry, transport, or ship in interstate or foreign commerce; sell or offer for sale such species; or violate any of the protective regulations. Other prohibited activities include hunting, dumping wastes, or heating waters near the threatened or endangered species.

Once every five years, a review of all threatened or endangered species is performed, and the list is modified as needed and published in the Federal Register. Protective regulations may be issued by either the DOI or the DOC in support of the ESA.

Exhibit 63: Red squirrels are protected under the Endangered Species Act. These animals are more like chipmunks than squirrels. (Photo: author)

International agreements

The ESA honors international treaties, such as migratory bird treaties with Canada, Mexico, and Japan; the Convention of Nature Protection and Wildlife Preservation in the Western Hemisphere; the International Convention for the Northwest Atlantic Fisheries; the International Convention of the High Seas Fisheries of the North Pacific Ocean; the Convention on International Trade in Endangered Species of wild Fauna and Flora; and other international agreements. Additionally, an international agreement was signed in 1973 requiring that all nations respect a treaty to protect the critical habitats of endangered species of fish, wildlife, insects, and plants.

The DOC and the DOI have program responsibilities for the ESA and cooperate with states, international governments, and other federal agencies.

Methods of managing endangered species

Recovery plans must be developed, adopted, implemented, and monitored to conserve and ensure the survival of endangered and threatened species. The plans must describe site-specific management requirements, measurable criteria, and estimates of the time required to carry out the actions needed to protect each species or habitat. A system must be developed to monitor the status of all at-risk species. Cooperative agreements are to be developed with appropriate state agencies, as needed, and land can be acquired by the federal government according to a recovery plan.

Each state must adhere to the ESA, and state laws cannot conflict with the ESA. When state regulations conflict with federal regulations, the more restrictive regulations apply. Exception to the ESA may be made for any declared disaster area. Civil and criminal enforcement can be applied, and penalties can be administered for violations of the ESA. Enforcement can range from substantial fines to imprisonment.

In order to review, critique, and approve recovery plans, an Endangered Species Committee has been established. At present, it is composed of the Secretary of the Interior (who serves as chairman of the committee), the Secretaries of Agriculture and the Army, the Chairman of the Council of Economic Advisors, Administrators of the EPA and the National Oceanic and Atmospheric Administration, the Administrator of the National Oceanic and Atmospheric Administration, and the President.[4]

Exhibit 64: *Still waters are contained by a dam constructed by beavers. Often it is difficult to assess the negative environmental effects of animal activities.*

Decisions on endangered species are to be made on the basis of the best scientific data available, economic impact, and any other relevant impact of identifying any particular area as critical habitat. Any areas of critical habitat can be excluded if it is determined that the benefits of such exclusion outweigh the commercial implications—as long as exclusion is based on the best data available.

An annual cost analysis is required to be performed by the Fish and Wildlife Service for species conservation costs, and all expenditures needed to conserve endangered or threatened species are considered in the study.[5]

Chronology of the Endangered Species Act (ESA)

1973, Endangered Species Act of 1973, Pub. L. 93–205, 16 USC 1531 et seq.

1978, Endangered Species Act Amendments of 1978, Pub. L. 95–632, 92 Stat. 3751

1979, Endangered Species Act Amendment, Pub. L. 96–159, 4(1)(C), 93 Stat. 1225,1226

1982, Endangered Species Act Amendments of 1982, Pub. L. 97–304

CHAPTER 33
Forests and Ranges: Forest and Rangeland Renewable Resources Planning Act (FRRRPA)

Overview

❖ The Forest and Rangeland Renewable Resources Planning Act is concerned with replacing and regrowing forests and maintaining ecological balance in rangelands.

❖ Long-term environmental benefits are the purpose of the Act.

❖ A National Forest System is created that is subject to land management plans.

❖ The National Forest System is composed of federally owned forest, range, and related lands that are combined into a nationwide whole.

❖ Land management and resource management are promoted by timber cutting restrictions, research programs, and surveys of conditions.

❖ Technical assistance is provided to the private sector.

❖ Extension service programs are developed.

Forest and Rangeland Renewable Resources Planning Act Acronyms

BLM—Bureau of Land Management

FRRRPA—Forest and Rangeland Renewable Resources Planning Act

USDA—U.S. Department of Agriculture

WRUA—Wood Residue Utilization Act

Purpose and Programs

The FRRRPA assesses renewable resources; inventories the national forest system; promotes guidelines for land management and resource management; establishes a scientific advisory committee; and requires the issuing of permits, contracts, and other legal instruments.[1]

A Reforestation Trust Fund, National Forest Transportation System, and the National Forest System are established under the FRRRPA.[2] Technical assistance is provided to both public and private sectors. Extension programs are established to disseminate information about renewable resources.

A National Forest System is created from individual units of federally owned forest, range, and related lands that are combined into a nationwide

262 ❖ The ABCs of Environmental Regulation

system. The National Forest System is dedicated to long-term public benefit. As an integral forest system, certain advantages are obtained.

The Forest Service of the U.S. Department of Agriculture (USDA) cooperates with other agencies to assess the nation's renewable resources and prepare a national renewable resource program, which is periodically reviewed and updated.[3] To meet this goal, the Forest Service must research the use of recycled and waste timber product materials, develop techniques for substituting secondary materials for primary materials, and promote using recycled timber product materials. Public involvement, as in most all federal acts, is a requirement—as is consultation with other governmental agencies.[4]

Managing and Reporting

Guidelines for land management plans must be environmentally sensitive and comprehensive. An interdisciplinary approach must be used to consider and integrate the sciences, such as physical, biological, and economic sciences. All regulations must be based on good science.

The forested lands must be maintained at appropriate rates of growth with appropriate forest cover and species of trees. Conditions of a timber stand or cluster of trees in an area for eventual harvesting are required to achieve maximum benefit for all species (multiple use) or sustained yield management (the capacity for relatively consistent levels of production of a wood product or products for an extended period of time).[5] Timber cutting limitations are established. A plant species cannot be obliterated through harvesting at the expense of another.

Both planning and re-planting for new growth forests is required by the FRRRPA. Periodic surveys and analyses of area conditions are required, as well as general and specific research programs and studies on different kinds of forests. Also, an annual report on the use of herbicides and pesticides in the National Forest System must be developed and submitted.

Temporary and permanent roads are major issues in the forest system, and one goal of the FRRRPA is to reestablish vegetative cover on roadways and on areas where that cover has been disturbed by the construction of roads.

Suitable lands must be identified for resource management. All national forest lands acquired through purchase, exchange, donation, or other means; the national grasslands; and land projects administered under other acts administered by the U.S. Forest Service are to be included in the system.[6] Non-federal lands are also protected. Inventories of these lands must include the different renewable resources, such as soil and water. The inventories must also contain maps, graphic material, and explanatory aids.

The Bureau of Land Management (BLM) is required to complete its own Forest Land and Resource Management Plans. The USDA may use the BLM assessments, surveys, and programs to assist states and other organizations in protecting and managing renewable resources on private land. Both forestry and range lands are concerns of the FRRRPA, and state and private lands are also controlled.[7]

Exhibit 65: In the lower right corner, a monitoring well is part of a plan required to prevent contamination of forests, ground water, and soils under the Forest and Rangeland Renewable Resources Planning Act.

Unit plans

All forest plans must have one integrated plan for each unit of the national system of forests. There must be one document set available to the public. They must contain maps and other information that address the proportion and methods of timber harvest to fulfill each plan. The unit plans must include work performed by an interdisciplinary team with public participation in the planning process and must be based on inventories of the applicable resources of that forest. Unit plans must be formally adopted and regularly revised as conditions change significantly—but at least every 15 years.

Research and Science

Environmental research must be performed to protect vegetation, including threatened flora, fauna, wood, and wood products. Fires must be prevented, and insects, diseases, noxious plants, air pollution damage, and other problems must be addressed. When biological, chemical, or mechanical control methods and systems are needed, they must be used in a way that protects people, resources, and property. A newer, related federal act, the Wood Residue Utilization Act (WRUA), makes information available about methods that can have potential commercial application for wood residues (those wood byproducts from timber harvesting and forest protection and management).[8]

USDA extension programs teach private forest and range landowners, processors, and users of forest and rangeland renewable resources important information about environmental protection. A wide range of subjects are taught in those extension programs ranging from urban forests, trees, and temperatures to shrubs as shelterbelts for erosion prevention. State and local programs are to be reinforced with USDA extension programs and funding.[9]

Chronology of the Forest and Rangeland Renewable Resources Planning Act (FRRRPA)

1974, Forest and Rangeland Renewable Resources Planning Act of 1974, Pub. L. 93–378, 16 USC 1601

1976, National Forest Management Act of 1976, Pub. L. 94–588

1978, Forest and Rangeland Renewable Resources Research Act of 1978, Pub. L. 95–307, 92 Stat. 353

1980, Wood Residue Utilization Act of 1980, Pub. L. 96–554, 94 Stat. 3257

1987, Renewable Resource Extension Act Amendments of 1987, Pub. L. 100–231, 101 Stat. 1565

1988, Forest Ecosystems and Atmospheric Pollution Research Act of 1988, Pub. L. 100–521, 102 Stat. 2601

CHAPTER 34

Soil and Water:
Soil and Water Resources
Conservation Act (SWRCA)

Overview

❖ The SWRCA is a soil and water conservation program.

❖ It protects agricultural and grazing lands and their waters.

❖ The Act provides for the collection of data about the land and its resources.

❖ The Act provides financial and technical support.

Soil and Water Resources Conservation Act Acronyms

SWRCA—Soil and Water Resources Conservation Act

USDA—U.S. Department of Agriculture

Purpose and Programs

SWRCA protects agricultural and private grazing lands. Under this act, an appraisal of the land must be performed to determine its physical condition and the actions needed to maintain natural use and prevent environmental degradation.[1]

SWRCA collects data to develop soil and water conservation programs.[2] Continued evaluation is required of soil, water, and related resources. Data reviewed must include the quality and quantities of soil, water, fish, wildlife, and the capabilities and limitations of those resources for meeting the current and projected demands of the land on the resource base.[3] Financial and technical assistance are provided for private grazing land conservation. Annual reports covering program effectiveness must accompany the submittal of annual budgets.

The USDA must develop, in cooperation with state and national organizations and the public, a national soil and water conservation program. This program guides land owners and users about soil and water conservation on both private and nonfederal lands. It gives direction to the future soil and water conservation efforts of the USDA. Updates to the program must be completed and reported to Congress by 2007.[4]

Chronology of the Soil and Water
Resources Conservation Act (SWRCA)

1977, Soil and Water Resources Conservation Act of 1977, 16 USC 2001–2009, Pub. L. 95-192

1985, SWRCA Amendments, Pub. L. 99–198

1994, SWRCA Amendments, Pub. L. 103–354

CHAPTER **35**
Ecosystem:
Antarctic Protection Act (AAPA)

Overview

❖ The Antarctic Protection Act (AAPA) builds upon international treaties to ensure that the minerals of Antarctica are not exploited, to monitor climate changes there, and to ensure continued natural laboratory study of stratospheric ozone depletion.

❖ It is unlawful for any person to engage in, finance, or provide assistance to an Antarctic mineral resource activity.

❖ The Act recognizes that that Antarctic continent has unique associated and dependent ecosystems that must be preserved.

Antarctic Protection Act Acronyms

AAPA—Antarctic Protection Act

Purpose and Programs

The habitats of the Antarctic continent are distinctive environments that have special ecosystems. Tourism, marine life, and oil spills are regulated in the region.

The Antarctic Protection Act recognizes the need to offer a natural laboratory to monitor critical aspects of stratospheric ozone depletion and global climate change. While Antarctica is protected by a series of international agreements, there have been poor waste disposal practices by the scientific stations of the different nations, oil spills, increased tourism, and over-exploitation of marine life. The waste products of researchers stationed at base camps have been building in volume and mass and have not been properly handled.

The Antarctic Treaty Consultative Parties agrees to a voluntary ban on mineral resource activities, which is legally binding in the AAPA.[1] No one can engage in, finance, or provide any assistance for any Antarctic mineral resource activity.[2]

Chronology of the Antarctic Protection Act (AAPA)

1978, Antarctic Conservation Act, Pub. L. 95–541, 92 Stat. 2048

1990, Antarctic Protection Act of 1990, Pub. L. 101–594, 16 USC 2461–2466

CHAPTER 36

Wetlands:
Coastal Wetlands Planning,
Protection, and Restoration Act (CWPPRA)

Overview

❖ The Coastal Wetlands Planning, Protection, and Restoration Act (CWPPRA) protects all coastal states with an emphasis on the Louisiana Coastal wetlands by declaring priorities for preserving, restoring, and conserving that state's wetlands.

❖ An appointed task force develops a prioritized list of coastal wetland restoration projects.

❖ The EPA, U.S. Army Corps of Engineers, U.S. Department of the Interior (DOI), and the State of Louisiana are designated stewards of the wetlands.

Coastal Wetlands Planning, Protection, and Restoration Act Acronyms

CWPPRA—Coastal Wetlands Planning, Protection, and Restoration Act

DOI—Department of the Interior

EPA—Environmental Protection Agency

Purpose and Programs

CWPPRA protects all coastal states' wetlands, particularly the Louisiana Coastal wetlands.[1] The Mississippi River, the largest river in the United States, deposits silt and debris carried from many other states and its tributaries into its delta and the Gulf of Mexico. Louisiana's wetlands—a sensitive coastal zone environment that serves as a purification area, transition zone, and a unique aquatic environment—needs protection from natural and man-made environmental threats. In about ten years, Louisiana will lose wetlands in an amount equal to the size of San Diego.

Priorities are declared for restoring and conserving state wetland areas with grants, planning, and specially designated projects.[2] A task force is created to identify, initiate, and prioritize a list of coastal wetlands restoration projects in Louisiana. All targeted wetland areas must be described, mapped, and designated. A single state agency must be designated to develop a wetlands conservation plan to form the basis for wetlands planning. The Fish and Wildlife Service has the lead role in updating and digitizing wetlands maps in

Texas. The Office of Coastal Restoration and Management in Louisiana identifies wetland trends, and plans, monitors, and coordinates activities with the EPA to conserve wetlands.

The U.S. Army Corps of Engineers, the EPA, the DOI, and the State of Louisiana are involved in implementing the requirements of this act. Existing plans are developed by each of these agencies and integrated and coordinated into an overall state conservation plan. Each project is given a

Exhibit 66: Slow moving and still waters act as filters to retard or purify both fresh and salt water. Eliminating wetlands by replacement with urbanized land creates many environmental problems, threatening the health, safety, and welfare of communities.

priority ranking. Projects must clearly indicate their benefits as a condition for funding. National coastal wetlands conservation grants are used for the wetlands protection projects and planning.[3]

There is a CWPPRA Task Force composed of five federal agencies—the Departments of Agriculture, Commerce, Army, Interior, and the EPA—and the state of Louisiana. Every three years the Task Force reports to Congress regarding the status and effectiveness of the plan. Authority is granted to the EPA and the Corps of Engineers to work with the state to achieve a goal of "no net loss of wetlands" in coastal Louisiana.

Exhibit 67: Swampy, marshy wetlands may be easily contaminated. Much of the vegetation in this wetland has been killed by soil or water contamination.

❖ Coastal Wetlands Planning, Protection, and Restoration Act

Coastal Basin Divisions

Basins are the basic geographic boundaries to be used in initiating restoration plan development. Lists of priorities are then developed. The Louisiana coastal zone is divided into nine hydrologic basins:

❖ Pontchartrain

❖ Breton Sound

❖ Mississippi River Delta

❖ Barataria

❖ Terrebonne

❖ Atchafalaya

❖ Teche/Vermilion

❖ Mermentau

❖ Calcasieu/Sabine[4]

Chronology of the Coastal Wetlands Planning, Protection and Restoration Act (CWPPRA)

1990, Coastal Wetlands Planning, Protection and Restoration Act, Pub. L. 101–646, 16 USC 3951–3956

CHAPTER 37
Non-native Species:
Nonindigenous Aquatic Nuisance
Prevention and Control Act (NANPCA)

Overview

❖ The ANPCA regulates the introduction of non-native species of fish and plants into established habitats.

❖ Diseases, parasites, or unexpected non-native species growth threatens native species, aquatic environments, and the economy of near-shore areas.

❖ Controls include prevention of unintentional discharges into waters; research, prevention, control, and information dissemination; development and execution of control methods; minimization of the economic and ecological impacts; and the establishment of a research technology program.

Aquatic Nuisance Prevention and Control Act Acronyms

ANPCA—Aquatic Nuisance Prevention Control Act

Purpose and Programs

ANPCA focuses on the problems created from introducing non-native species of fish and plants into established habitats.[1] When conditions are favorable, non-native species can become established and compete with, or prey upon, native species of fish, plants, or wildlife. Diseases or parasites can be introduced that could destroy the native species or disrupt aquatic environments and even the economy of near-shore areas.[2] Aquatic nuisance species can be unintentionally transported and introduced into inland lakes and rivers by recreational boaters, commercial barge traffic, and a variety of other pathways. Disruptions have been caused by the ruffe fish, mitten crab, green crab, brown tree snake, brown mussel, Eurasian watermilfoil, hydrilla, water hyacinth, and water chestnut. Species have also been harmed by the jettisoning and discharge of ship ballast.

As a result of non-native species causing problems, the ANPCA attempts to prevent unintentional discharges and introduction into waters; to coordinate federally-funded research, prevention, and control; to disseminate information; to develop and carry out control methods; to minimize the economic and ecological impacts; and to establish a program of research technology.[3]

Violations of ANPCA regulations can be subject to both civil and criminal penalties.

Non-native species

The zebra mussel, unintentionally introduced into the Great Lakes from ship ballasts, has infested vast areas of surface waters. In 1992, the zebra mussel was discovered at the northernmost reaches of the Chesapeake Bay watershed and posed an imminent risk of invasion of its main waters. Because the Chesapeake Bay is the largest recipient of foreign ballast water on the East Coast, there is a risk of further invasions of other nonindigenous species. Zebra mussels are only one example of thousands of nonindigenous species that have become unexpectedly established in waters of the United States causing economic and ecological degradation of the natural resources of waters. ANPCA recognized the potential economic disruption to communities affected by the zebra mussel because of its colonization on water pipes, boat hulls, and other hard surfaces. Quick action was required to stop infestation and retard the escalation of management costs. Still, the zebra mussel's economic disruptions to aquatic communities is estimated at over $5 billion.

Another biological threat to surface waters appeared earlier, in the early 1980s, in ballast water discharges. Ruffe is a non-native fish that caused severe declines in populations of other species of fish in Duluth Harbor (in Minnesota and Wisconsin). The ruffe spread quickly to Lake Huron and was expected to spread quickly to most other waters in North America if action was not taken promptly to control their spread. Other nonindigenous species that infest coastal waters of the United States and that have the potential to cause adverse economic and ecological effects are the mitten crab (Eriocher sinensis), which became established on the Pacific Coast; the green crab (Carcinus maenas), which became established in the coastal waters of the Atlantic Ocean; and the brown mussel (Perna perna), which became established along the Gulf of Mexico. Shellfish pathogens and aquatic nuisance vegetation species such as Eurasian watermilfoil, hydrilla, water hyacinth, and water chestnut have been introduced to waters of the United States from other parts of the world and cause or have the potential to cause adverse effects.

Requirements

Nuisance problems are addressed in the Great Lakes, Lake Champlain, the Columbia River system, and the Mississippi River system for the reasons noted. This Act requires coordination with Canada, Mexico, and International Maritime Organization of the United Nations. Regional research grants are made available for research on aquatic nuisance species prevention and control for the Chesapeake Bay, the Gulf of Mexico, the Pacific Coast, the Atlantic Coast, and the San Francisco Bay-Delta Estuary.

Ship ballast water is a major concern, so shipping studies are required to be performed to determine potential regulatory controls. A national ballast information clearinghouse is created at the Smithsonian Environmental Research Center.[4]

Chronology of the Aquatic Nuisance Prevention and Control Act (NANPCA)

1990, Nonindigenous Aquatic Nuisance Prevention and Control Act of 1990, Pub. L. 101–646, 104, 110 Stat. 4091, 16 USC 4701

1996, National Invasive Species Act of 1996, Pub. L. 104–332

Chapter 38
Land:
Federal Land Policy and
Management Act (FLPMA)

Overview

❖ Environmental quality is regulated on federally-owned lands to avoid negative spillovers to adjacent private lands.

❖ The FLPMA controls the public lands of the United States to help avoid environmental degradation.

❖ Public lands are defined and classified in this act. Most all public lands require a comprehensive long-range plan for their management, use, development, and protection.

❖ Systems and areas owned or controlled by the U.S. within the states are administered by the DOI through the Bureau of Land Management.

❖ The USDA has power to issue licenses and obtain permissions for rights-of-way through public lands.

Federal Land Policy and Management Act Acronyms

BLM—Bureau of Land Management

DOD—Department of Defense

DOI—Department of the Interior

FLPMA—Federal Land Policy and Management Act

USDA—U.S. Department of Agriculture

Purpose and Programs

FLPMA is the act which creates the Bureau of Land Management (BLM) to control the public lands of the United States.[1] Federal lands are vast; therefore, the need to control, manage, and regulate these lands is quite important. Careful control and management are necessary to ensure that these large undeveloped land areas do not degrade. The environmental quality of these lands is managed to prevent negative spillovers to adjacent private lands.

The FLPMA requires land-use planning, land acquisition, and disposition. It specifies administration by creating the BLM, which gives enforcement authority, establishes budgets, provides working capital, makes loans available to states, and requires annual reports.[2] Range management is promoted by this act by establishing grazing fees, requiring leases, and issuing permits for using federal lands and by establishing right-of-way restrictions

277

and requirements. Designated management areas are the National Forest System, National Park System, National Wildlife Refuge System, National Wild and Scenic Rivers System, National Trails System, National Wilderness Preservation System, California Desert Conservation Area, Yaquina Head Outstanding Natural Area (Oregon), the Fossil Forest Research Natural Area (New Mexico), and lands in Alaska.

These areas contain extremely fragile ecosystems that are easily damaged. The BLM conducts a wilderness study which identifies wilderness areas (roadless areas of 5,000 acres or more of public lands or roadless islands) that are to be designated special management areas. The study must be updated periodically.

Regulatory Requirements

Public lands and their resources must be regularly inventoried and land-use plans developed to guide present and future use. The land-use plans must be coordinated with state and local plans and other federal plans. The sale or lease of any federal parcel in these public lands must serve the national interest. Because there can be varying interpretations of the national and public interest, the disposal of these lands through sale or lease is not easily justified. For this reason, the Department of the Interior (administrator of the FLPMA) must develop rules and regulations for land disposition. Areas of critical environmental concern are designated within these land areas.

The Department of the Interior (DOI) is responsible for maintaining a current inventory of all public lands and their resources, including their value as scenic, recreational, or natural resources. Priority is given to areas of critical environmental concern. Land-use plans are developed with public participation. Interdisciplinary approaches to planning must include physical, social, and economic factors. Long-term benefits to the public must be evaluated, and all pollution control laws must be considered in the plans. The plans may designate new land areas for purchase, but sufficient reasons for such acquisitions must be included.[3] New land areas can be contiguous or away from the national forest system holdings. Conversely, the federal government may convey public lands into the state and local governments.

Detailed provisions of the FLPMA also include establishing trespass controls, fee schedules, a forest ranger force, and a working fund; delineating search and rescue responsibilities; lending to states; using Land and Water Conservation Fund to purchase lands; and managing ranges. Range management is a very important part of the FLPMA. Grazing fees are established on public lands in 11 western states. Leases are granted for grazing based on criteria, priorities, and allotment management plans.

Rights-of-way are granted or renewed for water use; pipelines; electric transmission and distribution lines; radio and telephone towers; roads and other transportation facilities; water storage, impoundment, transportation, or distribution; pipelines; slurry and emulsion systems and conveyor belts for transporting and distributing solid materials; systems to generate, transmit and distribute electric energy; radio, televisions, telephone, telegraph and other electronic signals and other means of communication; roads, trails, highways, railroads, canals, tunnels, tramways, airways, livestock driveways, or other transportation uses or systems in the public interest.[4]

Lands and resources are required to be periodically inventoried and their present land use documented. After the inventory, a future land use plan is to be developed in coordination with other federal, state, and local governments. Land use planning and management is expected to consider multiple use (many different uses on the land, such as housing, retail, industrial, tourist, and other uses) and sustained yield of natural resources. Multiple use takes into consideration the present and future use as well as natural resource protection and conservation, making judicious use of public lands.

Exhibit 68: Many different regulations require that soils be replaced according to specific requirements, such as back filling land areas to their same grade elevation to avoid standing water or improper drainage.

A number of factors must be considered during the land use planning: scientific, scenic, historical, ecological, environmental, air, water and archeological factors. Public lands must be preserved and protected in their natural condition so that they may be used for outdoor recreation. Also, the food and habitat of fish, wildlife, and domestic animals must be protected. Any public land areas of critical environmental concern must have plans developed to protect them.

Fair market values must be obtained in any sale of public lands. Any burdens created on local and state taxpayers must be paid by the federal government. Any moneys collected must be spent on the exact lands damaged that led to the collection of those funds. If there are remaining funds in excess of the amounts needed to repair damage, they may be used to repair other damaged public lands.

The California Desert Conservation Area requires a comprehensive, long-range plan for the management, use, development, and protection of its public lands.

Grazing on federal lands is controlled by livestock allotment management plans. Range conditions are monitored and inventoried also. Areas of public concern are those public lands where special management attention is required, such as when and if they are developed and protecting or repairing damage to important historic, cultural, or scenic resources or other natural systems or processes.[5]

Two areas of concern are the California Desert Conservation Area (Desert Lily Sanctuary) and the Dinosaur Trackway Area (Oklahoma and Texas). Prior to establishing such areas of concern, the DOI inventories public lands, develops land use plans, makes management decisions, and establishes potential geographic boundaries.

Chronology of the Federal Land Policy and Management Act (FLPMA)

1976, Federal Land Policy and Management Act of 1976, Pub. L. 94–579, 90 Stat. 2743, 43 USC 1701 et seq.

1988, Federal Land Exchange Facilitation Act of 1988, Pub. L. 100–409, 102 Stat. 1086

CHAPTER 39
Offshore:
Outer Continental Shelf Lands Act (OCSLA)

Overview

❖ The OCSLA regulates offshore oil and gas resources.

❖ Activities in the ocean must be managed to prevent accidents which cause pollution.

❖ Local and state governments affected by exploration, development, and production of oil or natural gas along the outer continental shelf must participate through this act.

❖ A Fishermen's Contingency Fund pays for the claims of fishermen when their equipment or catches are spoiled by oil or gas extraction.

❖ The transportation of natural gas in coastal waters requires a certificate of public convenience.

❖ The owner's identification must be color coded, stamped, and labeled on equipment and tools.

Outer Continental Shelf Lands Act Acronyms

CAA—Clean Air Act

CWA—Clean Water Act

FWPCA—Federal Water Pollution Control Act

MPRSA—Marine Protection Research and Sanctuaries Act

NAAQS—National Ambient Air Quality Standards

NRC—National Response Center

OCSLA—Outer Continental Shelf Lands Act

TSCA—Toxic Substances Control Act

Purpose and Programs

OCSLA regulates the exploration, development, and production of oil and gas located on the outer continental shelf beyond the shorelines of the United States.[1] The oil and gas resources of the Outer Continental Shelf must be managed to prevent pollution from accidents on offshore drilling platforms or along their ocean pipelines. The use of the most current technologies is promoted in the Act as a means to avoid spills.[2] States are to work closely with local governments to manage the Outer Continental Shelf for safety from offshore oil spills, natural gas spills, and the adverse activities of fishermen. Funds are provided to clean any oil or gas spills.[3]

Regulatory Requirements

Oil and gas in the oceans must be extracted with the greatest protection of the marine environment. The Fishermen's Contingency Fund is estab-lished to pay the claims of fishermen when equipment or catches are spoiled by the extractors of oil and gas.[4] An economic loss must be demonstrated in order to be awarded these funds.

The marine environment (fish and shellfish) is protected by the OCSLA through mandatory regulations that manage current extraction technology. In order to avoid potential hazards caused by any obstructions on the sea bottoms and on the surface, there must be color coding, stamping, and label-ing of equipment and tools with the owner's identification prior to their use.[5] (This provision for identification is designed to encourage care during sea operations. This provision supposes that careless owners and operators will be discovered more easily). For any gas distribution lines originating on the Outer Continental Shelf, the Department of Energy (DOE) must issue a cer-tificate of public convenience and necessity.[6]

More acts relating to ocean protection

A number of other ocean protection regulations relate to OCSLA. Some federal regulation provisions affect the Outer Continental Shelf but are not part of the OCSLA itself. For example, prohibitions on ocean dumping are clearly stated in the Clean Water Act (CWA)[7] and the Marine Protection Re-search and Sanctuaries Act (MPRSA).[8] The Clean Air Act (CAA) requires air pollution guidelines and restrictions which affect the waters above the conti-nental shelf. The National Ambient Air Quality Standards (NAAQS) are devel-oped to reduce air chemical deposits everywhere including the oceans of the world. The Federal Water Pollution Control Act (FWPCA)[9] and the Deepwater Ports Act of 1974[10] require that those responsible for a spill or other contami-nation immediately notify the National Response Center (NRC) as soon as they know about such spill or contamination from a vessel or operating facil-ity in or along navigable waters, in a deepwater port, or on or from a vessel transporting oil the outer continental shelf. To avoid the potential for spills, imports of foreign oil are to be reduced as much as possible by managing natural resource reserves.[11] Methods must be applied to facilitate natural gas distribution by local companies in lieu of using oil as a resource. Natural re-sources must be managed and crude oil and natural gas reserves must be protected. State and local governments can enact regulations equal to or more stringent than those of the OCSLA, and many cities, counties, and states do so.

Acts Relating to Marine Protected Areas

Clean Water Act of 1977 (33 U.S.C. 1251 et seq.)

Coastal Zone Management Act (16 U.S.C. 1451 et seq.)

Endangered Species Act of 1973 (16 U.S.C. 1531 et seq.)

Magnuson-Stevens Fishery Conservation and Management Act (16 U.S.C. 1801 et seq.)

Marine Mammal Protection Act (16 U.S.C. 1362 et seq.)

National Environmental Policy Act, as amended (42 U.S.C. 4321 et seq.)

National Historic Preservation Act (16 U.S.C. 470 et seq.)

National Marine Sanctuaries Act (16 U.S.C. 1431 et seq.)

National Park Service Organic Act (16 U.S.C. 1 et seq.)

National Wildlife Refuge System Administration Act of 1966 (16 U.S.C. 668dd-33)

Wilderness Act (16 U.S.C. 1131 et seq.) [12]

Chronology of the Outer Continental Shelf Lands Act (OCSLA)

1978, Outer Continental Shelf Lands Act, Pub. L. 95–372, 43 USC 1801 et seq.

1978, Outer Continental Shelf Lands Act Amendments of 1978, Pub. L. 95-372

1982, OCSLA Amendments, Pub. L. 97–212, 96 Stat. 143, 147

1988, Outer Continental Shelf Operations Indemnification Clarification Act, Pub. L. 95–372

Chapter 40
Undeveloped Land:
Wilderness Act (WA)

Overview
- ❖ A National Wilderness Preservation System is composed of federal wilderness areas.
- ❖ The Department of Agriculture (USDA) maps and develops legal descriptions for each wilderness area.
- ❖ The use of wilderness areas is limited to recreation and conservation and scenic, scientific, educational, and historical uses.
- ❖ Roads, motor vehicles, motorized equipment or motorboats, aircraft landing, or other forms of mechanical transport are prohibited in wilderness areas.
- ❖ Structures or installations are not allowed within any wilderness area.

Wilderness Act Acronyms
DOI—Department of the Interior

USDA—U.S. Department of Agriculture

WA—Wilderness Act

Purpose and Programs
A National Wilderness Preservation System is established composed of federally-owned areas designated as wilderness areas.[1] These areas are to be used and enjoyed in a manner that leaves them unchanged for future enjoyment. Wilderness areas are to be protected and preserved in perpetuity.[2] The USDA and Department of the Interior (DOI) prepare reports on the suitability of any area for preservation as wilderness and presents the reports to Congress and the President.

The USDA maps and develops legal descriptions for each wilderness area. Public records include any additions or deletions from the list of wilderness areas. Periodically each area in the national forests is assessed by the USDA for suitability for preservation as wilderness. Congress may increase each wilderness area in size by 1280 acres. Every roadless area of 5,000 contiguous acres or more in the national parks is periodically reviewed, along with every roadless island, national wildlife refuge, and game ranges. The DOI maintains the roadless areas within the national park system. The USDA may accept gifts of land for preservation as wilderness.[3]

Regulatory provisions

Public notice must be given concerning changes in wilderness area designations. Public hearings must be arranged. Decisions, plans, programs, and wilderness area designations are submitted to the Governor's office of each state, office of counties, or boroughs for their review and comment.[4]

The use of wilderness areas are limited to recreation and conservation, or scenic, scientific, educational, or historical uses. Wilderness areas can be used for prospecting for minerals only under certain conditions. Only those commercial services that support recreational or other wilderness purposes are allowed in wilderness areas.

Wilderness areas may be restricted to ingress and egress for exploration, drilling and production of oil, and use of land for transmission lines, waterlines, telephone lines, or mining and processing operations. Timber cutting is restricted to cutting under sound principles of forest management.[5]

Roads, motor vehicles, motorized equipment, motorboats, aircraft landing, structures, and installations are prohibited within any wilderness area.[6]

Chronology of the Wilderness Act (WA)

1964, Wilderness Act, Pub. L. 88–577, 78 Stat. 890, 16 USC 1131 et seq.

Chronology: 55 Years of Environmental Regulation

1947–1969

1947, Federal Insecticide, Fungicide, and Rodenticide Act, 7 USC 136 et seq.

1948, Federal Water Pollution Control Act (FWPCA), 62 Stat. 1155; Pub. L. 845

1948, Federal Water Pollution Control Act, Pub. L. 92–500

1952, FWPCA Amendments, Ch. 927, 66 Stat. 1155

1954, Atomic Energy Act of 1954, 42 USC 2014, 2012–2021d, 2022, 2111,2113, and 2114

1955, Air Pollution Control Act, Ch. 360, 69 Stat. 322

1960, FWPCA Amendments, Pub. L. 86–624, 74 Stat. 411

1963, Clean Air Act, Pub. L. 88–206, 77 Stat. 392

1964, Wilderness Act, Pub. L. 88–577, 78 Stat. 890, 16 USC 1131 et seq.

1965, FWPCA Amendments, Pub. L. 89–234, 79 Stat. 903

1965, National Emissions Standard Act, Pub. L. 89–675

1965, Solid Waste Disposal Act, Pub. L. 89–272, 90 Stat. 2795

1967, Air Quality Act of 1967, Pub. L. 90–148, 81 Stat. 465

1969, The National Environmental Policy Act of 1969, 42 USC 4321–4370e

1970–1979

1970, Clean Air Act Amendments of 1970, Pub. L. 91–604, 84 Stat. 1676, 42 USC 7401 et seq.

1970, Environmental Quality Improvement Act, 42 USC 4371–4375

1970, Federal Water Pollution Control Act Amendments, Title II of Pub. L. 224

1970, National Materials Policy Act of 1970, Pub. L. 91–512

1970, NEPA Amendment, Pub. L. 91–190, 42 USC 4321–4347

1970, OSHA Amendment, Pub. L. 91–596, 91st Congress, S. 2193, 29 USC 651 et seq.

1972, Coastal Zone Management Act (CZMA) of 1972, 16 USC 1451–1465

1972, Federal Environmental Pesticide Control Act of 1972, Pub. L. 92–516

1972, Federal Water Pollution Control Act of 1972, or the Clean Water Act, Pub. L. 92–240, 86 Stat. 47

1972, Marine Mammal Protection Act of 1972, Pub. L. 92–522;16 USC 1361–1407; 86 Stat. 1027

1972, Marine Protection, Research, and Sanctuaries Act of 1972, 33 USC 1401–1445; 16 USC 1431, 33 USC 1271

1972, Noise Control Act, 42 USC 4901–4918

1973, Endangered Species Act of 1973, Pub. L. 93–205, 16 USC 1531 et seq.

1973, FIFRA Amendments, Pub. L. 93–205

1974, Forest and Rangeland Renewable Resources Planning Act of 1974, Pub. L. 93–378, 16 USC 1601

1974, Safe Drinking Water Act of 1974, Pub. L. 93–523, 42 USC 300–300j–26

1975, FIFRA Amendments, Pub. L. 94–140

1975, NEPA Amendment, Pub. L. 94–52

1975, NEPA Amendment, Pub. L. 94–83

1976, Coastal Zone Management Act Amendments of 1976, 16 USC 1452

1976, Federal Land Policy and Management Act of 1976, Pub. L. 94–579, 90 Stat. 2743, 43 USC 1701 et seq.

1976, MMPA Amendment, Pub. L. 94–265; 90 Stat. 360

1976, National Forest Management Act of 1976, Pub. L. 94–588

1976, Resource Recovery and Conservation Act of 1976, (the RCRA Amendment), Pub. L. 94–580; 42 USC 6901 et seq.; 7 USC 1010 et seq.; 40 CFR 280 and 281

1976, Toxic Substances Control Act of 1976, Pub. L. 99–519, 15 USC 2601 et seq.

1976, Toxic Substances Control Act, Pub. L. 94–469

1977, Clean Air Act Amendments of 1977, Pub. L. 95–95, 91 Stat. 685

1977, Clean Water Act of 1977, Pub. L. 95–217, 33 USC 1251

1977, Executive Order 11991 42 FR 26967, 3 CFR, 1977 Comp.

1977, Safe Drinking Water Act of 1977, Pub. L. 95–190

1977, Soil and Water Resources Conservation Act of 1977, 16 USC 2001–2009, Pub. L. 95–192

1977, Surface Mining Control and Reclamation Act of 1977, Pub. L. 95–89, 30 USC 1201 et seq.

1977, TSCA Amendment, 15 USC 2601–2671

1978, Antarctic Conservation Act, Pub. L. 95–541, 92 Stat. 2048

1978, Atomic Energy Act Amendment, Pub. L. 95–604

1978, Endangered Species Act Amendments of 1978, Pub. L. 95–632, 92 Stat. 3751

1978, Federal Pesticide Act of 1978, Pub. L. 95–396, U.S.C. 136 et seq.

1978, Forest and Rangeland Renewable Resources Research Act of 1978, Pub. L. 95–307, 92 Stat. 353

1978, MMPA Amendment, Pub. L. 95–426; 92 Stat. 985

1978, Noise Control Act (Quiet Communities Act of 1978), Pub. L. 95–609, 92 Stat. 3079

1978, Outer Continental Shelf Lands Act Amendments of 1978, Pub. L. 95–372; 43 U.S.C. 1801 et seq.

1979, Endangered Species Act Amendment, Pub. L. 96–159, 4(1)(C), 93 Stat. 1225, 1226

1980–1989

1980, Act to Prevent Pollution from Ships, Pub. L. 96–478, 74 Stat. 2297

1980, Airport Noise Abatement Act, USC 47501–47510

1980, Coastal Zone Management Improvement Act of 1980, 16 USC 1453(17), 16 USC 1452(3)

1980, Comprehensive Emergency Response, Compensation, and Liability Act of 1980 (CERCRA) - "Superfund," 26 USC 4611–4682; Pub. L. 96–510, 94 Stat. 2797

1980, Solid Waste Disposal Act Amendments of 1980, Pub. L. 96–482, 42 USC 6901

1980, Used Oil Recycling Act of 1980, Pub. L. 96–482, 94 Stat. 2334

1980, Wood Residue Utilization Act of 1980, Pub. L. 96–554, 94 Stat. 3257

1981, MMPA Amendment, Pub. L. 97–58; 95 Stat. 979

1981, Municipal Wastewater Treatment Construction Grant Amendments of 1981, Pub. L. 97–117, 95 Stat. 1623

1981, Steel Industry Compliance Extension Act of 1981, Pub. L. 97–23, 95 Stat. 139

1982, Endangered Species Act Amendments of 1982, Pub. L. 97–304

1982, NEPA Amendment, Pub. L. 97–258, 4(b)

1982, Nuclear Waste Policy Act of 1982 (NWPA), 42 USC 10101–10270

1982, OCSLA Amendments, Pub. L. 97–212, 96 Stat. 143, 147

1982, EQIA Amendments, Pub. L. 97–258 4(b) 96 Stat. 1067 (established by NEPA (42 U.S.C. 4343)

1983, CERCLA Amendments, 42 USC 9601–9657; Pub. L. 98–802, 97 Stat. 485

1983, CWA Amendment, 33 USC Section 1251 (a)(2)

1983, Nuclear Waste Policy Act of 1982, Pub. L. 97–425

1984, Hazardous and Solid Waste Act (HSWA), 40 CFR 261, 262, 267, 268, 271, and 272

1984, Hazardous and Solid Waste Amendments of 1984, Pub. L. 98–616, 42 USC 6917 et seq. SWDA amended entirely as the Resource Conservation and Recovery Act (RCRA), 42 USC 6901, Subtitle D amended by 42 USC 6941–6949a

1984, MMPA Amendment, Pub. L. 98–364; 98 Stat. 440

1984, Standards for Treatment, Storage, and Disposal Facilities (TSDs), 40 CFR 264 and 265

1985, CWA Amendment, 33 USC Section 1251 (a)(1)

1985, SWRCA Amendments, Pub. L. 99–198

1986, Superfund Amendments and Reauthorization Act (SARA), Pub.L.99–499, 100 Stat. 1613

1986, Asbestos Hazard Emergency Response Act (AHERA), amended by TSCA, Pub. L. 99–519

1986, Asbestos Hazard Emergency Response Act of 1986, Pub. L. 99–519, 106 Stat. 3924

1986, Coastal Zone Management Reauthorization Act of 1985, Pub. L. 99–272, 100 Stat. 124

1986, Emergency Planning and Community Right-to-Know Act, Pub. L. 99–499, 42 USC 11001–11050

1986, MMPA Amendment, Pub. L. 99–659; 100 Stat. 3706

1986, Omnibus Low-Level Radioactive Waste Interstate Compact Consent Act, Pub. L. 99–240, 99 Stat. 1859

1986, Radon Gas and Indoor Air Quality Research Act of 1986, Pub. L. 99–499

1986, Safe Drinking Water Act Amendments of 1986, Pub. L. 104–182

1987, Marine Plastic Pollution Research and Control Act of 1987, Pub. L. 100–220

1987, Nuclear Waste Policy Amendments Act of 1987, Pub. L. 101–202

1987, Renewable Resource Extension Act Amendments of 1987, Pub. L. 100–231, 101 Stat. 1565

1987, Water Quality Act of 1987, Pub. L. 100–4, 33 USC 1254

1988, Amendments, Pub. L. 100–408

1988, Appalachian States Low-Level Radioactive Waste Compact Consent Act, Pub. L. 100–319, 102 Stat. 471

1988, Federal Insecticide, Fungicide, and Rodenticide Act Amendments of 1988, Pub. L. 100–532

1988, Federal Land Exchange Facilitation Act of 1988, Pub. L. 100–409, 102 Stat. 1086

1988, FIFRA Amendments, Pub. L. 100–532

1988, Forest Ecosystems and Atmospheric Pollution Research Act of 1988, Pub. L. 100–521, 102 Stat. 2601

1988, Marine Mammal Protection Act Amendments of 1988, Pub. L. 100–711; 102 Stat. 4755

1988, Massachusetts Bay Protection Act of 1988, Pub. L. 100–653, 102 Stat. 3835 1988, Medical Waste Tracking Act of 1988, Pub. L. 100–582, 102 Stat. 2950

1988, Mining and Mineral Resources Research Institute Amendments of 1988, Pub. L. 100–483, 102 Stat. 2341

1988, Ocean Dumping Ban Act of 1988, Pub. L. 100–688, Title I, 1001, 102 Stat. 4139

1988, Organotin Antifouling Paint Control Act of 1988, Pub. L. 100–333

1988, Outer Continental Shelf Operations Indemnification Clarification Act, Pub. L. 95–372

1988, Shore Protection Act of 1988, Pub. L. 100–688

1988, United States Public Vessel Medical Waste Antidumping Act of 1988, Pub. L. 100–688, 102 Stat. 4152

1989, Amendments, Pub. L. 100–220

1990–1999

1990, Abandoned Mine Reclamation Act of 1990, Pub. L. 101–508, 104 Stat. 1388–289

1990, Antarctic Protection Act of 1990, Pub. L. 101–594, 16 USC 2461–2466

1990, Clean Air Act Amendments of 1990, Pub. L. 101–549, 104 Stat. 2399

1990, Coastal Wetlands Planning, Protection and Restoration Act, Pub. L. 101–646, 16 USC 3951–3956

1990, Coastal Zone Act Reauthorization Amendments of 1990 (CZARA), 16 USC 1455(b)

1990, Great Lakes Critical Programs Act of 1990, Pub. L. 101–596, 1, 104 Stat. 3000, 33 USC 1269

1990, Great Lakes Oil Pollution Research and Development Act, Pub. L. 101–646

1990, MMPA Amendment, Pub. L. 101–627; 100 Stat. 4465

1990, Nonindigenous Aquatic Nuisance Prevention and Control Act of 1990, Pub. L. 101–646, 104, 110 Stat. 4091, 16 USC 4701

1990, Oil Pollution Act of 1990, Pub. L. 101–380, 33 USC 2701–2761

1990, OSHA Amendment, Pub. L. 101–552, Section 3101

1990, Pollution Prevention Act, Pub. L. 101–508, 42 USC 13101–13109

1991, Federal Agency Recycling and the Council on Federal Recycling and Procurement Policy, Executive Order 12780

1991, FIFRA Amendments, Pub. L. 102–237

1992, Community Environmental Response Facilitation Act, Pub. L. 102–426

1992, Federal Facility Compliance Act of 1992, Pub. L. 102–386, 106 Stat. 1505

1992, Federal Facility Compliance Act, Pub. L. 102–386, 106 Stat. 1505

1992, Lead-based Paint Exposure Reduction Act, Pub. L. 102–550, 1021(c) Stat. 3924

1992, Marine Mammal Health and Stranding Response Act, Pub. L. 102–587, 3001, 106 Stat. 5059

1992, MPRSA Amendments, Marine Mammal Health and Stranding Response Act, Pub. L. 102–587, 106 Stat. 5059

1993, Federal Acquisition, Recycling, and Waste Prevention, Executive Order 12873

1994, Abatement of Aviation Noise, Pub. L. 103–272 1(e), 108 Stat 1284

1994, Central Midwest Interstate Low-Level Radioactive Waste Compact Amendments Consent Act of 1994, Pub. L. 103–439, 108 Stat. 4607

1994, Marine Mammal Protection Act Amendments of 1994, Pub. L. 103–238, USC 1386 et seq.

1994, MPRSA Amendments, Marine Mammal Protection Act Amendments of 1994, Pub. L. 103–238

1994, NCA Amendments, Pub. L. 103–272, 108 Stat. 1379

1994, Ocean Pollution Reduction Act, Pub. L. 103–431, 108 Stat. 4396.

1994, SWRCA Amendments, Pub. L. 103–354

1995, Certain Commercial Space Launch Activities, Pub. L. 104–88

1995, Edible Oil Regulatory Reform Act, Pub. L. 104–55, 1, 109 Stat. 546, 33 USC 2704–2716

1996, Asset Conservation, Lender Liability, and Deposit Insurance Protection Act of 1996, Pub. L. 104–208, 2501, 110 Stat. 3009–462

1996, Coastal Zone Protection Act of 1996, Pub. L. 104–150, 110 Stat. 1380

1996, Food Quality Protection Act of 1996, Pub. L. 104–170, 110 Stat. 1489

1996, Land Disposal Program Flexibility Act of 1996, Pub. L. 104–119, 1, 110 Stat. 830

1996, National Invasive Species Act of 1996, Pub. L. 104–332

1996, Safe Drinking Water Act Amendments of 1996, Pub. L. 104–182, 110 Stat. 1613

1997, International Dolphin Conservation Program Act. Pub. L. 105–42, 111, Stat. 1122 USC 962 et seq.

1997, MPRSA Amendments, International Dolphin Conservation Program Act, Pub. L. 105–42, 111 Stat. 1122

1998, Border Smog Reduction Act of 1998, Pub. L. 105–286, 112 Stat. 2773

1998, National Ocean Survey Hydrographic Services Improvement Act of 1988, Pub. L. 106–541, 114 Stat. 2679

1998, Texas Low-Level Radioactive Waste Policy Act, Pub. L. 105–236, 112 Stat. 1542

1999, Chemical Safety Information, Site Security and Fuels Regulatory Relief Act, Pub. L. 106–40, 113 Stat. 207

2000–2002

2000, Alternative Water Sources Act of 2000, Pub.L. 106–457, 114 Stat. 1975

2000, ANAA Amendments, Pub. L. 106–181, 114 Stat. 178

2000, Beaches Environmental Assessment and Coastal Health Act of 2000, Pub. L. 106–457, 114 Stat. 1346 and 1375a

2000, Certain Alaskan Cruise Ship Operations, Pub. L. 106–554

2000, Chemical Safety Information, Site Security and Fuels Regulatory Relief Act, Pub. L. 106–40

2000, Chesapeake Bay Restoration Act of 2000, Pub. L. 106–457, 114 Stat. 1267

2000, Dry Bulk Cargo Residue Disposal on the Great Lakes; Study and Regulations, Pub. L. 106–554

2000, Estuary Restoration Act of 2000, or Estuaries and Clean Water Act of 2000, Pub. L. 106–457, 114 Stat. 1957

2000, Lake Ponchartrain Basin Restoration Act of 2000, Pub. L. 106–457, 114 Stat. 1273

2000, Long Island Sound Restoration Act, Pub. L. 106–457, 114 Stat. 1269

2000, MPRSA Amendments, Striped Bass Conservation, Atlantic Coastal Fisheries Management, and Marine Mammal Rescue Assistance Act of 2000, Pub. L. 106–555, 114 Stat. 2765

2000, Necessity of Military Low-Level Flight Training to Protect National Security and Enhance Military Readiness, Pub. L. 106–398, 317

2002, Small Business Liability Relief and Brownfields Revitalization Act, Pub. L. 107–118

APPENDIX 2:
ISO 14001 and Federal Regulation

An Overview of ISO Certification

ISO 9000 and ISO 14000 are quality control standards developed by the International Standards Organization (ISO) that may be implemented by organizations around the world to facilitate global commerce. Founded in 1946, the ISO historically had technical, product, and manufacturing standards as its focus. Today, however, quality control system standards and environmental standards are the thrust of the ISO.[1] The ISO comprises thousands of standards organizations in nations around the world; the American National Standards Institute (ANSI) is the member organization which represents the United States in the ISO.[2]

ISO 9000 is a quality assurance management system which encompasses health, safety, and the environment. In contrast to quality management systems such as ISO 9000, which deal with customer needs, environmental management systems such as ISO 14000 address the needs of employees, communities, customers, vendors, and the environment both today and also for the future by promoting pollution prevention and environmental protection.[3]

ISO 14000 is a voluntary program that organizations can use to "improve environmental performance,... reduce pollution, and minimize the adverse environmental impacts of their activities, products, and services."[4] It arose out the 1992 Global Environmental Initiative held in Rio de Janeiro, Brazil[5] and, after years of development by ISO's Technical Committee for Environmental Management, was established as a standard in 1996.[6] More than 18,000 businesses and organizations in over 40 nations around the world hold ISO 14001 certifications; more than half of the certifications are held by businesses and organizations in Japan, Germany, the United Kingdom, Sweden, and the United States.*[7]

ISO Certification and Federal Regulations

ISO 14001 certification differs from federal environmental regulations in that it is a voluntary and self-directed means of establishing Environmental Management Systems (EMS). Certainly, maintaining a ISO 14001 certification helps businesses and organizations meet or exceed the federal environmental regulations. It does not, however, take the place of technical or legal stan-

---

* As of July 2000.

dards, and certification does not assume compliance with federal laws and regulations.[8]

ISO 14001 Compliance

There are five main elements of ISO 14001 compliance:

❖ Environmental Policy

❖ Planning

❖ Implementation and Operation

❖ Checking and Corrective Action

❖ Management Review

Environmental Policy

In creating an environmental policy, consider the physical site(s) of operations and the direct and indirect impacts that a product, service, or waste product might have on the environment. This policy need not be detailed; rather, it should encourage those who use it to tailor the policy to individual products and services.[9] The environmental policy is the framework by which environmental objects and targets are set and reviewed. It should be documented, implemented, maintained, and communicated to all employees and should be made available to the public.[10] The environmental policy of any business or organization should be a part of and consistent with its strategic organizational plan; it should also be consistent with the environmental policies of other businesses or organizations which they depend upon for direction, resources, or technical support.[11]

Planning

In planning for ISO 14001 certification, consider legal and other environmental requirements; set objectives and targets for each process, product, or service and for all levels of operation (normal, shut-down, start-up, and emergencies); set a time frame for reaching targets and objectives; and consider environmental impacts for air, water, land, wetlands, and the use of natural resources.[12]

Implementation and operation

A single manual for implementation and operation of an EMS is not required. Collectively, organizational charts indicating EMS responsibilities, site emergency plans, and operations procedures are examples of documents that comprise an ISO 14001 "manual."[13] Tasks involved in implementation of an EMS include identifying resources, reporting progress, training of all persons, communicating pollution prevention efforts, identifying potential accidents and emergency situations, and planning to mitigate or remedy such situations.[14]

Checking and corrective action

This element includes monitoring, measuring, and evaluating the procedures included in the EMS; investigating nonconformance; recording all incidents of nonconformance and their remediation; and periodically auditing the EMS.[15] Audits are based on the results of previous audits as well the importance of the activity and its impact on the environment.[16] Documentation of this process is necessary for a third-party determination of ISO 14001 compliance.[17]

Management review

Periodic management review of the EMS is necessary to ensure that the EMS reflects the organization's current business strategy and is suitable, adequate, and effective for reducing and preventing pollution.[18]

Annexes

Annexes called "Guideline on the Use of the Specification" are included in the ISO 14000 Series Standard to provide clarification and are not intended for use in audits.[19]

Ten Steps for Implementing an ISO 14001 Certification Process[20]

W. M. von Zharen identifies ten steps for implementing an ISO 14001 certification process in her book, *ISO 14000: Understanding the Environmental Standards*.

Step One: Establish commitment

Step Two: Review where you are

Step Three: Develop and implement the environmental policy

Step Four: Know the applicable law

Step Five: Identify objectives and targets

Step Six: Say what you do (Training, workshops, seminars)

Step Seven: Do what you say (Oversee and report on the status of the EMS)

Step Eight: Prove it (Audits, certification)

Step Nine: Management review

Step Ten: Continual improvement... cycle through the steps; this is not the final step.

The Potential Benefits of ISO 14001 Compliance

Businesses and organizations that earn ISO 14001 certifications may experience improved performance and, consequently, reduced costs. Compliance may ease lending processes and "may become the standard by which organizations are judged regarding their ability to manage risk...."[21] ISO certification may someday become a way to "fast-track" federal environmental permit applications.[22] Although ISO 14001 certification is voluntary, earning a certification will position an organization to meet federal regulations more efficiently and avoid time-consuming, costly remediation processes.

---

[1] von Zharen, W. M. 1996. *ISO 14000: Understanding the Environmental Standard.* Rockville, MD: Government Institutes. 1–2.

[2] Bass, Ron. "Environmental Management Goes Global: What ISO 14001 Means to Local Governments." American Planning Association. 11 Oct. 2000. http://www.planning.org/info/iso.html.

[3] von Zharen, 12–13

[4] Bass

[5] von Zharen, 8

[6] Bass

[7] "The ISO Speedometer." www.inepm.org/htdocs/iso/speedometer. 14 Aug. 2002

[8] Bass

[9] von Zharen, 43–44

[10] Bass

[11] West, G. A., and J. G. Manta. 1996. *ISO 14001: An Executive Report.* Rockville, MD: Government Institutes

[12] Bass, von Zharen, 45.

[13] von Zharen, 47.

[14] Bass

[15] Ibid.

[16] von Zharen, 49.

[17] West, 23.

[18] Bass, Von Zharen, 49.

[19] von Zharen, 49.

[20] Ibid., 77-84.

[21] West, 52–53.

[22] Ibid., 53.

APPENDIX 3:
Number System for
Federal Laws and Regulations

Laws, Rules, and Regulations

Federal environmental acts and specific controls are the result of deliberate, careful consideration by lawmakers, public agencies, corporate professionals, and others. Many laws are passed along with policy actions by environmental agencies that create the federal framework.

Environmental rules and regulations are developed and recorded in the Federal Register as the Statutes at Large, United States Code, Code of Federal Regulations, Unified Agenda, and the Weekly Compilation of Presidential Documents. To clarify the process of enacting and numbering the environmental regulations, the general process for all regulations needs to be briefly reviewed. Although the federal agencies issue their own memoranda, clarifications, and bulletins which can have the effect of a formal regulation, they are not discussed here.

Enacting and Numbering the Laws

Federal environmental laws are enacted by the U.S. Congress and the President to support or enforce public policy. Bills which originate in the House of Representatives are given a number and the prefix "H.R."; bills which originate in the Senate are given a number with the prefix "S." Bills that are passed or are allowed to become law without the President's signature are transmitted by the White House to the Archivist of the United States for numbering.

When the law is approved, it may be called an "act." The text of the act is called a public statute. A public law number is assigned for the Statutes at Large volume that refers to that Congressional session.[1] Law numbers are sequenced starting at the beginning of each Congress by the number of Congress (103, 104, 105, etc.) such as Public Law 107–12 or Private Law 107–222. Private laws pertain to specific persons rather than a subject. All of the laws passed by that session of Congress have the same numerical prefix.

The first publication of the law is known as the "slip law." It is separately published as an unbound pamphlet. The Office of the Federal Register, National Archives and Records Administration prepares the slip laws with editorial notes that give citations to other laws and any needed details. These editorial notes are called "marginal notes" and give United States Code numbers and classifications. The slip law contains information about the legislative history of the law (committee report number, name of the committee, date of passing the Senate or House of Representatives, reference to the Congressional Record by volume, year, and date), as well as other information.

Public laws are transformed into other groups of documents and are given different names and numbers, edited or annotated with comments, and placed in categories. Sometimes comments that may change or amend the laws are added during the preparation of the different sets of documents or regulations.

Statutes at Large

United States Statutes at Large (example: 29 Stat. 491) contain the laws and any concurrent resolutions of Congress and reorganization plans or proclamations issued during each Congressional session. The Office of the Federal Register, National Archives and Records Administration prepares the United States Statutes at Large annually.

Supplemental volumes are issued which contain tables of prior laws that have been amended, repealed, or affected by other public laws enacted. Each volume has a table of contents and index. Each of the statutes are organized— that is, numbered—in chronological order and not by subject matter. In order to organize the laws by subject matter and show the changes made to those laws, the United States Code (example: 42 USC 6901) is assigned.

United States Code

United States Code is the compiled, written set of laws in effect on the day preceding the beginning of the session that follows the last session of Congress. The Code is prepared by the Law Revision Counsel of the House of Representatives. Complete, new editions are published every six years with supplements containing the latest revisions published every year.

There are 50 title headings numbered by alphabetical order according to subject matter. The purpose for this coding is to avoid the need for users to work with the Statutes at Large (numbered chronologically) and the later amendments to older laws. Through codification, one volume or title can contain all the current rules and regulations. In this manner, there can be "one-stop shopping" for users. The code is updated periodically, with changes annotated to sections. Those code versions containing comments, provisions, or additions for the sections are called United States Code Annotated. Titles may be changed as the editing is completed for each title. Changes in a section of the Code is made within five business days of enacting the law.

Federal Register

The Office of the Federal Register, National Archives and Records Administration publishes the Federal Register each workday. This daily publication contains sections that vary in length according to need. The Federal Register consists of notices, which are documents rather than proposed or final rules. Some examples of information announced in the notices are hearings and investigations, committee meetings, agency decisions and rulings, delegations of authority, issuance or revocation of licenses, grant application deadlines, availability of environmental impact statements, filing of petitions and applications, and agency statements of organization and functions. The Federal Register is available on the Internet.

Unified Agenda[2]

This semiannual agenda is a summary of those actions that are anticipated to be taken by federal agencies. Any regulations that have been adopted must be listed. Each agenda has a preamble and table of contents. Regulatory Identifier Numbers are assigned to the actions or proposals. It is published in April and October of each year and is also available on the Internet. The agenda is maintained by the Government Printing Office in a separate database.

Weekly compilation of presidential documents

Presidential documents include Proclamations, Executive orders (example: 12999) and Reorganization plans (example: 2002 Plan No. 7). This group of documents contains statements, messages, and other materials released by the Office of the President. Every Monday, the Office of the Federal Register publishes the past week's Presidential documents. The documents are compiled again annually in Title 3 of the Code of Federal Regulation. They can be viewed on the Internet.[3]

Details on the multiple numbering systems

Because environmental laws and their resulting programs can originate in many places within the federal government, they may start with different numbers in different places. A "bill" is the name given to a proposed law in the Senate or House. Prior to enactment, the House of Representatives or the Senate gives a number to the bill (example: S.B. 1203 or H.R. 1203). After a vote is taken that passes the bill, a public law number is assigned. If the President issues a proclamation, executive order, or reorganization plan, a document number is assigned (example: 12999) as well.

Each environmental law, as with any law, requires many instructions, requirements, assigned duties and responsibilities, and restrictions on behavior. The law may also designate penalties that can be changed over time. For these reasons, laws need further definition, and supplemental rules and regulations need to be written and changed to ensure that there will be no misunderstanding. When these additions are made, they are first announced in the Federal Register and may be given yet another number in order to provide a usable reference to receive comment from other public agencies who might be affected or the private sector. After the rules and regulations are published, revisions may be made to them prior to their official enactment. These details of a law are called "regulations."

Final rules and regulations published in the Federal Register serve as documents that have legal force or effect. Interim rules have immediate effect and are issued without prior notice. Most are issued in response to an emergency. Policy statements and interpretations are part of the Code of Federal Regulations (CFRs) but do not amend them. They can affect an agency's handling of its regulations or provide information to the public. Final rules, interim rules, and policy statements and interpretations are keyed by subject, numbered or renumbered, and codified in the CFRs.

Any changes in text of a rule or regulation is a change to the CFR and is given an effective date for its implementation. Each change begins with a heading which includes the issuing agency name, the CFR title and part affected, and a description of the subject of the document. Sometimes an agency docket number is included to key it to the internal filing system of an agency. The Regulation Identifier Number (RIN) may be added. After printing a regulation in the Federal Register as a final rule, it is given a number code. Under the CFRs numbering system of laws, the subject matter of each rule, regulation, or law is categorized under a "title" number. There are many titles that have constant numbers and subjects. Environmental laws are for the most part scattered among these 11 of the 50 title numbers:

5. Administrative Personnel
7. Agriculture
15. Commerce and Trade
16. Conservation
29. Labor
30. Mineral Lands and Mining
33. Navigation and Navigable Waters
40. Protection of the Environment
42. Public Health and Welfare
43. Public Lands
49. Transportation

Under each Public Law, United States Code, United States Statutes at Large, Code of Federal Regulations, title or chapter numbers (Arabic: 1, 2,...9, etc.) are assigned to further divide the subjects and guide the user to the desired section of the law. Subchapter numbers (upper-case Roman: I, II,...IX, etc.) are given to sub-items for additional directions. Finally, section numbers are assigned (1, 2,...999, etc.) and divided into lower-case letters (a, b,....z). For example:

Pub. L. 102-389, Title III, Oct. 6, 1992, 106 Stat. 1602

After a Public Law is codified in the United States Code, it receives another designation; for example, Title 42, The Public Health and Welfare, Solid Waste Disposal, Hazardous Waste Management is indicated as:

42 USC 6921

Every six years, public laws are incorporated into the United States Code, which is a codification of all general and permanent laws of the United States. The U.S. Code is arranged by subject matter, and it shows the present status of laws that have been amended on one or more occasions. It is maintained as a separate database on GPO Access.[4]

The United States Code has similar title numbers and names to the CFRs, but a notable exception is Title 40 which is named Public Buildings, Property, and Works in the U.S. Code. In the CFRs, it is Protection of the Environment. The CFRs have provisions that may contain rules and regulations developed over time to respond to needed changes in that law. As rules are developed, they are published in the federal register for review and comment by the public (including business and industry).

The subjects covered in the CFRs parallel those in the federal Public Laws. CFRs contain very specific rules for behavior with respect to protecting the public health, safety, and welfare; thus, protecting the environment.

The CFR numbering system is:

40 CFR 280

The first number, 40, indicates Title 40—Protection of the Environment. The last number, 280, indicates Part 280—Technical Standards and Corrective Action Requirements for Owners and Operators of Underground Storage Tanks (UST).

The CFRs are constantly changing. Some sections and parts are expanded, reduced, or deleted. Numbers are not always consecutive, and a system is maintained where some numbers in every sequence are skipped and reserved for future use by new topics. The EPA and other responsible environmental agencies regularly require fine tuning of subjects in the regulations or major revisions of entire sections. Access to the CFRs is available on the Internet; from the publisher of this book, Government Institutes; from the National Archives and Records Administration's Office of the Federal Register; and from the Government Printing Office (GPO). Paper editions of the CFR and Federal Register are available through Government Institutes and the Superintendent of Documents.

The Code of Federal Regulations is an annual publication that provides users with the detailed, permanent rules and regulations previously published for comment and interim or final rules found in the Federal Register. The purpose of the CFRs is to present the official and complete text of agency regulations in one organized publication. The CRFs have become the one comprehensive and convenient reference for the texts of the federal (environmental and other) regulations. To keep current, the CFRs must be used with the daily Federal Register. For most users, the most recent edition of the CFRs can be considered the major reference to most environmental regulations. The other compilations of documents must be studied to obtain the complete regulatory picture.

---

[1] The House of Representatives, Office of the Law Revision Counsel, is responsible for preparing and publishing the United States Code. The Code consolidates and organizes the subjects of laws. It does not include the regulations that are developed to implement the laws.

[2] The full name is Unified Agenda of Federal Regulatory and Deregulatory Actions

[3] http://www.access.gpo.gov; http://thomas.loc.gov

[4] http://www.access.gpo.gov

ACRONYMS

A

AAPA	Antarctic Protection Act
ACM	Asbestos containing material
AEA	Atomic Energy Act
AHERA	Asbestos Hazard Emergency Response Act
ANAA	Airport Noise Abatement Act
ANPCA	Aquatic Nuisance Prevention Control Act
AQRV	Air quality related value
ARAR	Applicable or relevant and appropriate requirements
AST	Aboveground storage tanks
ATSDR	Agency for Toxic Substances and Disease Registry

B

BACM	Best available control measures
BACT	Best available control technology
BART	Best available retrofit technology
BAT	Best available technology
BCT	Best conventional technology
BLM	Bureau of Land Management
BMP	Best management practices
BOD	Biological oxygen demand
BPCT	Best practical control technology
BPJ	Best professional judgment
BPT	Best practical control technology

C

CAA	Clean Air Act
CAIR	Comprehensive assessment information rule
CAMS	Continuous air monitoring system
CAMU	Corrective Action Management Unit
CBI	Confidential business information
CCL	Construction completion list
CCMP	Comprehensive conservation management plan
CEI	Compliance evaluation inspections
CEQ	Council on Environmental Quality
CERCLA	Comprehensive Emergency Response, Compensation, and Liability Act
CERCLIS	Comprehensive Emergency Response, Compensation, and Liability Information System
CFC	Chlorofluorocarbon
CO	Carbon monoxide
CSI	Common Sense Initiative
CSO	Combined sewer overflow
CTG	Control technique guideline
CWA	Clean Water Act
CWPPRA	Coastal Wetlands Planning, Protection, and Restoration Act
CZMA	Coastal Zone Management Act
CZMP	Coastal Zone Management Program
CZPA	Coastal Zone Protection Act

D

DHHS	Department of Health and Human Services
DLA-DRMS	Department of Defense Logistics Agency, Defense Reutilization and Marketing Service
DMR	Discharge monitoring report
DOC	Department of Commerce
DOD	Department of Defense
DOE	Department of Energy
DOI	Department of the Interior
DOJ	Department of Justice

DOL	Department of Labor
DOT	Department of Transportation

E

ELP	Environmental Leadership Program
EPA	Environmental Protection Agency
EPCRA	Emergency Planning and Community Right-to-Know Act
EQIA	Environmental Quality Improvement Act
EQR	Environmental Quality Report
ERA	Estuary Restoration Act
ESA	Endangered Species Act
ETS	Emergency temporary standard

F

FAA	Federal Aviation Administration
FDA	Food and Drug Administration
FDCA	Federal Food, Drug, and Cosmetic Act
FDF	Fundamentally Different Factors
FFCA	Federal Facility Compliance Act
FIFRA	Federal Insecticide, Fungicide, and Rodenticide Act
FIP	Federal Implementation Plan for a state
FLPMA	Federal Land Policy and Management Act
FOTW	Federally owned treatment works
FQPA	Food Quality Protection Act
FRRRPA	Forest and Rangeland Renewable Resources Planning Act
FWPCA	Federal Water Pollution Control Act

H

HAZCOM	Hazard communication
HCFC	Hydroclorofluorocarbon
HOV	High occupancy vehicle
HRS	Hazard ranking system

I

ICT	Individual Control Technologies
ISR	Interim Standards Rule
ITC	Intragency Testing Committee

L

LAER	Lowest achievable emission rate
LEPC	Local emergency planning committee
LEV	Low Emission Vehicle Program, or national LEV
LFD	Local fire department
LVE	Low volume exemption

M

MACT	Maximum achievable control technology
MARAD	U.S. Department of Transportation Maritime Administration
MCAN	Microbial commercial activity notice
MCLG	Maximum contaminant level goal
MCL	Maximum contaminant level
MMPA	Marine Mammal Protection Act
MOA	Memorandum of Agreement
MOU	Memorandum of Understanding
MPRSA	Marine Protection Research and Sanctuaries Act
MSDS	Material safety data sheets
MWe	Megawatts of potential electric output capacity

N

NAAQS	National Ambient Air Quality Standard
NAE	National Academy of Engineering
NASA	National Aeronautics & Space Administration
NAS	National Academy of Sciences
NCA	Noise Control Act
NCP	National Contingency Plan
NCRRDI	National Coastal Resources Research and Development Institute

NCZMA	National Coastal Zone Monitoring Act
NEPA	National Environmental Policy Act
NEP	National Estuary Program
NEPPS	National Environmental Performance Partnership System
NERRS	National Estuarine Research Reserve System
NIOSH	National Institute for Occupational Safety and Health
NOAA	National Oceanic and Atmospheric Administration
NO_x	Nitrogen oxides
NPDES	National Pollution Discharge Elimination System
NPL	National Priorities List
NRC	National Response Center
NRC	Nuclear Regulatory Commission
NRDA	Natural resource damage assessments
NRS	National Response System
NSF	National Science Foundation
NSPS	New source performance standards

O

OAPCA	Organotin Antifouling Paint Control Act
OCSLA	Outer Continental Shelf Lands Act
OEQ	Office of Environmental Quality
OPA	Oil Pollution Act
OSH Act	Occupational Safety and Health Act
OSHA	Occupational Safety and Health Administration
OSHRC	Occupational Safety and Health Review Commission

P

PACM	Presumed asbestos-containing material
PAIR	Preliminary assessment information rule
PA	Preliminary assessment
PBT	Lead and lead compound chemicals
PCB	Polychlorinated biphenyls
PIT	Permits Improvement Team
PMN	Premanufacture notice
PM	Particulate matter

POTW	Publicly owned treatment works
PPA	Pollution Prevention Act
PPS	Prevention of Pollution from Ships
PQL	Practical quantification level
PRP	Potentially Responsible Party
PSD	Prevention of significant deterioration

R

RACT	Reasonably available control technology
RCRA	Resource Conservation and Recovery Act
RD	Remedial design
RI/FS	Remedial investigation/Feasibility study
RMCL	Recommended maximum contaminant level
ROD	Record of decision
RQ	Reportable quantity

S

SDWA	Safe Drinking Water Act
SERC	State emergency response commission
SIP	State Implementation Plan
SMCRA	Surface Mining Control and Reclamation Act
SNUR	Significant New Use Rule
SPA	Shore Protection Act
SPCC	Spill Prevention Control and Countermeasure Plan
SRF	State revolving fund
SWDA	Solid Waste Disposal Act
SWRCA	Soil and Water Resources Conservation Act

T

TCLP	Toxicity characteristic leaching procedure
TDI	Toluene diisocyanate
TDS	Total dissolved solids
TIE	Toxicity identification evaluation
TRE	Toxicity reduction evaluation

TRI	Toxic Release Inventory
TSCA	Toxic Substances Control Act
TSD	Treatment, storage, and disposal facility
TSP	Total Suspended Particulates

U

UIC	Underground injection control
USDA	U.S. Department of Agriculture
USDW	Underground sources of drinking water
USGS	U.S. Geological Survey
UST	Underground storage tank

W

WA	Wilderness Act
WET	Whole effluent toxicity
WRUA	Wood Residue Utilization Act

X

XL	Excellence in Leadership

ENDNOTES

Chapter 1: Introduction

[1] Programs are implementation instructions that include enforcement procedures, funding mechanisms, and other directions.

[2] The Executive branch of the federal government is headed by the President and has the responsibility for carrying out the laws. The Legislative branch makes the laws, and the judicial branch of government judges or evaluates the fairness and constitutionality of the laws.

[3] For a list of addresses, see Headquarter/Regional Offices. www.epa.gov/epahome/postal.htm

[4] For example, land use is one area that has been left to the state and local governments.

[5] Lovins, A. B. 1979. *Soft Energy Paths: Toward a Durable Peace.* New York: Harper & Row.

[6] CERCLA is the Comprehensive Environmental Response and Liability Act. The Resource Conservation and Recovery Act (RCRA) refers to amendments—new sections, deletions, and changes—to the Solid Waste Disposal Act. 42 USCA 9601 to 9675; 42 USCA 6901 to 6992k; Pub. L. 94–580, Section 1.

Chapter 2: Summary Perspectives

[1] The Communicable Disease Center (CDC) is an agency within the U.S. Department of Health and Human Services.

[2] In some instances, a federal agency other than the EPA is given responsibilities for an environmental program, and there may be delegation of some duties to state and local agencies or even required cooperation with the EPA.

[3] Gallagher, L. M. 1997. Clean Water Act. In *Environmental Law Handbook*, Fourteenth Edition. T. F. P. Sullivan, ed. Rockville, MD: Government Institutes, Inc. 111.

[4] 42 USCA 6941; 4001.

[5] The SWDA may be cited as the "Resource Conservation and Recovery Act of 1976," Section 1; Pub. L. 94–580.

[6] By passing this act, Congress authorized a waiver of normally-granted sovereign immunity allowing the same civil fines and penalties for the private sector (or individuals) to be assessed on the federal government.

[7] 42 USCA 11002 (a).

[8] 42 USCA 11001 to 11050. The Emergency Planning and Community Right-to-Know Act (EPCRA) was enacted to further protect citizens from accidental releases of chemicals.

[9] 42 USCA 9601 to 9675. The first version of CERCLA was enacted in 1980. Subchapter IV and certain sections of CERCLA were included as amendments to the 1980 act with changes and additions to other federal acts and named the Superfund Amendments and Reauthorization Act (SARA) in 1986. In 1992, sections of CERCLA were added as the Community Environmental Response Facilitation Act; in 1996, sections were added as the Asset Conservation, Lender Liability, and Deposit Insurance Protection Act; and in 2002, sections were added as the Small Business Liability Relief Act and the Brownfields Revitalization Act.

Chapter 3: National Policy

[1] 42 USCA 4321 to 4370f.

[2] 42 USCA 4344, section 204.

[3] Pub. L. 101–617, 104 Stat. 3287, titled, "Environmental Research Geographic Location Information Act."

[4] 42 USCA 4331, section 101.

[5] 42 USCA 4333, section 103.

[6] 42 USCA 4342, section 201.

[7] Subtitle D of title I of the Workforce Investment Act of 1998 is to take effect in 2000 (section 4368a).

[8] 42 USCA 4366, sections (a)(1), (2), (3).

[9] 42 USCA 4366a, sections (a), (b).

[10] 4369, sections (a), (b). Pub. L. 106–398, s317, Necessity of Military Low-Level Flight Training to Protect National Security and Enhance Military Readiness, 2000.

Chapter 4: Environmental Quality

[1] 42 USCA 4371 to 4375. Environmental Quality Improvement Act of 1969.

[2] 42 USCA 4371, s202; 4372, s203; also, Executive Order 11991, 42 FR 26967, 3 CFR, Comp., 1977.

[3] 42 USCA 4371.

[4] 42 USCA 4370e.

Chapter 5: Preventing Pollution

[1] 42 USCA s13101 to 13109. Pollution Prevention Act of 1990, Pub. L. 101–508.

[2] "Source reduction," in the language of the EPA.

[3] 42 s13103; PPA s6604.

[4] 42 s13104; PPA s6605.

[5] 42 s13106; PPA s6607.

Chapter 6: Air Pollution

[1] 42 U.S.C. s7401 et seq. (1970).

[2] Clean Air Act. 1998 Amendments. Pub.L. 105-286, s1. 112 Stat. 2773. Portions of the CAA, particularly s7511b, may be referred to as the "Border Smog Reduction Act of 1998."

[3] 1967 Clean Air Act and its Amendments in 1970, 1977, and 1990.

[4] 40 CFR 63. 1998; 42 USC 7408.

[5] 49 CFR 192, 193, and 195.

[6] An initial list of 174 major source categories of hazardous air pollutants has been expanded over the years.

[7] 59 Fed. Reg. 21370 (1996).

[8] 42 USCA 7740; CAA Part C—Prevention of Significant Deterioration of Air Quality.

[9] defined as limits of 100 or 250 tpy.

[10] 40 CFR s52.21

[11] Brownell, F. W. 1997. Clean Air Act. In *Environmental Law Handbook*, Fourteenth Edition. T. F. P. Sullivan, editor. Rockville, MD: Government Institutes. 84.

[12] 42 USC 7412.

[13] 61 Fed. Reg. 31668 (1996).

[14] 42 USC 7651.

[15] The issue of regional haze is not addressed as a SIP requirement.

[16] Brownell, 95; CAA - Part C - Prevention of Significant Deterioration of Air Quality.

[17] Subchapter II—Emissions Standards for Moving Sources.

[18] OMB 2060-0345. 1998.

[19] Fed. Reg. 7716 (1994).

[20] 57 Fed. Reg. 32250 (1992), 40 CFR Part 70.

[21] Phase II sulfur dioxide requirements (CAA s405).

[22] CAA s405.

[23] http://utility.rti.org/part1/faqP1_3.cfm.

[24] The concentration of ozone in this region is about 10 parts per million by volume as compared to approximately 0.04 parts per million by volume in the troposphere.

[25] in wavelengths from 290 nm–320 nm.

[26] Such as aldehydes and ketones.

[27] Peroxyacyl nitrates are especially damaging photochemical oxidants that are very irritating to the eyes and throat.

[28] 43 s7511.

[29] Montreal Protocol on Substances that Deplete the Ozone Layer specifies certain substances produced in the U.S.

[30] 42 USC 7409, 7601(a). 50.7 Changes particulate matter in revisions, 1998.

[31] 40 CFR 68.

[32] Ayers, et al. 1994. Environmental Science and Technology Handbook. Rockville, MD: Government Institutes, 1994. 135.

[33] 40 CFR 50, 53, 58. 2.5 micrometers (PM2.5); and 10 micrometers (PM10).

[34] 40 CFR 51.100(O). Reasonably available control technology (RACT) is only used for secondary NAAQS, and can be used in State Implementation Plans as long as the secondary NAAQS are attained as quickly as possible. Primary and secondary NAAQS are required to be met by states as quickly as possible, and delays are only granted with "good cause" as defined by the EPA. See Administrative Procedures Act 553(b)(3)(B).

[35] 42 USC 7502.

[36] 42 USC 9602, 9603, 9604; 33 USC 1321, 1361. Unless the disturbances result in readings greater than 7.6 picocuries per gram or pCi/g of Uranium-238, 6.8 pCi/g of Thorium-232, or 8.4 pCi/g of Radium-226.

[37] Brownell, 85.

[38] 42 USC 7503.

[39] Any operating unit of a facility that burns any solid waste material from commercial or industrial establishments or the general public (single and multi family dwelling units, hotels, and motels)—and those that do not require a permit under the Solid Waste Disposal Act (SWDA) 42; USCA s6925—are called a "solid waste incineration unit."

[40] 56 Fed. Reg. 42216 (1991).

[41] 42 USC 7410.

[42] S. Rep. No. 91-1196, 91st Cong., 2d. Sess. 15-16(1970).

[43] 40 CFR Part 60.

[44] Brownell, 82-83.

[45] 43 s7511; 57 Fed. Reg. 32250 (1992); 42 USC 7661a.

[46] An affected state is defined as one whose air quality can be affected, is contiguous to the state containing the source, or is a state within 50 miles of the source.

[47] 42 USC 7661.

[48] If the change is made and the minor revision denied, then the source may be liable for violating its permit.

[49] CAA, Preamble. Title V.

[50] 42 USC 7661c.

[51] 40 CFR 73, E.

[52] Brownell, 106.

Chapter 7: Sound

[1] Noise Control Act of 1972, 42 USCA 4901 to 4918. (Quiet Communities Act of 1978, Pub. L. 950609, 92 Stat. 3079). 49 Appendix 1301.

[2] Subchapter IV—Noise Pollution, under the Clean Air Act Amendments; 42 s7641, P1569.

[3] 42 USCA 4913.

[4] 42 USCA 4904(b).

[5] 42 USCA 4909.

[6] 42 USCA 4907.

Chapter 8: Aircraft Sound

[1] Airport Noise Abatement Act, 1980, 40 USCA 4705 to 47510; Abatement of Aviation Noise, 1994 Pub. L. 103-272 1(e), 108 Stat. 1284; ANAA Amendments, 2000, Pub. L. 106-181, 114 Stat. 178.

[2] 49 USCA 47509.

[3] 49 USCA 47507.

[4] 49 USCA 47504.

[5] Pub. L. 106-181.

[6] 49 USCA 47504.

[7] 49 USCA 47507, 49 USCA 47508.

Chapter 9: Water Pollution

[1] Gallagher, L. M. 1997. Clean Water Act. In *Environmental Law Handbook*, Fourteenth Edition. T. F. P. Sullivan, ed. Rockville, MD: Government Institutes, Inc. 111.

[2] 33 USC 1311, Section 301.

[3] 33 USC 1342, Section 402.

[4] 33 USC 1341, 1342, Section 401, 402.

[5] 33 USC 1311, 1316, 1317, Section 301, 306, 307.

[6] 33 USC 1321, Section 311.

[7] 33 USC 1344, Section 404.

[8] 33 USC 1319, 1365, Section 309, 505.

[9] 40 CFR s122.2.

[10] The non-regulatory method of coordinating federal and state groundwater pollution control is the Comprehensive State Groundwater Protection Programs (CSGWPP). EPA had approved four of them by 1997: Alabama, Connecticut, New Hampshire, and Wisconsin.

[11] See the manual developed jointly by the Fish and Wildlife Service, Soil Conservation Service, and U.S. Army Corps of Engineers. *Federal Manual for Identifying and Delineating Jurisdictional Wetlands.* 1987.

[12] Gallagher, 112.

[13] Section 306(a)(2), 33 USC s1316(a)(2).

[14] Section 303(c)(2), 33 USC s1313(c)(2); 40 CFR s131.10(a).

[15] 33 USC 1314 (l) Section 304(l).

[16] Subchapter III - Standards and Enforcement.

[17] Water Quality Act, Public Law No. 100-4 (1987).

[18] Ibid.

[19] For a full discussion of the NPDES permit program, see *NPDES Permit Handbook*, Second Edition. Rockville, MD: Government Institutes, Inc. 1992.

[20] 33 USC 1342 (b), Section s402(b).

[21] 40 CFR s123.24.

[22] 40 CFR s123.25.

[23] 40 CFR 121.

[24] Section 304(e), 33 U.S.C. s1314(e).

[25] Section 402(o), 33 U.S.C. s1342(o).

[26] 33 USC 1314; Gallagher, 123.

[27] under Section 404 of the CWA.

[28] 40 CFR s230.10(a).

[29] 33 USC 1344 (g)(h); Gallagher, 144.

[30] NAIC codes are given to each land use. They are a uniformly accepted land use classification system intended to be a complete list of all possible uses.

[31] 60 Fed. Reg. 50804 (29 September 1995).

[32] 33 USC 1342; Gallagher, 133.

[33] 61 Fed. Reg. 41243 (9 September 1992).

[34] 33 USC 1326, Section 316.

[35] 40 CFR 228.12.

[36] Annex V of the International Convention for the Prevention of Pollution from Ships (MARPOL V) and the Marine Plastic Pollution Research and Control Act of 1987. Sewage form vessels is regulated under the Marine Sanitation Device Program. 40 CFR Part 140.

[37] 33 USC 1342.

[38] Subchapter VI—State Water Pollution Control Revolving Funds.

[39] Section 319(b), 33 U.S.C. s1329(b).

[40] 33 U.S.C.s1451-1464, as amended.

[41] Pub. L. 106-457, Title II, s202, 7 November 2000.

[42] Exemptions are facilities where the underground storage capacity is 42,000 gallons or less of oil, and the aboveground storage capacity is 1,320 gallons or less of oil, with no single container having a capacity over 660 gallons. 40 CFR s112.1(d)(2).

[43] Oil Pollution Act of 1990 (OPA); 33 USC 2701-2761.

[44] The National Response Center has additional duties to respond to pollution events under CERCLA, the Superfund Act. This center maintains the priority lists of Superfund sites (CERCLIS).

Chapter 10: Drinking Water

[1] Title 42. The Public Health and Welfare. Safety of Public Water Systems. Public Health Service Act (Title XII). PHSA. 42 USCA s300f–300j-26. Chapter 6A–Public Health Service. Pub. L. 93-523, 16 December 1974.

[2] 42 USC s6925(u)-(v); 42 USC 6928(h).

[3] 42 USC 300g.

[4] SDWA s1412(b)(1), 42 USC s300g-1(b)(1).

[5] Pub. L. 99–339, 100 Stat. 66 (1986).

[6] Pub. L. 104–182, 110 Stat. 1613 (1996).

[7] SDWA s1412(b)(3); 42 USC s300g-1(b)(3).

[8] There are no other environmental regulations that include assessments of costs and benefits.

[9] Williams, S. E. 1997. Safe Drinking Water Act. In *Environmental Law Handbook*, Fourteenth Edition. T. F. P. Sullivan, ed. Rockville, MD: Government Institutes. 202.

[10] SDWA s1412(e); 42 USC s300g-1(e).

[11] PQLs are used for carcinogens because the MCLG is zero and the PQL can represent the lowest feasible level.

[12] Enhanced Surface Water Treatment Rule, Disinfectant and Disinfection Byproducts Rule, and Ground Water Disinfect ion Rule.

[13] Williams, 212–217.

[14] Williams, 215; 42 USC 300g-l.

[15] SDWA s1412(b)(5), 42 USC s300g-1(b)(5)

[16] Williams, 217–223.

[17] Williams, 218.

[18] Ibid.

[19] Williams, 218–219.

[20] 40 CFR s144.26.

[21] Williams, 219.

[22] SWDA s3004; 42 USC 6924.

[23] Williams, 220.

[24] Williams, 221.

[25] Williams, 221–222.

[26] Williams, 206–209.

[27] RCRA s3004.

[28] Williams, 207.

[29] U.S. EPA. 2001. Office of Water. *SRT Fund Management Handbook*. EPA 832-B-01-003. April.

[30] Williams, 207; 42 USC 300 j-12

[31] Williams, 209–211.

[32] Williams, 223.

[33] Williams, 224.

[34] SDWA s1428(e); 42 USC s300h-7.

Chapter 11: Oil Spills into Water

[1] USC s2701-2761. Chapter 40 - Oil Pollution Act of 1990.

[2] Pub. L. 104-55 and Pub. L. 105-277 were enacted as part of the Edible Oil Regulatory Reform Act.

[3] Rosario Strait and Puget Sound, Washington and Prince William Sound, are waters where single hull tankers over 5,000 gross tons must be escorted by at least two towing vessels.

[4] Olney, A. P. 1997. Oil Pollution Act. In *Environmental Law Handbook*, Fourteenth Edition. T. F. P. Sullivan, ed. Rockville, MD: Government Institutes. 186.

[5] Ibid. 188.

[6] Ibid. 189.

[7] Ibid. 190–191.

[8] Ibid. 191–192.

Chapter 12: Ocean Dumping

[1] 33 U.S.C. 1401–1445. There are many amendments to the original act: Ocean Dumping Ban Act of 1988; Marine Mammal Health and Stranding Response act of 1992; Striped Bass Conservation, Atlantic Coastal Fisheries Management, and Marine Mammal Rescue Assistance Act of 2000.

[2] 33 USC 1342

[3] 33 USC 1413; www.epa.gov/OWOW/OCPD/oceans/update2.html. See the "Green Book," or "Evaluation of Dredge Material Proposed for Ocean Disposal - Testing Manual." (EPA-503/B-91/001). 1991.

[4] 16 USC 1431–1445(c)(1)

[5] 33 USC 1414

[6] 33 USC 1414(b)

[7] 33 USC 1412

[8] 33 USC 1414(a)(b)

[9] 33 USC 1417

[10] 33 USC 1442

[11] 33 USC 2738

Chapter 13: Ocean Dumping and Ships

[1] 42 U.S.C. s1901–1915. 1980. Chapter 33. Prevention of Pollution from Ships. In 1987 amendments, certain sections of this act along with sections of another title 42 may be cited as the "Marine Plastic Pollution Research and Control Act of 1987."

[2] Pub. L. 106-554, the Dry Bulk Cargo Residue Disposal on the Great Lakes; Study and Regulations, 2000.

Chapter 14: Oceans and Paints

[1] 33 USC s2401–2410. 1988, Chapter 37–Organotin Antifouling Paint Control Act; Pub. L. 100–333.

[2] as developed by the American Society for Testing and Materials.

Chapter 15: Shore Protection

[1] Public Vessel Medical Waste Antidumping Act of 1988. 33 USC s2501–2505.

[2] Shore Protection Act of 1988. 33 USC s2601–2623.

Chapter 16: Solid Waste

[1] 42 USC s6901–6992k, Chapter 82–Solid Waste Disposal Act.

[2] This does not include solid or dissolved material in domestic sewage, solid or dissolved materials in irrigation return flows, or industrial discharges that are point sources subject to permits defined as atomic energy. 42 USCA 6903; s1004(27)

[3] Funds are made available under Superfund to clean up those abandoned sites before prosecution.

[4] Even though they may be hazardous, some wastes are excluded from being called hazardous. These include mixtures of domestic sewage and other wastes passing through a sewer system to a publicly-owned treatment works; industrial wastewater discharges that are point source discharges under the Clean Water Act; irrigation return flows; and special nuclear or byproduct material regulated under the Atomic Energy Act.

[5] 40 CFR 265.352.

[6] 42 USCA 6908; FFCA, s109.

[7] 42 USCA; s6902; s1003(b).

[8] Final Rule, December 21, 2001

[9] 42 USC 9601 to 9675; 10 U.S.C. 2701 to 2810; and 26 U.S.C. 4671, 4672, 9507, and 9508.

[10] 42 USC 9607; Case, D. R. 1997. Resource Conservation and Recovery Act. In *Environmental Law Handbook*, Fourteenth Edition. T. F. P. Sullivan, ed. Rockville, MD: Government Institutes. 328–329.

Chapter 17: Hazardous Waste

[1] 42 USC 6901–6992k. The Resource Conservation and Recovery Act of 1976 (RCRA) and its 1984 Amendments.

[2] The National Biennial RCRA Hazardous Waste Report (Based on 1999 Data) - List of Treatment, Storage and Disposal Facilities. 06/01/2001.

[3] 42 USC 6915; SWDA, s2006.

[4] 42 USC 6924.

[5] 42 U.S.C. 6942(c).

❖ Endnotes

[6] 42 USC 6947.

[7] 42 USC 6933.

[8] 42 USC 6991b(c).

[9] 42 USC 6992a(a).

[10] 42 USC 6992d

[11] 42 USC 6925.

[12] 42 USC 6951.

[13] 42 USC 6983; There is an online library system (OLS) that connects the libraries of the EPA. OLS relates databases for books, reports, and audiovisual materials. Available online at: http://www.epa.gov/natlibra/ols.htm. 17 July 2002.

Chapter 18: Storage Tanks

[1] Nardi, K. J. 1997. Underground Storage Tanks. In *Environmental Law Handbook*, Fourteenth Edition. T. F. P. Sullivan, ed. Rockville, MD: Government Institutes. 360.

[2] EPA Office of Underground Storage Tanks. "FAQ 4: What Has EPA's Office of Underground Storage Tanks (OUST) Accomplished?" Available online at: www.epa.gov/swerust1/topfour.htm.

[3] EPA Office of Underground Storage Tanks. "UST Program Facts: Implementing Federal Requirements of Underground Storage Tanks" (EPA 510-B-96-007, December 1996). Also, cited in Sullivan, Jr. as Environmental Information, Ltd. "Underground Storage Tank Cleanup: Status and Outlook (1995)."

[4] "Health, safety, and welfare" are the very foundations of legislative protection granted under the U.S. Constitution. Governments at all levels operate under the premise that they are performing these sets of public services.

[5] Subchapter IX - Regulation of Underground Storage Tanks. 42 CFR 6991; SWDA 9001.

[6] 42 USC 6991h(f).

[7] EPA Office of Underground Storage Tanks. "State Authorization Status as of June 26, 2002." Available online at: http://www.epa.gov/swerust1.

[8] EPA delegates primary responsibility for implementing the RCRA hazardous waste program to individual states. This devolution of power "with strings connected to EPA" ensure nationwide consistency of standards and flexibility to states. In 2002, 50 states and territories had been granted authority to implement the basic RCRA program. Many of the 50 states are also authorized to implement additional components of RCRA, such as its Land Disposal and Corrective Action Restrictions. State RCRA programs must be at least as stringent as the federal requirements, but they can be more stringent. A State Authorization Tracking System (STATS) gives information about the authorization status for all states. Available online at: http://www.epa.gov/epaoswer/hazwaste/state/index.htm. 15 July 2002.

[9] 40 CFR 280.20(a)(4).

[10] 40 CFR 280.20(c)(l)(ii).

[11] 40 CFR 2809.30.

[12] 40 CFR 280.43.

[13] 40 CFR 280.40(a)(3).

[14] After December 1998, the tanks must be upgraded or permanently closed. 40 CFR 280.41.

[15] 40 CFR 280.41.

[16] RSPA, 173.8(b). 1998.

[17] 40 CFR 280.11 and §280.10(c); 42 USC 6991b.

[18] Such as the Natural Gas Pipeline Safety Act of 1968; Hazardous Liquid Pipeline Safety Act of 1979; and any state laws for gas and liquid pipelines.

[19] 42 USC s6991; 40 CFR, s280.12.

[20] This term is determined on a case-by-case basis, and regulated substances in very small quantities in a tank may be excluded from RCRA requirements.

[21] Such as under the Atomic Energy Act of 1954.

[22] Such as those regulated by the Nuclear Regulatory Commission. See 10 CFR 50, Appendix A.

[23] 42 USC 6991e(b).

[24] One of the objectives of EPA is to include each set of state regulations into the U.S. Code of Federal Regulations. U.S. EPA, Region 6 offices; August 4, 1998.

[25] 42 USC 6991(a)(2)(b).

[26] 40 CFR 280.2.

[27] 40 CFR 280.50.

[28] 40 CFR 302.

[29] 40 CFR 280.101.

Chapter 19: Federal Compliance

[1] 42 USC 6961. Section 6001 of the Solid Waste Disposal Act. Federal Facility and Compliance Act of 1992, Pub. L. 102–386, 106 Stat. 1505. Also, see Federal Acquisition, Recycling, and Waste Prevention, Executive Order 12873, 1993.

[2] 42 USC 6961 Section 6001.

[3] Chapter 82, Solid Waste Disposal. Section 6908. Also see FFCA Section 109. Small Town Environmental Planning.

Chapter 20: Workplace

[1] 29 CFR 1977.12.

[2] Pub. L. 105–198.

[3] 29 USC 660, s22(c).

[4] Pub. L. 105-241 amended sections 3(5) and 19(a) of the Act to include the United States Postal Service as an "employer" subject to OSHA enforcement.

[5] Executive Order 12196, 26 February 1980.

[6] 29 USC 567.

[7] 29 USC 655(b).

[8] 29 USC 655(c)(1).

[9] 29 USC 654(a)(1).

[10] 29 USC 1057.

[11] 29 CFR, 1910.20.

[12] Pub. L. 105–197.

[13] 29 CFR 1910.1200.

Chapter 21: Chemicals

[1] 15 USC 2601–2692.

[2] 15 USC 2604.

[3] 15 USC 2609.

[4] 15 USC 2607.

[5] 15 USC 2604.

[6] 40 CFR, s710.26.

[7] 15 USC 2603.

[8] Ibid.

[9] 15 USC 2610, 2615; Landfair, S. W. 1997. Toxic Substances Control Act. In *Environmental Law Handbook*, Fourteenth Edition. T. F. P. Sullivan, ed. Rockville, MD: Government Institutes. 580–2.

[10] 60 Fed. Reg. 66,706. 1995; Landfair, 274–275.

[11] Landfair, 249.

[12] 15 USC 2601–2692. Toxic Substances Control Act. Chapter 53, Toxic Substances Control. Subchapter III–Indoor Radon Abatement.

[13] 15 USC 2681–2692. Subchapter IV–Lead Exposure Reduction. 1992. Lead-based Paint Exposure Reduction Act. Pub. L. 102–550. Title X. Sec. 1021(c).

[14] 15 USC 2681–2692 and amendments to 2206, 2610, 2612, 2615, 2616, 2618, 2619. Lead-based paint activities is defined as housing risk assessment, inspection, and abatement; and any public buildings constructed before 1978, commercial building, bridge, or other structure or superstructure, identification of lead-based paint and materials containing lead-based paint, de-leading, removal of lead from bridges, and demolition.

Chapter 22: Pesticides

[1] 1996 Amendments, Pub. L. 104-170, 110 Stat. 1489, and Title 21, Food and Drugs, are called "Food Quality Protection Act of 1996."

[2] 7 USC 136 to 136y.

[3] 7 USC 136a.

[4] An application must include standard chemical descriptions, specific mention of pests and hosts, and extensive testing data. If not provided, the EPA can demand additional testing.

[5] 7 USC 136a(e).

[6] Subpart D, 159.152; 152.50(f)(3).

[7] 7 USCA 136 to 136y; s20; Integrated Pest Management.

[8] Miller, M. L. 1997. Pesticides. In *Environmental Law Handbook*, Fourteenth Edition. F. T. P. Sullivan, ed. Rockville, MD: Government Institutes. 315

[9] See EPCRA mentioned earlier in this Chapter.

[10] 21 USC 342.

[11] 42 USC 6923.

Chapter 23: Land

[1] 30 USC 1201, 1202, 1211. Surface Mining Control and Reclamation Act of 1977.

[2] Ibid.

[3] 30 USC 1202, 1291.

[4] 30 USC 1231.

[5] 30 USC 1233.

[6] 30 USC 1236.

[7] 30 USC 1256.

[8] 30 USC 1268.

[9] 30 USC 1272.

[10] 30 USC 1221. Mining and Mineral Resources Research Institute Act of 1984 (MMRRIA).

Chatper 24: Nuclear Safety

[1] Development and Control of Atomic Energy. Atomic Energy Act of 1954 (AEA). In later years amendments created Low-Level Radioactive Waste Policy Act (LLRWPA).

[2] 42 USC 2014, 2021 to 2021d, 2022, 2111, 2113, 2114.

[3] 42 USC 2022.

[4] 42 USC 2021.

[5] 42 USC 2021a.

[6] 42 USC 2021d. Low-Level Radioactive Waste Policy Act (LLRWPA).

[7] 42 USC 2113.

Chapter 25: Public Notice and Spill Planning

[1] Superfund Amendments and Reauthorization Act (SARA), enacted as a part of the CERCLA amendment in 1986. 42 USC 11001 et seq.

[2] 42 USC 9602, 11002; There are 360 extremely hazardous substances that require reports to state and local agencies if released from their sources. These substances are reportable quantities (RQs), and they are identified according to their acute lethal toxicity. RQs are adjusted to one of five levels: 1, 10, 100, 1,000, or 5,000 pounds. EPA bases the adjustments on concerns such as acute and chronic toxicity, aquatic toxicity, ignitability, and potential carcinogen reactivity. An RQ value is assigned for each of those characteristics. The most stringent RQ value or the lowest quantity of a substance requires reports of its release.

[3] 42 USC 304; 11004.

[4] 42 USC 313; 11023.

[5] 42 USC 323; 11043.

Chapter 26: Hazardous Waste Spill Cleanup

[1] Comprehensive Emergency Response, Compensation, and Liability Act of 1980. 42 U.S.C. 9601–9675. Chapter 103–Comprehensive Emergency Response, Compensation and Liability. Sections of CERCLA may be cited as the "Asset Conservation, Lender, Liability, and Deposit Insurance Protection Act of 1996."

[2] 42 USC 9622(b).

[3] 40 CFR 302.4.

[4] 42 USC 9601(8)(B).

[5] 42 USC 9601 (16).

[6] 42 USC 9602, 9601 (14).

[7] 42 USC 9602, 9603.

[8] Similar requirements are stated in the FWPCA 33 USC 1251 et seq.

[9] 42 USC 9607.

[10] 42 USC 9608.

[11] 42 USC 9617, 2239.

[12] Lee, R. T. 1997. Comprehensive Environmental Response, Compensation and Liability Act. In *Environmental Law Handbook*, Fourteenth Edition. T. F. P. Sullivan, ed. Rockville, MD: Government Institutes. 474.

[13] 42 USC 7420.

[14] 40 CFR 300.

[15] Executive Order 12580; 52 Fed. Reg. 2923, 1987.

[16] 40 CFR 300.

[17] 62 Fed. Reg. 504422; 40 CFR 300.425.

[18] U.S. EPA National Priorities List. NPL Site totals by States and Milestone. September 2002. http://www.epa.gov/superfund/sites.

[19] 40 CFR 300.400(g)(2).

[20] 42 USC 9604.

[21] 42 USC 9605.

[22] Public Law 107-118. Small Business Liability Relief and Brownfields Revitalization Act.

Chapter 27: Asbestos in Buildings

[1] 15 USC 53—Subchapter II. Asbestos Hazard Emergency Response. 2641–2656.

[2] 15 USC 2601–2692. Subchapter II: Asbestos Hazard Emergency Response; 15 USC 2641–2656 was enacted in 1986.

[3] 15 USC 2641 (a)(b).

[4] http://www.epa.gov/earth1r6/6pd/asbestos/asbestos.htm

[5] Asbestos in Shipyards Standard; Extension of the Office of Management and Budget's Approval of Information-Collection (Paperwork) Requirements. 1915.1001. 31 October 2000.

Chapter 28: Extinction

[1] Pub. L. 106–555 s1, 114 Stat. 2765. Certain portions and sections of this act may be cited as the "Striped Bass Conservation, Atlantic Coastal Fisheries Management, and Marine Mammal Rescue Assistance Act of 2000."

[2] 16 USC 1361, 1362, 1371–1389, 1401–1407, 1411–1418, 1421–1421h. The Marine Mammal Protection Act protects animals, creates a marine mammal commission, prohibits certain tuna harvesting, and responds to marine mammal health and stranding.

[3] 16 USC 1401.

[4] 16 USC 1373.

[5] 16 USC 1411; Driftnets are restricted under "Driftnet Impact Monitoring, Assessment, and Control Act of 1987."

[6] 16 USC 1372.

[7] 16 USC 1383.

[8] 16 USC 3812, 1383b.

[9] Pub. L. 105–42, s1(a), 111 Stat. 1122. May be cited as the "International Dolphin Conservation Program Act."

[10] Pub. L. 106–555, Title II, s201, 114 Stat. 2767. May be cited as the "Marine Mammal Rescue Assistance Act of 2000."

Chapter 29: Shoreline

[1] 16 USC 1451–1465.

[2] 16 USC 33 Sections 1451–1465. 1996 Amendments; Pub. L. 104–150, Section 1; Stat. 1380. This act and amendments may be cited as the "Coastal Zone Protection Act of 1996." It can be called either CZMA or CZPA.

[3] 16 USC 1451.

[4] 16 USC 1452, 1456.

[5] 16 USC 1452, 544f.

[6] 16 USC 1455(e).

[7] 16 USC 1455(b).

[8] 16 USC 1456(c).

[9] 16 USC 1461.

[10] A new short title: "Harmful Algal Bloom and Hypoxia Research and Control Act of 1998."

Chapter 30: Coastal Ecosystem

[1] 33 USC Section 2801 to 2805. Chapter 41—National Coastal Monitoring.

Chapter 31: Estuaries

[1] 33 USC 2901–2909. Chapter 42—Estuary Restoration. "Estuary Restoration Act of 2000." Pub. L. 106–457.

[2] 33 USC 2905.

[3] 106 Pub. L. 256, Oceans Act of 2000.

[4] 106 Public Law 284—Beaches Environmental Awareness, Cleanup and Health Act of 1999 (B.E.A.C.H.)

Chapter 32: Species Protection

[1] 16 USC Chapter 35, Section 1531 to 1544. Endangered Species Act of 1973.

[2] All federal departments must protect these species. Section 1531.

[3] 16 USC 1531–1534.

[4] 16 USC 1536(e).

[5] Pub. L. 106–201, 1(a), 1(b), Amendments require cost analyses for endangered species in annual reports from the DOI to Congress.

Chapter 33: Forests and Ranges

[1] 16 USC 1600–1614.

[2] 16 USC 1604.

[3] 16 USC 1641.

[4] 16 USC 1612.

[5] 16 USC 1601(d).

[6] Such as Title III of the Bankhead-Jones Farm Tenant Act (7 U.S.C. 1010 et seq.)

[7] 16 USC 1604.

[8] 16 USC 1681.

[9] 16 USC 1672.

❖ Endnotes

Chapter 34: Soil and Water

[1] 16 USCA 2001-2009. Soil and Water Resources Conservation Act of 1977. November 18, 1977, as amended 1985 and 1994.

[2] 16 USCA 2005.

[3] Ibid.

[4] 16 USCA 2006.

Chapter 35: Ecosystem

[1] 16 USCA 2461–2466, Antarctic Protection Act of 1990, November 16, 1990, as amended 1996.

[2] 16 USCA 2463.

Chapter 36: Wetlands

[1] 16 USC 3951–3956, Coastal Wetlands Planning, Protection, and Restoration Act. Chapter 59A. Wetlands.

[2] 16 USC 3951.

[3] 16 USC 3956, s307.

[4] North American Wetlands Conservation Act; 16 USCA 4401–4414, December 13, 1989, as amended 1990 and 1994.

Chapter 37: Non-native Species

[1] 16 USC 4701–4751.

[2] 16 USC 4701.

[3] 16 USC 4741(f).

[4] 16 USC 4712, s 1102.

Chapter 38: Land

[1] 43 USCA 1701–1785. Federal Land Policy and Management Act of 1976. Chapter 35—Subchapter I. Section 1701.

[2] 43 USC 1712 and 1731.

[3] 43 USC 1732.

[4] 43 USC 1752–1761.

[5] 43 USC 1702.

Chapter 39: Offshore

[1] 43 USCA 1801–1866. Outer Continental Shelf Lands Act of 1978. Chapter 36—Outer Continental Shelf Resource Management.

[2] 43 USC 1843(b), 1801, 1802.

[3] 43 USC 1348, 1845.

[4] 43 USC 1842

[5] 43 USC 1843(b)

[6] 43 USC 1862(b).

[7] On January 19, 2001, Environmental Protection Agency Administrator Carol Browner signed a prepublication version of the rulemaking to revise the Clean Water Act 403(c)—Ocean discharge criteria to better protect our beaches, coasts, and ocean resources from pollution.

[8] 3 USC 1401.

[9] Federal Water Pollution Control Act. Section 311(b)(5)

[10] Pub. L. 104–324.

[11] 16 USC 1852. Regional Fishery Management Councils.

[12] Executive Order. Office of the President. 26 May 2000.

Chapter 40: Undeveloped Land

[1] 16 USC 1131–1136.

[2] 16 USC 1132(2)(c) et seq.

[3] 16 USC 1135.

[4] 16 USC 1132 (3)(c).

[5] 16 USC 1133.

[6] 16 USC 1132 (3)(c).

Index

B

C